Instructor's Resource Manual

Public Speaking
Concepts and Skills for a Diverse Society

SEVENTH EDITION

Clella Jaffe
George Fox University

D1457730

Prepared by

Miri Pardo
St. John Fisher College

WADSWORTH
CENGAGE Learning

Australia • Brazil • Japan • Korea • Mexico • Singapore • Spain • United Kingdom • United States

WADSWORTH
CENGAGE Learning

ISBN-13: 978-1-133-48946-7
ISBN-10: 1-133-48946-X

Wadsworth
20 Channel Center Street
Boston, MA 02210
USA

Cengage Learning is a leading provider of customized learning solutions with office locations around the globe, including Singapore, the United Kingdom, Australia, Mexico, Brazil, and Japan. Locate your local office at: **www.cengage.com/global**

Cengage Learning products are represented in Canada by Nelson Education, Ltd.

To learn more about Wadsworth, visit
www.cengage.com/wadsworth

Purchase any of our products at your local college store or at our preferred online store
www.cengagebrain.com

Printed in the United States of America
1 2 3 4 5   19 18 17 16 15

CONTENTS

Part I

GENERAL CONSIDERATIONS

This section addresses pertinent issues that an instructor—especially a first-time instructor—can use to structure an effective introductory public speaking course. It first considers some theoretical foundations for pedagogy. Then it turns to more practical matters of grading, testing, syllabus construction, and student assignments.

1

PUBLIC SPEAKING AND A DIVERSITY PERSPECTIVE

You (or someone in your department) probably selected *Public Speaking: Concepts and Skills for a Diverse Society, 7/e,* because you want students to be aware of cultural issues that affect public speaking. However, this is not a modified anthropology course; your major intention, like mine, is to empower students to speak and listen effectively in the existing institutions of an increasingly pluralistic society and world.

The preface in the text that explains why I wrote the book and how diversity skills are additional competencies for public speakers. Briefly, the text includes many examples from other speaking traditions--both from within the United States and from other countries. They are there to help students understand that norms are simply norms. There are other ways to speak, listen, and reason, and in an electronically connected world we increasingly encounter diverse traditions.

Although I include cultural issues in every chapter, the text still aims to prepare students for public speaking within institutions in the US. Consequently, I cover the basic units—audience analysis, listening, informative speaking, persuasive speaking, delivery, research, and so on—that will help your students prepare effective speeches. I write from a liberal arts perspective that incorporates historical principles of rhetoric as well as modern dialogical theories of communication into the discussion. By providing knowledge, skills, and (hopefully) the motivation students need to be competent public communicators, we together enable your students to participate successfully in the dominant institutions of this culture.

While some instructors have diversity within a single classroom, many teach largely homogeneous, Euro-American students. I have taught in both settings. At George Fox and Oregon State University, students are fairly homogeneous in background; in contrast, classes at St. John's University include Italians, Greeks, West Indians, African Americans, Puerto Ricans, Chinese and Irish students, Koreans, and more—a real reflection of the diversity that is New York City. The materials in this text work well in either setting.

CHANGES IN THE SEVENTH EDITION

In each new edition I update examples and research. I also revise the entire text for readability and clarity. If you used the sixth edition, you'll find the following additional changes, made in response to feedback from reviewers:

Here are some highlights of what's new:

- **New terms and emphases.** In response to reviewer requests, you'll find new material on civic engagement (Chapter 1 and throughout the text), collectivist and individualist cultures (Chapter 1 and additional references), systematic desensitization (Chapter 2), and oral style (Chapter 12).

- **Additional figures that summarize information.** Reviewers noted the value of visuals, such as Figure 2.1, that summarizes the canons of rhetoric. This edition includes several additional summary tables. For example, one in Chapter 7 compares Internet research to library research; a table in Chapter 12 compares oral to written style, and Chapter 17 includes a table that summarizes several major fallacies.

- **Revised organization within chapters.** In response to reviewer feedback, material from Chapter 10 (the section on connectives) and Chapter 11 (the section on supporting main points) is now in Chapter 9 (organizing main points). Chapter 17 (foundations for reasoning) now precedes Chapter 18 (persuasive speaking). Chapter 18 is substantially reorganized around speeches to convince (about facts, values, and policies) and speeches to actuate behaviors.

- **Updated box features.** New **Practically Speaking** boxes include a Native American activist (Chapter 1), a Korean American businesswoman (Chapter 9), a discussion of Wikipedia (Chapter 7), and a student who organized a civic engagement project on her campus (Chapter 14). A new **Ethics in Practice** box in Chapter 3 discusses research on Facebook and civility.

- **New sample speeches.** I have replaced or updated many sample speeches for currency, variety, and even greater effectiveness. Here are three examples: Chapter 7 (research) highlights a "civic engagement speech" in which a student explains a problem and then identifies an organization that works to solve it. Chapter 13 (presentation aids) uses visuals from a speech on artificial gills throughout the chapter. Chapter 16 (informative speaking) features a Chinese student explaining his culture's version of Valentine's Day.

- **Updated research.** Communication scholars continue to expand our understanding of listening and reasoning. Information on historical rhetorical traditions (Diversity in Practice, Chapter 1), gender and anxiety (Chapter 2), and dual coding theory (Chapter 12) are just a few examples of research updates.

- **Update references to cultural and social issues.** Rapid developments in politics, technological innovations, the influence of social media and the like require updating in each new version. Here are just two examples: You'll find a brief excerpt from President Obama's speech at the memorial service for the people killed when Representative Gabrielle Gifford (D-AZ) was shot in Arizona (Chapter 3). Ted Sorenson's death was noted, and the famous Inaugural Address he helped President Kennedy write is featured at the end of Chapter 12.

TEACHING PHILOSOPHY

Helping students become more informed critical thinkers is a major goal for speech students. Thousands of instructors use some version of Benjamin Bloom's Taxonomy of Thinking Skills when they plan courses. Bloom worked with a group of scholars who identified three domains of learning: cognitive, affective, and psychomotor. Within the cognitive domain, he identifies the following six levels of thinking, each of which builds on the preceding ones. A group of scholars, led by one of his former students, revised the taxonomy for the twenty-first century by renaming the levels and reordering levels 5 and 6. Their revised terminology is in parentheses.)

- Level 1: Knowledge (Remembering)—learners acquire knowledge of vocabulary terms, theories, definitions, and similar basic information that is foundational to understanding of a subject. (*key terms:* cite, list, identify, define)

- Level 2: Comprehension (Understanding)—learners understand the material well enough to translate, paraphrase, or explain it in their own words. (*key terms:* explain, give examples, illustrate, rephrase, summarize)

- Level 3: Application (applying)—building on the previous levels, learners begin to apply what they have learned to specific instances. (*key terms:* classify, predict, relate, demonstrate)

- Level 4: Analysis (analyzing)—learners examine a phenomenon and explain why or why not a particular strategy or behavior works in the specific instance. (*key terms:* diagnose, differentiate, examine, outline, conclude)

- Level 5: Synthesis (creating)—using a combination of the learned principles, strategies, ideas, and techniques, the student draws together the materials to create a unique product. (*key terms:* combine, compose, plan, integrate, expand)

- Level 6: Evaluation (evaluating)—the learner understands the concepts well enough to judge and rate a specific phenomenon. (*key terms:* compare and contrast, judge, weigh, assess, critique)

Bloom, B. S. (Ed.). (1956). *Taxonomy of educational objectives: the classification of educational goals. Book I: Cognitive domain*. New York, NY: Longman.

Forehand, M. (2005). Bloom's taxonomy: Original and revised. In M. Orey (Ed.). Emerging perspectives on learning, teaching, and technology. Retrieved October 15, 2011, from http://projects.coe.uga.edu/epltt/

With these skills in mind, I try to incorporate exercises and activities that will challenge students on each level. Consequently, these course components target Bloom's six categories of thinking.

Knowledge and Comprehension. Textual readings, lectures, classroom discussions, instructional videos, supplementary activities, and tests build these two components.

Application. **Stop and Check** and **Build Your Speech** exercises within the chapters as well as the end-of-the-chapter activities were written with application in mind. When students create a speech, they put course principles into practice.

Analysis. I have students give peer feedback—both written and verbal—after their classmates' speeches. (See the note "Giving Feedback" for details.) Additional ideas include:

- A journal is one way for students to analyze what they see and hear around them. The essay questions located in the test bank for each chapter and some **Application and Critical Thinking Exercises** at the end of each chapter can be adapted for journaling.

- Or set aside three to five minutes at the end of class sessions and have students write a response paper about some aspect of the day's class.

- Classroom discussions and **Stop and Check** features give additional opportunities for students to analyze a specific example of reasoning, a public speech, the delivery skills of a speaker, and so on. Videos, especially of their own speeches, are also useful.

- Look over the essay questions in the test bank. Some would make good discussion ideas. If you use a course management tool, such as Blackboard or Moodle, you can set up a forum, chat, or wiki where students can contribute their ideas.

- I often give an essay final—both when I teach single sections and when I coordinate a 425 person course. (You'll find it described under "Testing Issues.") This is a further opportunity for students to analyze a public speech. Look for the critique form on the final page in the test bank.

Synthesis (Creating). Students who produce unique, creative speeches are integrating elements of course content into new creations. The **Build Your Speech** features within chapters help students with synthesis.

Evaluation. Providing opportunities for self-evaluation and for making judgments about their classmates' speeches and outlines are two ways to help students use this thinking skill. In addition, the **Stop and Check** features ask students to weigh ideas and form judgments.

DIVERSITY AND LEARNING STYLES

Students bring to our classrooms a variety of individual learning preferences. Some learn best from reading; others from observation and modeling. Some prefer group discussions; others like to learn alone. Some appreciate concrete material presented in a sequential fashion; others learn more randomly. The literature on learning styles is voluminous and fascinating, and there are literally millions of webpages on the topic. Chapter 11 also has a section on cognitive diversity.

Cultural factors also influence learning styles. The following essay written by a communication scholar provides a good overview of factors to consider when you teach in a classroom with students from diverse cultural backgrounds:

4

Stefani, L. A. (1999). The influence of culture on classroom communication. In L. Samovar and R. E. Porter (eds.) *Intercultural communication: A reader* (9th ed.). Belmont, CA: Wadsworth.

I wrote the text and this manual with a number of learning styles in mind. For instance, mind maps, alternative outlines, and suggestions for multiple ways of recording research information are all designed for students whose thinking styles are less linear.

GRADING

Wouldn't it be nice if we could just eliminate grades? However, we must give feedback in the form of a grade or an evaluation of some sort. Students want to know in advance what is expected of them—and then to be judged on those expectations. For this reason, assignments at the end of Part I in this manual list specific skills required for each speech, give guidelines for doing them well, and supply rubrics followed by evaluation forms based on those skills. The evaluation forms are not "weighted," making them adaptable to several grading systems.

Early in the term, duplicate and distribute the criteria for speech evaluation endorsed by the National Communication Association. You'll find these criteria on page 15 in this manual. The criteria show that a "C" speech meets the basic requirements of the assignment. (Many students feel they should get an "A" because "I worked so hard on this speech.") If you want to eliminate a point grading scale, you can use these criteria to assign a letter grade—A, C+, etc.—that you'll eventually convert to percentage points for the final grade.

I arrange to make a video of each speech. Many types of cameras are available—from built-in cameras on laptops, iPhones, iPads, or MP3 players, to the Flip camera, which makes it easy to record each speech, then email a copy to them and download a copy to my desktop. Students can watch their speeches and evaluate their performances; this virtually eliminates grade protests.

DIALOGICAL TEACHING: GIVING FEEDBACK

A major theme of this text is dialogical speaking and listening, and feedback—both written and verbal—as a major way for you to engage in a dialogue with your students.

Written Feedback

Use the evaluation form provided with each speech assignment to write comments about the speech as you listen. Follow the D-R-E Method described in Chapter 4. **D**escribe what they do (especially in the area of delivery). **R**espond by providing your reactions. **E**valuate by looking for effective and less effective aspects of the preparation and the performance. Here are some examples:

- I didn't hear you establish credibility. What links you to your topic?
- I liked the details in your example. They made me care about your characters—and your topic.
- Referring to frustrations about registration is a good way to establish common ground.
- Citing your sources for these statistics would make them stronger as evidence.
- You cited the *National Review* and the *Nation*—quite different in philosophy. This gives balance.
- You looked out the window during your introduction. As you progressed through your main points your eye contact became more inclusive. Your gestures function to illustrate your points. Be careful not to use too many.

The ***book CourseMate***, available for the seventh edition, includes speech critiquing guidelines and an opportunity for students to interactively critique several speech videos. They can compare their checklist and speech improvement plan with my feedback.

5

Verbal Feedback

I verbally point out one *effective* element of the speech to the entire class. I don't give negative feedback publicly unless a student asks for it—and never during the early speeches. All my suggestions for improvement are written.

In advance of the speech, I assign a student to give verbal feedback—which I direct. (Otherwise, they'll say, "I liked it. It was a good speech.") Consequently, I say something like, "Teresa, after Josef's speech, talk to him about his evidence—what kinds did he use? Did it pass the tests?" This way, she listens specifically, and the class has something concrete to discuss afterwards. Sometimes I ask the speaker, "Josef, what challenge did you face as you prepared this speech? What do you want Teresa to talk to you about later?"

Are you familiar with the book, *The One Minute Manager*? The author discusses one minute reprimands and one minute compliments. One minute conferences are useful. They work like this: If five people speak that day, dismiss everyone but the speakers five minutes early; then sit by the speakers one by one and open by saying, "How'd you think it went?" Amazingly, they often say what you would "nail" them on. Examples:

- Student: "I think I looked out the window too much." Me: "I noticed that too. How do you plan to change that on your next speech?"
- Student: "I really didn't have time to prepare." Me: "And how do you think that affected your performance?"

Right then, I "ballpark" a grade—"Somewhere between C+ and B-." After the class, I review the speech, write a couple more comments, and assign a final grade.

TESTING ISSUES

Although we need to assess our students' knowledge, comprehension, ability to apply, analyze, synthesize, and evaluate, there is a considerable amount of debate about the best way do this. Generally, introductory courses include at least one objective test; some include essay evaluations.

Objective Tests

Recognition and recall are two common ways to assess knowledge.

- *Recognition.* Multiple-choice, true-false, and matching are typical recognition questions. Students must choose from alternatives or determine the accuracy of a given statement. Recognition questions typically deal with knowledge and comprehension. Matching questions sometimes test ability to apply information.

- *Recall.* Fill in the blank questions, in contrast, require students to recall specific information. This means they must search their memories and come up with facts, theories, and so on. They typically assess knowledge of basic information.

   Cultural Considerations. Some students (especially foreign students) do poorly on objective tests. Nonnative speakers of English find it difficult to discriminate between shades of meaning in true-false or multiple-choice questions. If you use objective tests, consider allowing these students to use a dictionary so they can look up confusing words—both on objective and essay tests.

   Learning Style Considerations. Another category of students finds it difficult to answer some true-false questions because they can see so many shades of meaning inherent in the question. I allow students to justify their answers on each question, and typically they write, "This could be true if you look at it this way . . . but if you consider . . . then it is probably false." (Generally they select the correct answer in the first place, but if they don't, I evaluate their explanation.)

Essay Tests

Essay questions are a type of recall questions that assess all the levels of thinking: Knowledge, comprehension, and ability to apply information. Moreover, they give students opportunities to demonstrate their abilities to analyze, synthesize, and evaluate.

Consider giving an essay final (2 hour time span). For example, record a typical student speech. Show the speech in the first few minutes of the class. Have students take notes on it and begin planning their essays. Show the speech again about 20 minutes later; this gives an opportunity to look for additional aspects to evaluate. Then, they settle into writing. Show the speech the third time at the beginning of the second hour. This provides a final opportunity to confirm conclusions and to identify elements missed in the first showings.

THE COURSE SYLLABUS

Constructing a Syllabus

Your course syllabus is a written document that informs students of the course content and of your expectations regarding their performance. During the first or second class, distribute your syllabus and go over it orally, answering any questions that students might have. When your policies are in writing, you can refer back to them in the event that a student questions a final grade.

Include these components in your syllabus:

1. The course title, number, section number, and meeting time
2. Prerequisites, if any
3. Information about yourself including your name, title, office location, office hours, and campus telephone number, email address, and if applicable, course website address.
4. A course description. (Some institutions require you to include the description from the course catalog.)
5. Learning outcomes (measurable objectives) you will focus on
6. Required and recommended materials
7. Class procedures
8. Attendance requirements, policies for make-up work
9. Grading system
10. Assignments
11. A schedule

The following pages show a sample syllabus and two course schedules: One for use with a 15-week semester course; one to use with a 10-week quarter system.

SP 111C: INTRODUCTION TO PUBLIC SPEAKING

MWF 1:25-2:20, room
Fall Semester 2012

name   office hours
office location   email
telephone extension

Course Description: Basic principles of purposive speaking concentrating on content, organization, audience motivation, and language. Students apply these principles to several oral presentations with primary emphasis on extemporaneous public speaking.

<u>Course Objectives</u>: This course will help you

- develop an understanding of the process of speechmaking
- know terminology related to public speaking
- prepare speeches that are appropriate to your audience given a purposive situation
- develop skill in listening to public speeches
- sharpen your critical thinking abilities through evaluation of evidence and reasoning
- develop skills in delivery
- understand the role of culture in public speaking and the role of public speaking in culture
- appreciate diversity in speaking traditions

<u>Required Materials.</u> Jaffe, C. I. (2012). *Public speaking: Concepts and skills for a diverse society, 7th ed.* Belmont, CA: Wadsworth. Purchase at the campus bookstore or through the publisher's website where you can rent or purchase an electronic copy—often saving you money.

<u>Course Policies</u>

Attendance: Because Speech 111 is a discussion and performance class, your attendance is vital. You are allowed three (3) "free" absences for the inevitable doctor's visits, court appointments, funerals, and illnesses that come up during a semester. After that, points may be deducted.

- <u>Do not</u> miss a scheduled performance. All of your speech dates are announced in advance, and you must arrange for any schedule conflict at the time the speech is assigned. The only allowable make-up speeches or exams require <u>documented</u>, <u>legitimate</u> excuses.
- Each tardy (more than ten minutes) counts as 1/2 an absence.

Grading: Five (5) graded speeches, three (3) graded written assignments, and two (2) major tests: a midterm and a final combine with a number of short quizzes or in-class responses over assigned readings make up the grade. Quizzes are announced at least two class periods in advance.

Assignments:		
	Telling a Modern Legend	30 pts.
	Tribute (audio taped)	50 pts.
	Audiovisual Aid Speech	100 pts.
	Content Outline	20 pts.
	Current Issue Speech	150 pts.
	Content Outline	25 pts.
	Persuasive Speech	150 pts.
	Content Outline	25 pts.
Exams:	Midterm	75 pts.
	Quizzes, in class writing	75 pts.
	Final	100 pts.

Your accumulated points will be converted to percentages; final grades will be assigned as follows:

90%	=	A
80-89.9%	=	B
70-79.9%	=	C
60-69.9%	=	D
below 60	=	F

Course Calendar: Topics, Readings, and Assignment Due Dates
(15-week semester)

Week 1:	Course Introduction & Overview	Chs. 1 & 2
	SPEECH #1 (self-introduction)	Appendix B
Week 3:	Ethics & Listening	Chs. 3 & 4
	Narrative; Narrative speech assignment made	Ch. 15
Week 4:	Audience Analysis	Ch. 6
	Delivery	Ch. 14
Week 5:	**NARRATIVE SPEECHES**	
Week 6:	Informative Speaking; assign audiovisual speech	Chs. 16 & 5
	Organizational Patterns	Ch. 9
	Introductions and Conclusions, Outlines	Chs. 10, 11
Week 7:	Research	Ch. 7
	Supporting Materials	Ch. 8
	Visual Aids	Ch. 13
Week 8:	**AUDIOVISUAL SPEECHES**	
Week 9:	Finish **SPEECHES**, review for midterm	
	MIDTERM EXAM; assign current issue speech	
Week 10:	Language	Ch. 12
	Speaking in Small Groups	Appendix A
Week 11:	**CURRENT ISSUE SPEECHES**	
Week 12:	Finish **SPEECHES**	
	Foundations for Persuasion; assign persuasive speeches	Ch. 17
Week 13:	Persuasive Speaking	Ch. 18
Week 14:	**PERSUASIVE SPEECHES**	
Week 15:	Finish **SPEECHES**; course review	
Finals		

Adaptations for a 10-Week Quarter System

<u>Five Assignments.</u> It is possible to assign five speeches during a 10-week quarter, as the following course schedule on the next page demonstrates. Students make a video of their second speech, and give the fourth in a panel or symposium format. (Each panel takes 1/2 of a period. This allows the speeches to be completed in two days rather than the more typical four.)

<u>Four Assignments.</u> You may want to assign only four presentations—all delivered "live"—and make adjustments in the schedule to give a little more breathing space. Here are some suggestions.

Speech #1: Telling a modern legend.

Speech #2: To emphasize diversity, discuss the chapter on language at an earlier date, and choose an assignment that is particularly good for discussing cultural topics such as the following:

- a tribute
- a speech of definition
- a narrative speech (exemplum pattern)

Speech #3: Keep the visual aid speech of demonstration, biography, or explanation. Present the chapters on research, supporting materials, organization, and visual aids earlier.

Speech #4: Persuasive Presentation. Keep this speech, but use more time before it to discuss reasoning.

<u>The revised syllabus might read like this:</u>

<u>Grading:</u> There are four (4) graded speeches, three (3) graded written assignments, and two (2) major tests: a midterm and a final. In addition, there will be a number of short quizzes and in-class writing responses over assigned readings. (Quizzes will be announced at least two class periods in advance.)

<u>Assignments:</u>		
	Telling a Modern Legend	25 pts.
	Speech of Definition	30 pts.
	Content Outline	10 pts.
	Audiovisual Aid Speech	100 pts.
	Content Outline	15 pts.
	Persuasive Speech	100 pts.
	Content Outline	20 pts.
<u>Exams:</u>	Midterm	50 pts.
	Quizzes	50 pts.
	Final	100 pts.

Course Calendar
Topics, Readings, and Assignment Due Dates

Week 1:	Introduction to Public Speaking and Culture	Ch. 1
	Speech #1 assigned and discussed	
	Overview of the Speechmaking Process	Ch. 2
	Narrative	Ch. 15
Week 2:	Listening	Ch. 4
	SPEECH #1	
Week 3:	Audience Analysis	Ch. 6
	Speech #2 assigned and discussed	
	Language & Delivery	Chs. 12, 14
Week 4:	**SPEECH #2** (audio taped)	
	Informative Speaking; choosing topics	Chs. 16 & 5
	Speech #3 assigned and discussed	
	Research and Supporting Materials	Chs. 7, 8
Week 5:	Organizational Patterns, Introductions, Conclusions	Chs. 9, 10
	Outlining	Ch. 11
	Visual Aids	Ch. 13
Week 6:	**SPEECH #3**	
Week 7:	Finish Speech #3, assign Speech #4 (Group Speech)	
	MIDTERM EXAM	
	Speaking in Small Groups (Investigative Report)	Appendix A
Week 8:	**SPEECH #4** (two groups)	
	SPEECH #4 (two groups)	
	Reasoning	Ch. 17
	Assign Speech #5	
Week 9:	Persuasive Speaking	Ch. 18
	(Review of Chapters 7 and 8.)	
	SPEECH #5	
Week 10:	**SPEECH #5**	
Finals		

11

STUDENT SPEECH ASSIGNMENTS

Student speech assignments on the following pages include a description of the speech, a list of specific skills to be developed, and guidelines for preparing the speech. All (with the exception of the video speech) are followed by at least one outline or script that exemplifies the speech.

A rubric and an evaluation form follow each assignment. These forms are designed to reflect the specific skills in the assignment. If you use them to assess your students' grades, have students tear them out and hand them to you with their outline. If you prefer forms of your own making, students can use the ones in the workbook as preparation guides or checklists.

Telling a Modern Legend (1 ½ to 3 min.). Students introduce themselves to the class by telling a legend that has been handed down from either their family or from a significant group to which they belong.

Birth Date Speech (1 ½ to 3 min.). Students introduce themselves by researching the date they were born and finding something that relates to their interests or personality.

Single Point Speech (2 to 3 min.). The speaker presents only one major idea and develops it with several pieces of supporting information.

Drawing a Speech of Introduction. The speaker introduces a classmate by interviewing that person and producing a drawing that represents the other's characteristics. The drawing becomes the visual aid.

Speech of Tribute (2 to 3 min.). A tribute is a special kind of ceremonial speech that praises the characteristics of people who exemplify important cultural traits.

Visual Aid Speech (5 to 6 min.). This informative speech requires skillful use of audio or visual support. Options include a process speech (or demonstration speech), a biography, or an explanation or description. Scripts of visual aid speeches can be found in the text and in the *Jaffe Connection CD-ROM* and videos available from Wadsworth.

Speech of Definition (2 to 3 min.). Students define an English word or a term from another language. (There may not be an exact equivalent or translation directly into American English.). They then support the definition with additional information or with a narrative.

Video Recorded Speech. Students video record one of their speeches such as the tribute, the speech of definition, or the exemplum. (They may also choose a speech from Appendix B such as a farewell, an announcement, nomination, or introduction.)

Thirty-Second Videotaped Speech. Students prepare the script for an opinion speech that they write on cue cards or a teleprompter (if available) and then deliver before a camera. The single point speech or a modified Monroe's Motivated Sequence work well.

This speech often helps students evaluate their presentational skills. Some colleges and universities have media centers that are available for classroom taping. More and more students have access to equipment to make their own videos.

Exemplum (3 to 5 min.). This narrative form uses a narrative to illustrate a quotation. Chapter 15 in the text provides an explanation and example.

Narrative Speech (3 to 5 min.). The purpose of this assignment is to tell a story or explain a proverb that reinforces an important cultural resource. This may be a belief, a value, an attitude, or an action. The speech may be humorous. Sample student speeches are found at the end of Chapter 15, in Appendix C, and on the *Jaffe Connection CD-ROM.*

Current Issue Speech (Informative) (6 to 7 min.). Think of this speech as an investigative news report. A major goal of this assignment is to handle a current controversial or problem topic in an objective manner.

Speech to Persuade (6 to 7 min.). The purpose of this speech is to reinforce attitudes, values, beliefs, or actions of the audience. Students will find sample speeches at the end of Chapters 17 and 18 and in Appendix C in the text.

Panel Discussion: Controversial Issue (20 to 25 min. total). Students work with a group to discuss a controversial or problematic topic in depth. They choose a panel or symposium format to present their information.

Panel or Symposium Discussion: Movie Reality vs. Print Reality (20 to 25 min. total). A group of students watches a movie based on a historical character or event. Then they do historical research to assess the accuracy of the movie. They then compare and contrast the print reality and the movie reality.

Other Possibilities. Appendix B provides guidelines and samples for the following special occasion speeches that can be given throughout the term:

> Introductions
> Farewells
> Announcements
> Award presentations
> Acceptance speeches
> Nominations
> Commemorative speeches
> Eulogies

STUDENT SPEECH ASSIGNMENTS, EXAMPLES, RUBRICS, AND EVALUATION FORMS

Criteria for Evaluating Speeches

Self-Evaluation Form

Telling a Modern Legend
Sample Speech: A Modern Legend (self-introduction), by Derek Reamy
Rubric and Evaluation Form: Telling a Modern Legend

Birth Date Speech
Sample Speech: Birth Date (self-introduction), by Bob Pettit
Rubric and Evaluation Form: Birth Date Speech

Single Point Speech
Sample Speech: Come Watch Lacrosse, by Andres Lucero
Rubric and Evaluation Form: Single Point Speech

A Tribute
Sample Speech: A Tribute to the Dog, by George Graham Vest
Rubric and Evaluation Form: A Tribute

Exemplum
Sample Speech: Tenacity, by Bradley Christensen
Rubric and Evaluation Form: Exemplum Speech

Narrative Speech
Sample Speech: Lee Johnson's Revenge, by Michael Henderson
Evaluation Form: Narrative Speech

Presentation Aids Speech
Sample Outline (Explanatory Speech, cultural topic): The *Dun Dun* Drum, by Josh Valentine
Rubric and Evaluation Form: Presentation Aids Speech

Definition Speech
Sample Speech: Endurance, by Effie Mills
Rubric and Evaluation Form: Definition Speech

Audio Recorded Speech
Rubric and Evaluation Form: Recorded Speech

Thirty-Second Videotaped Speech
Sample Thirty-Second Speech: Tinnitis, by Patrick Barbo
Rubric and Evaluation Form: Thirty-Second Speech

Current Issue Speech
Rubric and Evaluation Form: Current Issue Speech

Persuasive Speech
Sample Outline (Persuasive Speech to Actuate): Organ Donation, by Danielle Schutz
Rubric and Evaluation Form: Persuasive Speech (General Form)
Rubric and Evaluation Form: Persuasive Speech (Monroe's Motivated Sequence)

Panel Discussion: A Current Controversial or Problematic Issue
Group Presentation: Movie Reality vs. Print Reality
Evaluation Form: Panel Discussion or Group Presentation

Below you'll find a list of criteria that speech instructors throughout the country routinely distribute. These guidelines will help you understand typical grading requirements.

Adapted from guidelines of the National Communication Association

CRITERIA FOR EVALUATING SPEECHES

The average speech (grade "C") should meet these criteria:

1. Conform to the kind of speech assigned (informative, persuasive, etc.)
2. Be original.
3. Be appropriate to the audience.
4. Meet time requirements (assigned date, time limits).
5. Fulfill the assignment's requirements such as use of a visual aid.
6. Have an identifiable introduction, body, and conclusion.
7. Have a clear central idea.
8. Be reasonably direct and competent in delivery (<u>extemporaneous</u>, NOT read).
9. Be free of errors in grammar, pronunciation, and word usage.
10. Use at least three sources (where required).

The above average speech (grade "B") should also:

1. Deal with a challenging topic, adapted to the audience.
2. Fulfill all the major requirements of introduction and conclusion.
3. Demonstrate research through use of at least 5 sources, clearly identified in the speech.
4. Create and sustain attention.
5. Exhibit proficient use of connectives such as transitions.
6. Be direct and competent in style and delivery.

The superior speech (grade "A") should also:

1. Genuinely contribute to the knowledge and beliefs of the audience.
2. Demonstrate greater research (7 sources).
3. Use vivid language, maintaining special interest.
4. Be delivered extemporaneously in a commendable manner.

The below average speech (grade "D" or "F") is seriously deficient in the criteria required for the "C" speech.

D = unrehearsed, biased, or unsupported opinions.
F = fabricated evidence, distorted evidence, plagiarized.

15

SELF-EVALUATION FORM

Name _____ Speech _____

Write B (before), D (during) or A (after) if you experienced any of these reactions as you presented your speech.

Physical Symptoms
_____ Heart pounding
_____ Constriction of throat
_____ Voice not normal? How? _____
_____ Trembling? Where? _____
_____ Feeling too warm, face flushed, blushing
_____ Dry mouth
_____ Increased perspiration
_____ "Butterflies" in the stomach
_____ Other _____

Physical Preparation
_____ Got a good night's sleep
_____ Limited my caffeine
_____ Consciously relaxed
_____ Ate sensibly

Mental Preparation
_____ Knew physical symptoms were normal
_____ Took preparation and rehearsal time
_____ Assumed my audience was positive
_____ Assured myself I would do OK
_____ Thought how interesting my topic was
_____ Focused on my personal strengths
_____ Kept the speech in perspective
_____ Visualized myself giving a great speech

- I noticed that my listeners . . . .

- Other speakers . . .

- My goals for this speech were . . .

- In this speech, my strengths and weaknesses were . . .

- My instructor can help me improve by . . .

16

SPEECH ASSIGNMENT: Telling a Modern Legend

Time: 1 1/2 to 3 minutes

Description: Introduce yourself by telling a legend that's been handed down from either your *family* or from a *significant group* to which you belong such as your sports team, living group, religious group, club, or place of work. The speech consists of two parts:

- **Part 1** is composed of the story itself, and will take most of the time of the speech.
- **Part 2** identifies the main lesson of the story in which you reveal some of your personal traits or the values you believe are important.

Skills
- Select a story that's appropriate to the assignment and time limitations.
- Identify the point of the story and link that point to yourself.
- Introduce and conclude the story in an interesting manner.
- Survive!!

Guidelines

1. Select an appropriate legend. Consider the complexity of the story. Can it be told within the short time period? Does your audience have enough background knowledge so the story will make sense to them? What does the story reveal about your personality?

2. List the events of the story in chronological order. Include relevant details the audience needs in order to understand your narrative. After your main events are in order, edit out irrelevant details that do not contribute to the point of the story.

3. Write out the point of the story and the characteristics it reveals about your family or group. Link those characteristics to yourself.

4. Plan an opening statement that draws the audience's attention to your topic. DO NOT say, "I'm gonna tell a story about my grandma." Here are a few suggestions:

   - Start your story with a specific time and place. "When my grandmother was 12 years old, she sailed to the United States alone."

   - Start with a short quotation that tells the moral of your story. "They say that only the good die young; one of my soccer team's heroes proves that saying."

5. Write key <u>words</u> on a note card so that you can jog your memory during your speech. Do not write out the speech word-for-word. Don't try to memorize the speech.

6. Rehearse the main ideas of the speech. Select the exact wording only as you speak. Your speech should sound just a little bit different each time.

SAMPLE SPEECH: A Modern Legend (self-introduction)

by Derek Reamy, Loyola University, Maryland

I'm from the South; and if you come from the South, or know anything about the South, you'll know how important good cooking is to a Southerner. Eating meals together is a tradition in my family. Every holiday of my childhood was spent over a meal at my grandparents' home, enjoy-ing my grandmother's cooking. Hand in hand with the meal was storytelling—my grandfather being the center of storytelling attention. He told stories about everything: The family murders, people in the neighborhood, his childhood, and even stories about food!

One story I remember in particular was one he told about some of his experiences as a child during the Great Depression. After our meal was finished, he'd push back his chair, look at me, and begin.

"Boy," he'd say, "let me tell you 'bout when I was comin' up. You think you got it hard now, but I say you all got it easy. When I was a boy—during the Depression—we didn't have none of this here fancy food. Just potatoes!

Baked potatoes,

      boiled potatoes,

            creamed potatoes,

                  mashed potatoes,

                      potato salad,

                          potato soup . . .

"Biscuits too, if we was lucky. Nothin' better than momma's warm biscuits with a bit of butter. Course, no one had butter then. But IF you did, you gave thanks. You gave thanks to the good Lord no matter what you had," he'd tell me.

"Give thanks," he commanded me throughout my life, and accompanying this advice was the example of his life lived in thanks. His thankfulness never stopped when the meal was finished and the food cleared away. Instead, he was grateful throughout all aspects of his life. My grandfather's life—and this story he tells—illustrates for me what it is to be thankful. Through his example, I have learned to be grateful for what I am given.

Telling a Modern Legend
Rubric

Remained within time limits (1 ½ to 3 minutes)   Yes _____   No _____
Used one note card only, no complete sentences   Yes _____   No _____
Memory – obviously well rehearsed   Yes _____   No _____

Criteria	Exemplary	Satisfactory	Inadequate	Points Possible	Score
Content/Topic Selection— Selected an appropriate legend (Story handed down by *family* or from a *significant group*).	Story can be told in a short amount of time; audience has enough background knowledge to make sense of story.	Audience has some background, but story cannot be told in a short amount of time and audience unable to fully make sense of story.	Story cannot be told in short amount of time; audience lacks background knowledge to make sense of story.	5	
Introduction— Planned an opening statement that draws the audience's attention to your topic.	Started story with a mention of specific time and place, or used a quotation that illustrated the moral of the story.	Had some plan to gain attention, but did not provide sufficient detail to fully capture audience's attention.	Did not plan an opening statement; used stock beginnings such as "I'm gonna tell a story about my grandma."	5	
Body— Content development.	Listed the events of the story in chronological order & included sufficient relevant details the audience needs in order to understand your narrative.	Listed some events of the story and included some detail, but did not fully or clearly develop enough for the audience to understand your narrative.	Did not list events of the story in chronological order or included insufficient relevant details or failed to edit out irrelevant details so audience could understand your narrative.	10	
Purpose	Clearly explained the point of the story, and the characteristics it reveals about your family or group, & link those to yourself.	Somewhat explained the point of the story, the characteristics it reveals, but failed to develop fully or link those to yourself.	Did not clearly explain the point of the story, or the characteristics it reveals about your family or group. Did not link those to yourself.	5	
Delivery				5	

Comments:

EVALUATION FORM: Telling a Modern Legend

Time: 1 1/2 to 3 minutes

Name _____ Time _____

Speech Content

_____ Story appropriate to the audience and assignment

_____ Interesting opening statement

_____ Understandable order of events

_____ Edited; all material relevant

_____ Point of story is clear

_____ Point is linked to speaker

Delivery

(Your instructor will describe your behaviors such as eye contact, posture and gestures, use of your voice.)

Memory

_____ Obviously well rehearsed

_____ Use of one note card only; no complete sentences   Grade _____

SPEECH ASSIGNMENT: Birth Date Speech

Time: 1 to 1 1/2 minutes

Description: In this brief self-introduction use something that happened on the day, week, or month of your birthday to reveal important information about yourself.

Skills
- Research in the periodicals section of the library or a reputable database.
- Identification of an important personal characteristic or value.
- Success in extemporaneous delivery

Guidelines
1. Go to the periodicals section of the library and find a newspaper or magazine published on your birthday, or birth week or month. Or find an archived periodical in an online database. For instance, find a *New York Times* published on the exact date of your birth. Or look at a *Rolling Stone* magazine published in your birth month. Browse until you find an interesting article, advertisement, sports feature, movie review, television guide, etc.

2. Use something from this article or feature to tell about one of your significant personal characteristics.

3. Prepare a short speech that identifies your birth date, describes the contents of the article or feature, and explains the personal characteristic that made this article or feature significant to you.

4. Write key words on note cards to use in your delivery.

    Point A: Key words from your introductory statement.

    Point B: Key words that describe your selected feature.

    Point C: Key words that describe your personal characteristic.

Examples:
Margo found an advertisement that featured a woman stating, "The way to a man's heart is through his stomach." She contrasted the slogan to her own views of gender relationships.

Micah was born on the day of the Challenger spacecraft disaster. He used this event to explain his interest in space exploration.

Other students have used sporting events, television programs, dance reviews, political news, merchandise prices, and so on to introduce themselves.

SAMPLE SPEECH: Birth Date (self-introduction)

Bob Pettit, Oregon State University

Bob skimmed a newspaper from the day he was born. Since no single article "leaped out" as significant, he combined elements of several to reveal some of the experiences that led him to return to college after many years.

I read the *Oregonian* from the day of my birth—November 28, 1952—and I was struck by how much the world has grown right along with me.

The news was unspectacular that day—a collage of things, many foreshadowing events yet to come—growing pains, if you will, of a world struggling to figure out how it's really done. How to live without war and racism. How to know and be ourselves. How to confront the dishonesty of governments to their people and of people to themselves.

The tantrum of war was evident. The Korean peace talks had bogged down. Ho Chi Min wanted a truce with France. Americans still gloated in self satisfaction at having won the "Big One." The Cold War was chilly indeed. McCarthyism was in full swing.

A front page headline told of a busload of "Negro" soldiers in South Carolina who were sentenced to jail and fined $1570, because one of them sat next to a white girl. This article was countered by another headline—the U. S. Attorney General's call for the end of racial segregation in the public schools.

Reading that paper also struck me by what was not there.

There was nothing about me. It would have been nice to have seen something, you know, nothing much really, maybe a little box in the corner of the front page, "Bob Pettit has arrived." But no, nothing was mentioned. Nothing that really gave a clue to my future nature—my likes and dislikes—the essence of me. There should have been something about rattlesnakes and sawmills, cab driving and rock and roll, about world travel, alcohol, Alcoholic Anonymous, but there was none of it, these growing pains yet to come, unforeseen.

And this reinforces my belief that in order to grow there must be a place from which to grow; that part of growing up is—well, growing up. And that we all have had the need to let out a whoop and a yell.

Birth Date Speech
Rubric

Remained within time limits (1 ½ to 3 minutes) Yes _____   No _____
Used one note card only, no complete sentences Yes _____   No _____
Memory – obviously well rehearsed   Yes _____   No _____

Criteria	Exemplary	Satisfactory	Inadequate	Points Possible	Score
Introduction — Planned an opening statement that draws the audience's attention to your topic.	Components are adequately addressed in the introduction.	Not all the components are adequately addressed in the introduction.	Components are inadequately addressed in the introduction.	5	
Research — Find a newspaper or magazine published on your birthday, birth week or birth month. Share this with the audience.	Fully discussed the newspaper or magazine article; cited it (gave its title), discussed its content (ideas, phrases, photographs, etc.)	Mentioned the newspaper or magazine article, but did not fully discuss its content.	Did not cite or reference the newspaper or magazine article; did not discuss its content.	10	
Purpose — Use something that happened on the day, week or month or your birthday to reveal important information about yourself.	Reveal one of your significant personal characteristics, drawn from the article. For example, your personal interests, or views on current issues.	Hinted at significant personal characteristics, but did not explicitly connect research and self.	Did not clearly state a purpose; failed to connect research to self.	10	
Delivery				5	

Comments:

EVALUATION FORM: Birth Date Speech

Time: 1 to 1 ½ minutes

Name _____Time _____

Speech Content

_____   Effective introductory statement

_____   Description of research item(s)

_____   Explanation of personal characteristic

Delivery

(Your instructor will describe your behaviors such as eye contact, posture and gestures, use of your voice.)

Memory

_____   Obviously well rehearsed

_____   Use of one note card only; no complete sentences

Grade _____

SPEECH ASSIGNMENT: Single Point Speech

Time: 2 to 3 minutes

Definition: In a single point speech, you present only one major idea and develop it with several pieces of supporting information.

Skills

- Ability to state a major idea
- Ability to state and explain reasons that support the idea
- Interesting introduction
- Memorable conclusion
- Selection of appropriate language
- Extemporaneous delivery

Guidelines

1. Select one major idea that you can support with several reasons. <u>Suggestions</u>: Vacations are important. Volunteering to coach in the Special Olympics enriched my life. There are three good reasons NOT to cohabitate before marriage.

2. Provide reasons to support your major idea. Use such materials as examples, facts, and statistics to explain your reasons for making that statement. You may have to do library research, interview a knowledgeable person, draw from your own experiences, or use electronically stored data as you gather your supporting materials.

3. Plan a brief introduction to orient your audience to your topic.

4. Think the speech through to a concluding statement.

5. Rehearse the speech. Don't memorize exact wording; instead, learn only the major ideas and the relationship between them. Put key words on note cards to use as you speak.

SAMPLE SPEECH: Come Watch Lacrosse

by Andres Lucero, St. John's University, New York

Introduction Have you ever sat and watched a long, boring baseball game? You all know the deal: ball . . . strike . . . ball. . . strike. . . ten minutes later, a pop up. Well, if you've endured such "entertainment," and agree that there might be more exciting things to do with your time, you should try watching a sport created by Native Americans—one that is fast and exciting, hard hitting, and very strategic. A sport like lacrosse. As you may know, I play lacrosse for the university.

[Single point] Today, I will explain why you should watch a lacrosse game.

First Reason Lacrosse is fast and exciting. In fact, it's called the fastest sport in the world, because the clock runs constantly and only stops for a few seconds when the ball goes out of bounds. Unlike baseball or football, players never have time to rest. For that reason, there are many substitutions during the game. Since there is always action on the field, there is never a boring moment. Watching lacrosse is similar to watching a long rally in a tennis match, yet the game itself is as hard hitting as football.

Second Reason Lacrosse is a very physical game. Since it's a contact sport, not surprisingly, there is lots of right contact. If I'm not careful, I can be seriously injured. I know this from experience. In my first month of college play, I had a painful introduction to Division I lacrosse. On too many occasions, I found myself lying flat on my back, with nothing but sky in view. I discovered that many lacrosse players set up a kill and look to just cream a guy. However, a player doesn't have to be roughed up. Some players—myself included—try to use strategy to outsmart the opponent.

Third Reason Good players and good teams do not just go out and run around the field, they plan what they will do; then they execute their plan. When you watch a game, you can see how the entire team works together to make goals. Most of the finesse teams, those who concentrate on strategy, win more often than those who look for ways to injure their opponents.

Conclusion You now have three good reasons to watch a lacrosse game—it is a fast, hard-hitting sport that requires much strategy to win. So the next time you find yourself sitting in front of the TV watching a ball . . . then a strike . . . then a ball. . . then ten minutes later, a pop up, get up and go experience a lacrosse game first hand!

Single Point Speech
Rubric

Remained within time limits (2 to 3 minutes)   Yes _____   No _____
Minimal use of note cards   Yes _____   No _____
Memory – obviously well rehearsed   Yes _____   No _____

Criteria	Exemplary	Satisfactory	Inadequate	Points Possible	Score
Introduction — Planned an opening statement that orients the audience to the topic & draws the audience's attention to your topic.	Components are adequately addressed in the introduction.	Not all the components are adequately addressed in the introduction.	Components are inadequately addressed in the introduction.	5	
Purpose — State the major idea of the speech.	Explicitly stated the major idea or purpose (I.e., "Today I will explain why you should watch a lacrosse game.")	Mentioned main idea but did not explicitly state the purpose.	Failed to clearly identify the major idea of the speech.	5	
Body — Content Development & organization. Offer reasons to support the major idea (3).	Supported the major idea with reasons and evidence (facts, examples, statistics). Cited sources.	Offered some support for the ideas, but did not fully develop support for all the reasons.	Failed to develop support for the ideas. Did not offer evidence (facts, examples, statistics) or cite sources.	10	
Conclusion — concluded memorably.	Clearly summarized the reasons offered.	Attempted a summary, but did not narrow down the focus.	Ended abruptly, failed to summarize the reasons.	5	
Delivery				5	

Comments:

EVALUATION FORM: Single Point Speech

Time: 2 to 3 minutes

Name _____Time _____

Speech Content

_____ Gains attention in introduction

_____ Single point clearly stated

_____ Reasons clearly stated

_____ Each reason explained

_____ Memorable concluding statement

_____ Appropriate language

Delivery

(Your instructor will describe your behaviors such as eye contact, posture and gestures, use of your voice.)

Memory

_____ Evidence of practice

_____ Minimal use of note cards   Grade _____

SPEECH ASSIGNMENT: A Tribute

Time: 2 to 3 minutes

Definition: A tribute is a special kind of ceremonial speech that praises the characteristics of people who exemplify important traits that make society better.

Skills
- Identify an important cultural belief, value, attitude, or behavior.
- Identify a person or who embodies that cultural resource.
- Prepare a speech that praises the chosen trait.
- Prepare an introduction and conclusion for your speech.

Guidelines
1. Choose a worthy subject, contemporary or historical, whose characteristics and values are worthy of admiration. Heroes—famous or lesser known—come from many fields such as medicine, education, politics, and religion.

2. Arrange your speech into an introduction, body, and conclusion as the following guidelines explain.

3. Introduce your subject by planning an interesting opening line. For example, instead of saying, "Today I am going to talk about Bill Gates who is an important American," one student stated the number of people employed at Microsoft, people who depend on Mr. Gates' creativity for their livelihood. Another began his tribute to the late dancer Martha Graham with a quotation from a *New York Times'* review, which praised the creativity and energy Ms. Graham brought to the world of dance. After your opening statement, provide enough information for the audience to understand who your subject is and why she or he deserves praise.

4. The body of your speech reveals worthy characteristics including some or all of these elements:
   - <u>Background</u>: parentage, hardships, or ethnic roots, and so on.
   - <u>Education</u>: educational background, whether positive or negative.
   - <u>Achievements:</u> character traits in three areas: personality (such as friendliness or curiosity), physical attributes (such as speed or endurance), and characteristics of the spirit (such as courage or perseverance). Use examples that demonstrate your points. Summarize the subject's lasting achievements or enduring legacy.

5. Conclude with impact. Think your speech through to the very end. End with a summary of the major values embodied in the life of your character, values that other people can emulate. Finish, as you began, with a memorable statement.

SAMPLE SPEECH: A Tribute to the Dog

George Graham Vest (1830-1904)

Tributes can focus on ideas such as "justice" or "liberty" as well as animals who exhibit valued traits. This speech praises a dog. The speaker, a lawyer in a small Missouri town, represented one man who sued another for killing his dog. This is Vest's summation speech to the jury. (As you might guess, his client won the case.) Vest went on to become United States senator from Missouri from 1879-1903.

This speech is more than 100 years old. As you read through it, notice the changes in language that have occurred in the century. For one thing, Vest uses "he" to mean people in general. In addition, compare the lawyer's formal style to the informality you'll find in some of the speeches in your text.

GENTLEMEN OF THE JURY: The best friend a man has in the world may turn against him and become his enemy. His son or daughter that he has reared with loving care may prove ungrate-ful. Those who are nearest and dearest to us, those whom we trust with our happiness and our good name may become traitors to their faith. The money that a man has, he may lose. It flies away from him, perhaps when he needs it most. A man's reputation may be sacrificed in a moment of ill-considered action. The people who are prone to fall on their knees to do us honor when success is with us, may be the first to throw the stone of malice when failure settles its cloud upon our heads.

The one absolutely unselfish friend that man can have in this selfish world, the one that never deserts him, the one that never proves ungrateful or treacherous is his dog. A man's dog stands by him in prosperity and in poverty, in health and in sickness. He will sleep on the cold ground, where the wintry winds blow and the snow drives fiercely, if only he may be near his master's side. He will kiss the hand that has no food to offer; he will lick the wounds and sores that come in encounter with the roughness of the world. He guards the sleep of his pauper master as if he were a prince. When all other friends desert, he remains. When riches take wings, and reputation falls to pieces, he is as constant in his love as the sun in its journey through the heavens.

If fortune drives the master forth an outcast in the world, friendless and homeless, the faithful dog asks no higher privilege than that of accompanying him, to guard him against danger, to fight against his enemies. And when the last scene of all comes, and death takes his master in its embrace and his body is laid away in the cold ground, no matter if all other friends pursue their way, there by the graveside will the noble dog be found, his head between his paws, his eyes sad, but open in alert watchfulness, faithful and true even in death.

Discussion Questions

- What characteristics of the dog does Vest praise? What would our society be like if more people behaved as Vest argues a dog behaves?

- Do you know of a person who would be a good speech subject because he or she embodies the characteristics that Vest praises here?

Tribute Speech
Rubric

Remained within time limits (2 to 3 minutes)   Yes _____   No _____
Minimal use of note cards   Yes _____   No _____
Memory – obviously well rehearsed   Yes _____   No _____

Criteria	Exemplary	Satisfactory	Inadequate	Points Possible	Score
Introduction — Planned an opening statement that draws the audience's attention to your topic.	Used a statistic or quotation to draw audience in to the topic.	Not all the components are adequately addressed in the introduction.	Did not plan an opening statement; used stock beginnings such as "Today I'm going to talk about Bill Gates, an important American."	6	
Purpose — Identifies an important cultural belief, value, attitude or behavior.	Explicitly states the cultural resource, the person embodies.	Suggests the cultural resource, but does not explicitly state it.	Fails to identify the cultural resource.	6	
Body, content development, organization. Identifies a person who embodies that cultural resource.	Provides sufficient information for audience to understand who the subject and why the subject is worthy of praise. Includes information on the background, education, and achievements of the subject.	Provides some information about the subject and why the subject is worthy of praise, but background, education and achievements could be more fully developed.	Does not provide sufficient information for audience to understand the subject and why the subject is worthy of praise.	18	
Conclusion — highlighted cultural values.	Summarized and connected to the purpose, cultural value.	Attempted to summarize but did not connect to the cultural value.	Did not offer a conclusion; failed to highlight the cultural value.	5	
Delivery — Vocal	Conversational & fluent.	Somewhat conversational & fluent.	Not conversational or fluent.	5	
Delivery — Physical	Posture & gestures appropriate	Somewhat effective posture & gestures.	Posture or gestures inappropriate or distracting.	5	
Delivery — Eye contact.	Direct eye contact.	Direct eye contact most of the time.	Lack of direct eye contact.	5	

Comments:

EVALUATION FORM: A Tribute

Time: 2 to 3 minutes

Name _____ Time _____

Speech Content

_____ Creative opening

_____ Subject introduced clearly

_____ Background information adequate

_____ Education described

_____ Achievements

        _____ of the spirit

        _____ of the body

        _____ of fortune

_____ Conclusion highlighting cultural values

Editing

_____ All points relevant?

_____ Unity of speech

Cultural Values

_____ Clearly identified

_____ Relevant to this audience

_____ Demonstrated in the tribute

Delivery

_____ Minimal use of note cards

_____ Direct eye contact

_____ Posture and gestures appropriate

_____ Conversational and fluent   Grade _____

SPEECH ASSIGNMENT: Exemplum

Time: 3 to 5 minutes

Description: The purpose of this assignment is to tell a story to explain a proverb that reveals important values of a culture. Humor may be your best strategy.

Skills
- Identify a cultural value.
- Use a story or example that illuminates that value.
- Begin with impact.
- Edit: use economy, unity, and definiteness of characterization
- End with impact.

Guidelines

1. Locate a quotation. Consult the reference section of your library and find a book such as *Bartlett's Familiar Quotations* that classifies quotations by major theme and by author. Another option is to search for quotations on the Internet on a site such as www.bartleby.com, which provides links to many sources for quotations, including *Bartlett's*.

2. Once you have found your quotation, develop it in four ways. Use page 265 in your text for further information.

    - Describe the author or source. For author information, consult a second reference book such as an encyclopedia, a dictionary of authors, or a *Who's Who* type of book. If your source is anonymous, state that fact. However, consider adding an explanation of why you think the quotation was important enough for people to repeat so often that it has become a cultural proverb.

    - Paraphrase the quotation in your own words. Put simply, translate it into everyday English.

    - Illustrate the major point of the quotation with a narrative drawn from your personal experiences, a historical text, an inspirational book, and the like.

    - Apply the point of the quotation and the story to the audience.

SAMPLE SPEECH: Tenacity

Adapted from a speech by Bradley Christensen, George Fox University
February 2003

Quotation: "Nothing in this world can take the place of persistence. Talent will not; nothing is more common than unsuccessful people with talent. Genius will not; unrewarded genius is almost a proverb. Education will not; the world is full of educated derelicts. Persistence and determination alone are omnipotent. The slogan 'press on' has solved and will always solve the problems of the human race."

Source: Calvin Coolidge, the 30th President of the United States (1923-1929) was born July 4, 1872, in Plymouth, Vermont. The son of a village storekeeper, he graduated from Amherst College with honors, entered law and politics in Northampton, Massachusetts, and slowly but determinedly climbed the political ladder from town councilman to Governor of Massachusetts. Warren Harding chose him to be vice-president; and when Harding died in office, Coolidge became president.

Paraphrase: The most valuable attribute is persistence. A tenacious attitude takes one farther than talent, genius, or education. I agree that tenacity is vital to a person in a difficult situation or to someone who is pursuing a goal. However, Coolidge also believed that those who "press on" will solve the problems of the human race. Tenacity is not necessarily the solution to the world's problems. In fact, a persistent despot can go far with little talent or moral fiber.

Narrative: I realized the importance of tenacity when I was assigned to military duty at the Prince Sultan Air Base in the Kingdom of Saudi Arabia. First came the notification of deployment. In preparation for departure I had an anthrax shot. The actual trip was long, with stops in the United States, Germany, and finally the air base.

Our first day of work lasted 18 hours; we endured 70-hour work weeks in sandstorms and 120 degree heat. Needless to say, we daily returned to the compound exhausted. My first roommate (who will remain nameless) went crazy after two days and was sent back to the states. My only relief was with three co-workers: Boyd from Kansas, Mullins from Missouri, and Nordhoff from Illinois. Our managers worked us hard! And we took ice cream trips to the Coalition Compound stand when one of us got paperwork sending us out of the situation.

This went on for three months. One day, word arrived that I could leave — on my 20th birthday. The long ride home seemed somehow shorter, and a two week island vacation was my reward. A second reward was development of my character: this experience was life changing and showed me I could get through a very unpleasant situation by "pressing on."

Application: Now, most of you won't go to Saudi Arabia. However, tenacity or perseverance is important in all situations — even when there's no promise of reward. At the very least, hard times improve character.

Exemplum Speech
Rubric

Remained within time limits (3 to 5 minutes)	Yes _____	No _____
Minimal use of note cards	Yes _____	No _____
Memory – obviously well rehearsed	Yes _____	No _____

Criteria	Exemplary	Satisfactory	Inadequate	Points Possible	Score
Purpose — Locate a quotation/proverb that reveals important cultural values.	Explicitly stated.	Mentioned main idea but did not explicitly state the quotation.	Failed to clearly identify the quotation.	5	
Body — Content Development & organization. Describe the author or source.	Provides sufficient information for the audience.	Provides some information but is not fully developed.	.Fails to provide information about the author or source.	5	
Paraphrase the quotation in your own words.	Clear paraphrase in own words.	Attempts a paraphrase but unclear, doesn't quite catch the meaning.	Fails to paraphrase the quotation.	5	
Illustrate the major point of the quotation with a narrative.	Narrative is clear, and clearly connects to the quotation.	Narrative somewhat clear, connection to the quotation could be stronger.	Fails to illustrate the quotation with a narrative.	5	
Apply the point of the quotation to the audience.	Explicitly states the cultural value, and connects it to the audience.	References the cultural value but does make it relevant to this audience.	Fails to identify the cultural resource.	5	
Delivery	Posture and gestures appropriate; conversational; direct eye contact.	Postures and gestures mostly appropriate; delivery mostly conversation; direct eye contact most of the time.	Posture and gestures inappropriate or distracting; delivery lacks fluency; lack of direct eye contact.	5	

Comments:

EVALUATION FORM: Exemplum Speech

Time: 3 to 5 minutes

Name _____Time_____

Exemplum Pattern

_____ Quotation clearly stated

_____ Source identified and described adequately

_____ Quotation paraphrased

_____ Narrative that illustrate it

_____ Application to the audience

Cultural Value

_____ Clearly identified

_____ Relevant to this audience

_____ Demonstrated in the narrative

Editing

_____ All points relevant?

_____ Characters clearly defined

_____ Unity of speech

Language

_____ Constructed dialogue (if appropriate)

_____ Effective placement of details

Delivery

_____ Minimal use of note cards

_____ Direct eye contact

_____ Posture and gestures appropriate

_____ Conversational

_____ Fluency of thought   Grade _____

SPEECH ASSIGNMENT: Narrative Speech

Time: 3 to 5 minutes

Description: The purpose of this assignment is to tell a story with a significant core theme regarding a cultural belief, value, attitude, or action. A humorous story may present your point effectively.

Skills
- Identify an important cultural belief, value, attitude, action.
- Use a story or example to illustrate your core idea.
- Begin with impact.
- Choose a pattern that effectively organizes the main points.
- Edit to achieve economy, unity, definiteness of characterization.
- End with impact.

Guidelines
1. Choose a narrative function—that is, decide if you want to explain a belief, provide an example, persuade your audience, or offer possibilities (see Chapter 15) that are as yet unrealized. Remember that reinforcing a value is a form of persuasion.

2. Identify your characters. What personality characteristics do they have? How do they look? speak? act?

3. Sketch out your plot—what happens in the story? What crisis or crises do the characters face?

4. Identify the theme or major idea your story conveys.

5. Select an organizational pattern that meets your needs. Choose from the spiral pattern (Chapter 9) or the exemplum pattern (Chapter 15). In some speeches, the chronological pattern (Chapter 9) may be most appropriate.

6. Polish the language in your speech. Select vivid, descriptive words. Include enough details at the beginning of your speech to set your narrative in place and time. Make sure your points of conflict are described in vivid detail. Use lists and constructed dialogue between characters where appropriate.

SAMPLE SPEECH: Lee Johnson's Revenge

Michael Henderson, KBOO radio, Portland, Oregon.

It might, like many another racial incident, have left the community and the victim embittered.

J. Lee Johnson, 34, a black entrepreneur in Lawrence, New Jersey, arrived at his computer company to find racial slurs painted on the walls and a dead bird lying on the doorstep. He had just opened a new company in the neighborhood.

The graffiti contained references to the KKK, a drawing of a painted cross and a slur that read, "No Nigir," As the local paper wrote, "The green spray-painted words were crude and one was even misspelled, but their meaning was clear: blacks are not welcome."

Johnson, whose parents were raised in the South and who knew first hand the racism they had undergone, did not feel welcome. "At first I didn't know what to do," he says. "This was like a cold slap in the face. It knocked a little bit of the wind out of my sails."

But Johnson is tough. His parents had also brought him up never to hate anyone because of their race or religion. "Most people thought I would be in a retaliatory mood," he told me. "But we can't afford to let these things rip our communities."

Local residents and business people rallied round, telling him what had happened was deplorable and didn't reflect the feeling in the neighborhood. "They told me to hang in there." The mayor came by, expressing her horror and the commitment of the community that such actions would not be tolerated. Churches and other community groups, aware that racial incidents although uncommon were not unknown in the area, set up support networks. Johnson's mailbag was "stuffed" with letters from caring people.

Five days after the incident the police had charged the vandal—a ten-year-old boy. "I was floored," Johnson told a racist sensitivity training session at the local Episcopal church. "You really can't say it's the parents' fault. Kids are exposed to hatred and violence on television every day. It's what we are as a community. It's coming out in small children, and it's got to stop."

He decided to reach out to the young man as others had done to him earlier in life, believing that America cannot afford to lose a generation to hatred and bias.

The white youngster had never met a black man. Johnson gave him a tour of his business, meeting blacks, whites, Hispanics, working there. He introduced him to the inside of computers. They sat and talked on the very spot where the boy had left the dead bird.

Today, Johnson says, the boy is doing better at home and school. "He has found a place to channel energies which had gone astray. I like to visualize ten years down the road, what would be his mindset if we don't reach out and show him the beauty of differences in people."

The blotches of paint on the wall that cover over the graffiti still remain. Johnson can't yet afford to paint the building. They are a constant reminder of the past. But the friendship he has built with a young boy who knew no better is a stake in a different future and part of the cure to what he calls the threatening disease of prejudice. A community is the richer for his action.

38

Narrative Speech
Rubric

Remained within time limits (3 to 5 minutes)	Yes _____	No _____
Minimal use of note cards	Yes _____	No _____
Memory – obviously well rehearsed	Yes _____	No _____

Criteria	Exemplary	Satisfactory	Inadequate	Points Possible	Score
Purpose — Tell a story whose theme reveals a cultural belief, value, attitude or action.	Selected a story worth telling. Story's purpose explicitly stated.	Story could be worthwhile. Mentioned main idea but did not explicitly state the value.	Story was inappropriate or did not fulfill the assignment. Failed to clearly identify cultural resource.	5	
Body — Content Development & organization. Character/s.	Fully developed the character's personality and mannerisms.	Somewhat developed the character's personality and mannerisms.	Failed to develop the character's personality or mannerisms.	5	
Plot	Understood and communicated the action.	Somewhat understood and communicated the action.	Failed to understand or communicate the action.	5	
Organizational pattern — Spiral, exemplum, or chronological.	Clear and effective.	Somewhat clear and effective.	Unclear or ineffective.	5	
Language	Effective, sufficient details, constructed dialogue.	Somewhat effective, details or dialogue could be clearer.	Unclear or ineffective.	5	
Delivery	Posture and gestures appropriate; conversational; direct eye contact.	Postures and gestures mostly appropriate; delivery mostly conversation; direct eye contact most of the time.	Posture and gestures inappropriate or distracting; delivery lacks fluency; lack of direct eye contact.	5	

Comments:

EVALUATION FORM: Narrative Speech

Time: 3 to 5 minutes

Name _____Time_____

Invention

_____ Purpose is clear

_____ Story characters clearly defined

_____ Plot developed—climax, change in characters

_____ Adequate development throughout

_____ Narrative merit (story is worth telling)

Cultural Significance

_____ Point of story reveals significant cultural value, attitude, behavior or belief

_____ Relevant to this audience

_____ Demonstrated in the narrative

Disposition

_____ Effective conclusion

_____ Organizational pattern clear

_____ Effective introduction

_____ Parts of speech effectively connected

Language

_____ Constructed dialogue (if appropriate)

_____ Effective placement of details

_____ Listing (where appropriate)

Delivery

_____ Minimal use of note cards

_____ Direct eye contact

_____ Posture and gestures appropriate

_____ Conversational

_____ Fluency of thought   Grade _____

SPEECH ASSIGNMENT: Presentation Aids Speech

Time: 5 to 6 minutes

Description: This informative speech requires skillful use of presentation aids that support, rather than substitute for, the main ideas of the speech. Choose support such as objects, charts, video clips, graphs, or drawings. Your instructor may require you to create slides using presentation software such as PowerPoint.

Skills
* Fully developed introduction and conclusion
* Clearly stated main points
* Support for each main point
* Use of signposts
* Use of at least two research sources
* Skillful use of audio or visual aids

Informative Options

Process or Demonstration A speech clarifying a process by which something is done, is created, or occurs. You may actually demonstrate the process. (See text pages 276-278.) Topics should add to the knowledge of a college-level audience.

    <u>Examples:</u> how the lottery system works; stages of grief; how to analyze handwriting; the progress of a disease; how to do calligraphy; the process of learning in senior adults.

Report about a Person A speech giving the main life events and accomplishments of a famous individual who has made significant contributions to society. (See text pages 280-281.)

    <u>Examples:</u> subjects who contributed positively—or negatively—to society; Supreme Court justices, politicians, artists, entertainers, military officers, and so on make good subjects. Consider a subject from another culture or another time.

Explanation or **Description** A speech that explains a complex idea or describes a place, event, or object—how it is made, how it works, its significance, and so on. (Text pages 281-285 give more detail.)

    <u>Examples:</u> lucid dreaming, noninvasive medications, a wedding in another culture, a Romanian orphanage, an ostrich.

SAMPLE OUTLINE: Presentation Aids Speech (Explanatory, cultural topic)

Josh Valentine, George Fox University

Topic:	The *Dun Dun* Drum
General Purpose:	To inform
Specific Purpose:	To inform my audience about the *dun dun* (which most will not have heard of), and to describe how and why it is used.
Central Idea:	The *dun dun* is an African drum with an interesting history that is used both musically and linguistically.

Introduction

I. Imagine that your friend asks you what you did over the weekend, but instead of using words, your friend beats a drum.

II. You will probably never have such an encounter, but in some cultures, music is used for purposes that are different from those we are accustomed to.

    A. *Webster's Dictionary* defines language as "any system of symbols, sounds, or gestures used for communication."

    B. Our culture does not have instrumental sounds that represent English words, but in other cultures around the world, sounds have meaning.

III. I have been playing percussion since junior high, and I first learned about the *dun dun* (pronounced doon doon) drum while attending a percussion workshop two years ago.

IV. Today, I will explain the history of the *dun dun* as well as its linguistic use and its musical use.

Body

I. The Nigerian talking drum actually talks in the Yoruba language.
[Display photograph of *dun dun* drum, downloaded and used with permission from http://media.dickinson.edu/gallery/Sect5.html]

    A. This drum originated during the Oyo Empire of Yoruba-land in the fifteenth century AD for the purpose of worship.

    B. Drums are constructed from trees located near roads where many people pass, which allows the tree to hear human speech (DeSilva).

    C. The Yoruba language is easily communicated on the *dun dun*.

        1. Yoruba is a tonal language.

        2. Yoruba speakers use three basic pitches or tones, connected by glides, as an essential element of pronunciation (How bata drums talk . . .).

            a. Listen to this sound clip and try to identify the three main tones.
[Play a sound clip downloaded for one-time use from the Internet.]

            b. If you have a sharp ear, you may also be able to pick out some slides essential to the Yoruba language.

        3. Melody is the basis for the Yoruba language since the same word pronounced with a different melody means something different.

    D. The *dun dun* functions by changing the tension of two skin heads using the leather straps that hold the heads in place.
[Point out the straps on the PowerPoint slide]

II. The *dun dun* was originally created to communicate.

    A. The Yoruba from southwestern Nigeria have used drums for spiritual communication throughout their history.
[Show carved drum downloaded from www.hamillgallery.com . . . YorubaDrum01.html]

        1. The *dun dun* was originally created as a tool for worship of the gods.

        2. Songs and hymns of praise were created entirely on *dun dun* drums and are still recited today.

        3. Listen to the intensity of this spiritual worship song played on talking drums.

[Play example, downloaded for one-time use from the Internet from www.world-beats.com/instruments/dundun.htm]

B. The Yoruba also use drums for social communication.

   1. The *dun dun* has been a part of day-to-day casual conversation.

      a. "A master drummer can maintain a regular monologue on a talking drum, saying 'hi' to different people, cracking jokes, and telling stories" (Plunkett).

      b. *Dun dun* drummers often speak the names of friends and family on their drums as a greeting and sign of respect.

      c. The *dun dun*'s secondary, yet most obvious, use is as a musical instrument.

   2. It became a musical instrument because of its use in worship.

      a. At first it was used mainly to communicate ideas, but since worship in the Yoruba culture is a corporate activity, people began coming together and music on the *dun dun* was born.

      b. Religious songs are still recited today, although often only for their musical value.

   3. Even everyday speech becomes song when the Yoruba use the *dun dun*.

      a. The word *kabo*, which means welcome, is only a two-syllable word, so a more common phrase "spoken" on a *dun dun* is, "Welcome, we are happy that you arrived safely" (Drum Talk, Ltd.).

      b. "Speech" on the *dun dun* is always made rhythmic, even when the spoken word would not be rhythmic.

   4. The *dun dun*'s use as a musical instrument has spread far beyond Nigeria.

      a. After the *djembe*, the *dun dun* is the most well-known and recognizable African drum used in America.

      b. "[It] fares well in jazz blues, R&B, rock and roll, reggae, classical music, even choral music" (Awe).

      c. This clip comes from a song by African American musician Francis Awe.

      [Play sample clip downloaded from the Internet from www.nitade.com/html/ cd1.html]

Conclusion

I. Whether in language or in song, the *dun* dun's sound is always unusually beautiful.

II. Today, we have seen the origins of the Nigerian talking drum (*dun dun*), its uses as a linguistic tool, and its uses as a musical instrument.

III. So next time you hear music as simple as a beating drum, you might remember that the drummer may be communicating much more than you think.

References

Awe, Francis. (1999). Talking drum drum clinic by Francis Awe. Retrieved March 20, 2002, from www.after-science.com/awe/clinic.html

BataDrum.com. (2002). How Bata drums talk and what they say. In Understanding the purpose and meaning behind the rhythms. Retrieved March 21, 2002, from www.batadrums.com/understanding_rhythms/talk.htm

DeSilva, Tamara. (1997). Lying at the crossroads of everything: Towards a social history of the African drum. Research, writing, and culture: The best undergraduate thesis essays, 1998–2000 (2). Retrieved March-20, 2002, from www.artic.edu/saic/programs/depts/undergrad/Best_Thesis_Essay.pdf

Drum Talk Ltd. (2000). Background information. Retrieved March 20, 2002, from www.drumtalk.co.uk/drum_background.html

Plunkett, A. (2002). Nigeria (Africa) Dun dun. World Beats. Retrieved March 21, 2002, from www.world-beats.com/instruments/dundun.htm

Presentation Aids Speech
Rubric

Remained within time limits (5 to 6 minutes)	Yes _____	No _____
Minimal use of note cards	Yes _____	No _____
Memory – obviously well rehearsed	Yes _____	No _____
Appropriate visual aids	Yes _____	No _____
Skillful use of visual aids	Yes _____	No _____

Criteria	Exemplary	Satisfactory	Inadequate	Points Possible	Score
Topic — appropriate to the assignment.	Speech about a process, person, evaluation or description.	Topic somewhat appropriate to the assignment.	Topic did not fit the assignment.	5	
Purpose —	Clearly informative.	Somewhat informative.	Purpose did not fit the assignment.	5	
Introduction — Gained attention, related to audience, established credibility, previewed the body.	Components are adequately addressed in the introduction.	Not all the components are adequately addressed in the introduction.	Components are inadequately addressed in the introduction.	15	
Body — Organization clear.	Organizational pattern used effectively.	Somewhat organized but could be improved.	Organizational pattern missing or not used effectively.	20	
Body — content development. Main point supported with evidence.	Main points fully developed and supported with evidence. Cited sources explicitly.	Main points developed and somewhat supported with evidence.	Failed to fully develop main points or support them with evidence. Did not cite sources.	20	
Conclusion	Summarized and ended with impact.	Somewhat of a summary and impact, but could be improved.	Failed to summarize or end with impact.	10	
Delivery	Spoke at appropriate volume, rate, with sufficient variety; appropriate posture and gestures; fitting appearance, eye contact.	Somewhat appropriate volume, rate, and somewhat appropriate variety; posture, gestures appearance or eye contact could be improved.	Failed to speak at appropriate volume, rate, with sufficient variety, inappropriate posture or gestures; unfitting appearance, lack of eye contact.	25	

Comments:

EVALUATION FORM: Presentation Aids Speech

Time: 5 to 6 minute   Name _____Time_____

Disposition

_____ Attention gained

_____ Related to audience

_____ Credibility established

_____ Previewed

_____ Organization clear

_____ Main points clear

_____ Signaled conclusion

_____ Tied to introduction

_____ Summarized

_____ Ended with impact

Invention

_____ Topic of significance (need)

_____ Informative purpose

_____ Audience related

_____ Speaker credibility demonstrated throughout

_____ Adequate supporting material

_____ Evidence of research

_____ All details relevant

_____ VISUAL AID

Style

_____ Precision of language

_____ Jargon defined

Delivery

_____ Voice: rate, volume, variety, quality

_____ Posture and gestures

_____ Other: appearance & eye contact

Memory

_____ Minimal use of note cards

_____ Fluency of thought   Grade _____

SPEECH ASSIGNMENT: Definition Speech

Time: 2 to 3 minutes

Description: Words are linguistic symbols that allow humans to communicate. Words as symbols have meaning only because a group of people agrees that the symbols represent an object, thought, or feeling. Often we hear the phrase, "Meanings are in people, not in words." Even within the same cultural context, you'll find many variations in the meaning of a single word.

You may choose to define a word or term from another language or a term with no exact equivalent or translation directly into U. S. English.

Skills
- Define an abstract term so that it's meaning and your interpretation of that meaning become clear to your audience.
- Clearly define the term in a well-organized manner based on careful and thoughtful analysis.

Guidelines
1. <u>Main Point I:</u> Focus on the denotation of the term found in various reference books such as a thesaurus or etymological dictionary.

    - One of your references must be the *Oxford English Dictionary* or any unabridged dictionary.

    - You must select two of the following methods of defining a term.

        ➢ Synonym and antonym
        ➢ Use and function
        ➢ Etymology and historical example
        ➢ Comparisons

2. <u>Main Point II:</u> Focus on the connotation of the term according to your own life experience. Be as creative as you wish in clarifying the term.

    - Option: explain what the term means to you based on a personal experience.

    - Option: quote other people as to what the term means to them.

    - Additional options:

        ➢ Telling a story.
        ➢ Giving examples.
        ➢ Referring to a person who exemplifies the term.
        ➢ Relating the term to a political, social, or moral issue.
        ➢ Anything else you can think of that may give your audience greater insight into the meaning of the word.

Beth Von Till and associates at San Jose State University.

SAMPLE SPEECH: ENDURANCE

Effie Mills, George Fox University

When you think of the word ENDURANCE, the image of a marathon runner enduring a 26-mile course is probably what comes to mind. But *Webster's Dictionary* defines it as "a bearing or suffering; a continuing under pain or distress without resistance or without sinking or yielding to pressure; sufferance; patience." The *Encarta Dictionary* says the word endurance came from the 14th century French word *endurer* which in turn came from the Latin root word *durus* which means hard.

In order to explain what the word *endurance* means to me I need to describe a surgery I recently went through because of TMJ. TMJ is a very painful condition in which the jaw joint deteriorates and can't work properly. I had to have bite plane and braces before I could under go the surgery, which gave me time to come to grips with the surgery process. My oral surgeon explained how they would reconstruct my joints and then cut and extend my lower jaw to prevent future problems. I would also be having my wisdom teeth removed during the same process. After surgery, my jaw would be wired shut for two months while things healed.

Unfortunately, my head knowledge did not prepare me for the reality of the experience. What should have been a four-to-five hour surgery became nine. Waking up from anesthesia was terrifying. I could hear people talking to me telling me to do different things, but I was unable to open my eyes or respond in any way. I had black-outs and nausea even after I came home. The eight weeks on baby food, soup broth, and milkshakes quickly went from "doable" to "an eternity." I changed from sleeping on my side to sleeping in a recliner at a 45-degree angle.

Some of this ordeal took place over the summer, but two weeks overlapped with the beginning of my senior year in high school. During that time I sipped liquids or squirted baby food into my mouth with a syringe.

Even after my jaw was unwired, there were experiences I wasn't prepared for. As the wires came off, I felt like my jaw would fall apart. I wasn't allowed to chew for a year, which meant everything I ate went through the food processor first. Imagine what that meant for parties, school lunches, and Thanksgiving and Christmas dinners. When I was finally able to chew again, I had to relearn the process. I had to start slow with only softer foods and even had to consciously make myself chew or I'd forget and just swallow.

There were definitely times that I wanted to give up. But, logically, that was impossible. So I made the best of the situation—trying to keep a positive attitude. This was not something I could control, so why fight it?

There were benefits to this process. My constant jaw pain is gone; my faith increased; I learned that I can't control everything. I also grew a lot as a person and discovered important lessons. Once my friends saw me wired shut and swollen up like a chipmunk, I was no longer too concerned about my image!

As a result of this experience, my definition of ENDURANCE is not letting the inevitable beat you; instead, rise above it for the better.

Definition Speech
Rubric

Remained within time limits (2 to 3 minutes)	Yes _____	No _____	
Minimal use of note cards	Yes _____	No _____	
Memory – obviously well rehearsed	Yes _____	No _____	

Criteria	Exemplary	Satisfactory	Inadequate	Points Possible	Score
Purpose — Define an abstract word or term so that its meaning becomes clear for your audience	Clearly fulfilled the purpose.	Attempted to fulfill the purpose but missing some elements.	Failed to fulfill the purpose.	5	
Introduction	Strong opening statement.	Somewhat strong opening.	Weak or insufficient opening.	5	
Define the term Using 2 — from OED or unabridged dictionary, synonym, & antonym; use and function; etymology & historical example; comparison.	Clearly defined denotative meaning using at least 2 required methods:	Denotative meaning could be clearer.	Failed to use at least two methods.	10	
Connotative meaning — Choose at least one: own experience, tell a story, give examples; refer to person who exemplifies; relate to social, political or moral issue; other.	Related the term to self. Clearly described the connotative meaning.	Related term to self somewhat. Connotative meaning could be clearer.	Failed to describe connotative meaning or relate term to self.	10	
Delivery — Eye contact, gestures, extemporaneous.	Components are adequately addressed in the speech	Components are somewhat addressed in the speech.	Components are not addressed in the speech.	5	

Comments:

48

EVALUATION FORM: Definition Speech

Time: 2 to 3 minutes

Name _____

Word Selected _____

Invention and Disposition

_____ Strong opening statement

_____ Denotative definition

　　　　_____ Dictionary definition

　　　　_____ 1st method of definition

　　　　_____ 2nd method of definition

_____ Connotative definition

　　　　_____ Term related to speaker

　　　　_____ Interpretation clearly illustrated

_____ Memorable ending

Style

_____ Language appropriate

_____ Concise

_____ Interesting language

Delivery

_____ Eye contact

_____ Gestures

_____ Extemporaneous delivery

Memory

_____ Evidence of rehearsal

_____ Minimal use of note cards　　　　　　　Grade _____

SPEECH ASSIGNMENT: Audio Recorded Speech

Time: 1, 2, or 3 minutes

Description: You will record a speech. Because recorded speeches such as radio commentaries often require exact time limits, your instructor may ask you to time the speech at exactly 1, 2, or 3 minutes in length.

Skills
- Effective use of vocal variety.
- Manuscript delivery, read in a conversational manner.
- (opt.) Exact timing

Guidelines
1. Choose an assignment from the text, Appendix B. An announcement, tribute, speech of definition, exemplum, farewell, or introduction work well.

2. Organize your speech carefully according to guidelines given in the text. Pay special attention to connectives.

3. (Opt.) Edit your material so that it is exactly one *or* two *or* three minutes in length.

4. Write out your speech using capital letters and triple spacing.

5. Because you must convey shades of meaning through vocal variation alone, pay special attention to pauses, accents, rate, and volume to enhance your message. Then mark your script accordingly.

   - Circle or use a colored highlighter on words you plan to stress.
   - Put // (slash) marks where you intend to pause.
   - Put a   where you want your tone to rise and an Ø where you want it to fall.

6. Practice reading your script until you are satisfied that your delivery sounds conversational. Speak as if you were conversing with only one person. Mentally visualize a typical listener and then speak directly to that individual.

7. Record your speech. Replay the recording, listening carefully to your voice. If you don't like what you hear, simply re-record the speech until you are satisfied.

8. Bring the final version of your recording to class.

Recorded Speech
Rubric

Remained within time limits (1 or 2 or 3 minutes)   Yes _____   No _____
Manuscript delivery   Yes _____   No _____

Criteria	Exemplary	Satisfactory	Inadequate	Points Possible	Score
Purpose	Clearly of the speech is clear.	Purpose is somewhat clear.	Failed to identify the purpose.	5	
Introduction	Components are adequately addressed in the introduction.	Components are not completely addressed.	Components are inadequately addressed.	5	
Body — Organization and content development.	Clear organizational pattern, transitions, previews and summaries.	Organizational pattern, transitions and previews are not completely addressed.	Organizational pattern, transitions and previews are incomplete or inadequate.	10	
Delivery	Conversational; well rehearsed.	Somewhat conversational.	Not conversation, not rehearsed.	10	

Comments:

EVALUATION FORM: Audio Taped Speech

Time: 1, 2, or 3 minutes

Name _____Time_____

Invention

_____ Appropriate topic

_____ Purpose clear

_____ Main ideas clear

_____ Main ideas supported

Disposition

_____ Organizational pattern clear

_____ Transitions, internal previews, and summaries

_____ Effective introduction

_____ Strong conclusion

Style

_____ Language appropriate, clear

_____ Interesting language

Delivery

_____ Appropriate rate

_____ Volume

_____ Vocal variety

_____ Effective use of pauses

_____ Conversational delivery

Grade _____

SPEECH ASSIGNMENT: Thirty-Second Video Recorded Speech

Description: Prepare and video record a thirty-second speech. You can find this type of speech on some local news broadcasts that allow citizens to voice their opinions in short speeches.

Skills
- Choose an appropriate speech purpose—to convince, reinforce, inform, or actuate your audience.
- Deliver a speech effectively using cue cards or a TelePrompTer.
- Use nonverbal skills to deliver your speech effectively on camera.
- Edit your material to fit precisely into a time frame.

Guidelines

1. Choose a single idea that you can convey in a short period of time.

    - Examples of TV editorials: A woman who had adopted racially mixed children told the audience that she is happy to discuss adoption, but urged them not to ask, "Where did you get your children?" in the child's presence. A man urged people not to purchase a book by a convicted criminal. He argued that people shouldn't profit from their crimes.

    - Examples of student topics: One announced a community clean up day and urged the audience to participate in it. Another reinforced the cultural value of reaching out to others by urging listeners to donate to the food bank. A third student rhymed his speech urging the audience to put on shorts and enjoy the last few days of autumn.

2. Organize your ideas. The single point speech (Part I of this manual), a simplified Monroe's Motivated Sequence (pages 328-329 in the text) and one of the speeches in Appendix B would be appropriate.

3. Edit your speech to exactly thirty seconds. Transfer your script to a teleprompter, if one is available. If not, use large cue cards that you read as someone holds them near the camera.

4. Videotape your speech, using the cue cards or a teleprompter.

5. After you view all the speeches in the class, discuss the following questions:

    - What was the easiest part of this assignment? What was most difficult?

    - What topics did you consider and discard as possibilities? Why?

    - What can be "covered" in 30 seconds? What cannot?

SAMPLE THIRTY-SECOND SPEECH: Tinnitis

Patrick Barbo modified his longer speech on tinnitis for this short speech.

YOU ONLY HAVE TWO HANDS, AND I BET YOU DON'T TAKE A HAMMER AND SLAM THOSE HANDS EVERYDAY THEN EXPECT THEM TO WORK PROPERLY.

SIMILARLY, YOU ONLY HAVE TWO EARS. YET MOST PEOPLE SLAM THEM EVERYDAY WITH LOUD NOISE WITHOUT EVEN THINKING TWICE ABOUT POSSIBLE PERMANENT DAMAGE BEING DONE.

TURNING DOWN THE VOLUME ON YOUR MUSIC CAN REDUCE SOME DAMAGE TO YOUR HEARING.

IMAGINE YOURSELF AS AN OLDER PERSON WITH PERMANENT WHISTLING IN YOUR EARS AND THEN IMAGINE YOURSELF WITHOUT HEARING PROBLEMS.

YOU CHOOSE. IT'S UP TO YOU TO KEEP THE VOLUME DOWN NOW TO AVOID PROBLEMS LATER.

EVALUATION FORM: Thirty-Second Speech

Name _____ Time _____

Invention and Disposition

_____ Topic appropriate to the time limit

_____ Purpose clear

_____ Major idea clear

_____ Supporting material to the point

_____ Organized well

_____ Edited well

Style

_____ Language appropriate, clear

_____ Interesting language

Delivery

_____ Timing

_____ Pleasant facial expressions

_____ Appropriate gestures

_____ Camera-appropriate clothing

_____ Camera-appropriate grooming

_____ Vocal variety

_____ Appropriate speaking rate

_____ Volume

_____ Conversational-sounding delivery   Grade _____

SPEECH ASSIGNMENT: Current Issue Speech

Time: 6 to 7 minutes

Definition: Think of this speech as an investigative news report. Select a <u>current</u> problem or controversial topic and present it as objectively as you can. Visual aids may accompany this speech in a supporting role.

Consult at least three sources for this speech—one from within the last six months. (An "A" speech should have seven sources.) Be prepared to discuss any source you cite or list on your bibliography.

Skills
- Informative purpose
- <u>Invention</u>: examples, statistics, testimony, audience analysis, speaker credibility, cited sources from library research
- <u>Disposition</u>: use of transition statements, internal preview/internal summary. All organiza-tional skills from the audio-visual speech.
- <u>Style</u>: language that is accurate, appropriate, clear, and interesting
- <u>Delivery</u>: extemporaneous delivery from a key word outline

Guidelines
1. **Invention.** Topic choice sometimes causes stress. Select a subject that doesn't bore you to sleep, but one that does not make you so angry you cannot present an informative speech. Because of the nature of the assignment, you will probably not be an "expert."

   - Read newspapers, news magazines, and other sources such as the Voter's Pamphlet. Broadcasts such as the *PBS NewsHour* or *All Things Considered* (National Public Radio) include more in-depth coverage than the typical network shows.

   - Present information that is not widely known. Most people know all they care to about abortion and other common controversial topics.

   - Do research using <u>current</u> oral, print, or electronic materials. Define the problem. Iden-tify its components. Gather statistics, examples, and testimony to support your main points.

2. **Disposition**. Select an organizational pattern that will help the audience get the most from your speech. Pro/con is often effective.

   - Write your intro. Gain attention and reveal your topic. Relate to the audience. Provide your qualifications for this topic. Preview your main points.

   - Write your conclusion. Signal the end is near. Review main points. Refer to the intro-duction. Provide a memorable ending.

   - Polish the speech by writing transition statements, internal summaries and/or internal previews.

   - Outline the speech, writing rhetorical labels in the margin. Type and proofread your work.

3. **Style.** Evaluate word choices and word combinations. Choose vivid words. Check pronun-ciation of words of which you are unsure.

4. **Memory and Delivery.** Put speaking outline on note cards. Write single cue words only—no complete sentences. Practice the speech. Time yourself. Edit.

Current Issue Speech Rubric

Remained within time limits (6 to 7 minutes)   Yes _____   No _____
Minimal use of note cards   Yes _____   No _____
Memory – obviously well rehearsed   Yes _____   No _____

Criteria	Exemplary	Satisfactory	Inadequate	Points Possible	Score
Purpose — Inform the audience about a current problem or controversial issue.	Clearly fulfilled the purpose	Attempted to fulfill the purpose but missing some elements.	Failed to fulfill the purpose.	10	
Introduction — Gain attention, reveal your topic, relate to the audience, provide your qualifications for this topic, preview your main points.	Strong opening statement. Clearly fulfilled the purpose	Somewhat strong opening. Attempted to fulfill the purpose but missing some elements.	Weak or insufficient opening. Failed to fulfill the purpose.	5	
Organization	Clear organizational pattern used.	Attempted to use organizational pattern but missing some elements.	Weak or insufficient organization.	10	
Topic Development	Defined the problem, identified its components, used a wide variety of recent sources (at least seven).	Attempted to define the problem and identify its components, but missing some elements. Used at least three recent sources.	Failed to define the problem and identify its components. Failed to cite recent sources.	25	
Topic Development — Develop the issue with evidence from several sources.	Offered statistics, examples, and testimony to support your main points.	Attempted to offer statistics, examples and testimony to support your main points but missing some elements.	Failed to offer statistics, examples and testimony to support your main points.	25	
Conclusion — Signal the end; review your main points; refer to the introduction; provide a memorable ending.	Strong closing. Clearly fulfilled the purpose.	Somewhat strong closing. Attempted to fulfill the purpose but missing some elements.	Weak or insufficient closing. Failed to fulfill the purpose.	10	
Delivery — Eye contact, gestures, extemporaneous.	Components are adequately addressed in the speech.	Components are somewhat addressed in the speech.	Components are not addressed in the speech.	15	

Comments:

EVALUATION FORM: Current Issue Speech

Time: 6 to 7 minutes

Name _____Time_____

_____ Topic choice (significant)
_____ Informative purpose

Disposition

_____ Attention gained
_____ Related to audience
_____ Established credibility
_____ Previewed

_____ Organization clear
_____ Main points clear
_____ Main points supported
_____ Transition/internal summary/preview

_____ Signaled speech conclusion
_____ Tied to intro
_____ Review of main points
_____ Ended memorably

Invention

_____ Adequacy of support
_____ Statistics
_____ Example
_____ Testimony
_____ Relevant data
_____ Cited sources

Style

_____ Precise language
_____ Vivid style

Memory

_____ Evidence of practice
_____ Fluency of thought
_____ Minimal use of notes

Delivery

_____ Voice: rate, pitch variation, volume, pauses
_____ Eye contact
_____ Posture
_____ Gestures

Grade _____

SPEECH ASSIGNMENT: Persuasive Speech

Time: 6 to 7 minutes

Definition: The purpose of this speech is to alter or reinforce attitudes, values, beliefs, or actions.

Skills
- All previous skills of invention and disposition
- Use of proofs: audience (pathos), speaker (ethos), and rational (logos)

Examples of Persuasive Topics and Purposes
- **To actuate behavior**: The average American's junk mail adds up to 1 1/2 trees worth of paper annually; save trees by writing to a specific address and having your name removed from junk mail lists.

- **To convince/policy**: Because Americans need to conserve fossil fuels, and because cars automobiles get better gas mileage at slower speeds, the nation should return to the 55 mph speed limit.

- **To convince of a value**: Educational choice is good, because it allows people to have personal control over their lives.

- **To reinforce a belief or value**: Democracy continues to be the best system of government in the world today.

Guidelines
1. Select a topic, using the suggestions found on pages 306-307 of the text. What do you believe or feel strongly about? What will create a better society or better, more fulfilled individuals?

2. Decide on a claim of fact, value, or policy.

3. Analyze your audience's current beliefs and behaviors, attitudes and values as they relate to your topic.

4. Plan how you will intertwine appeals to logic, to emotion, and to your credibility in order to be more persuasive.

5. Choose an organizational pattern that is appropriate for the subject matter and purpose of your speech. Prepare an introduction, conclusion, and connectives that make your speech "flow."

6. Pay attention to language choices, checking for clarity, accuracy, and interest.

7. Outline the contents of your speech. Type your outline. Make a speaking outline on note cards using key words only.

8. Rehearse.

SAMPLE OUTLINE: Persuasive Speech to Actuate

Topic: Organ Donation
General Purpose: To persuade
Specific Purpose: I will prove that there is a shortage of organs in the United States that can be
                                eliminated if individuals will donate their organs.
Central Idea: A shortage of organs exists in the U. S., but we can solve the problem if each
                                person agrees to donate.

I. **Introduction**

   A. At eighteen, Kevin, the high achiever of his senior class, had a bright future when he suddenly
       died of a brain aneurysm.

      1. His parents faced a choice thrust upon thousands of families: to keep Kevin's body
          functioning long enough for transplant teams to remove his organs, corneas, and bone
          marrow, or to allow him simply to die.

      2. Kevin's parents chose to donate his organs—fortunately, an increasingly common practice.

   B. There is a nationwide shortage of available organs; you or one of your loved ones may join the
       thousands of people who desperately need transplants.

   C. I became interested in this subject this summer when my cousin was hit in the head with a
       baseball and declared brain dead; his organs were removed and flown to various parts of the U.
       S. to give renewed life to many people.

   D. Today, I'll discuss the problem of organ scarcity and its causes; then I will show how each of you
       can be part of the solution.

II. **Body**

   A. Organ donating is basically a problem of supply and demand.

      1. Every day more than 80,000 people wake up needing an organ donation (Frequently asked
          questions [FAQ], 2005).

         a. This many people would fill the Rose Bowl (Greve, 2005).

         b. Today, 63 will receive a transplant , 17 will die, and an additional name per minute will
             be added to the list (FAQ, 2005; Gupta, 2005).

         c. Minorities include about 50% of this number (MOTTEP Facts and Figures, 2005).

      2. About 30% of the needy receive an organ annually; 70% are waitlisted (PR Newswire, 2005).

         a. Nearly 25% of wait listed patients are Hispanics; their wait period is 26-58% longer than
             for whites (Office of Minority Health, 2005).

         b. Nearly 27% of all wait listed patients are African Americans; for kidney transplants it is
             36% (Office of Minority Health, 2005).

         c. According to the American Kidney Fund nearly 61,000 people are waiting for kidney
             transplants; only 16,000 will get them (Facts about kidney disease, 2005).

   B. It is easy to see that there are not enough organs, and there are several reasons for this.

1. According to a Gallup survey 85% of respondents approved of organ donation, but only 69% said they were likely to donate; 25% said they were very unlikely to do so – and 47% of these people gave no reason or said they had given the matter little thought (2000).

2. Another cause of the shortage may be reluctance to deal with death.

   a. However, the Organ Procurement and Transplantation Network (2003) says donation is about life — giving someone a chance at life.

   b. Traditional Chinese and Jewish people, as well as many Native Americans, believe the body should remain intact (Palliative Care Council, 1999).

3. Dean Kappel of the Mid-America Transplant Association says that doctors and nurses are reluctant to get involved (Maier, 1990).

   a. Some feel uncomfortable imposing on grieving families.

   b. No physician will consider transplantation without consent of next-of-kin—even if the patient had a donor card, due to fear of lawsuits.

4. A lesser factor is the fear that someone will terminate life-supports inappropriately to take organs (FAQ, 2005).

5. Many people do not realize that, with advances in medical science, they don't have to die to donate.

   a. In 2001, 6485 living donors provided bone marrow, kidneys, and other organs ("Gift of Life," 2002).

   b. In April 2001, Secretary Thompson launched a national campaign to encourage Americans to "Donate the Gift of Life" and this has resulted in increased donations (Greve, 2005).

TRANSITION: Although there is a desperate shortage right now, it doesn't have to be that way.

C. Nearly 70 organs and non-organs can be donated.

   1. Donations include: skin grafts to burn victims, heart valves, corneas, ligaments, and even bone.

      a. You can donate bone marrow any time, like you donate blood.

      b. The average bone donor can help 51 people.

   2. The federal Department of Human Health and Services organ donor Web site (FAQ, 2005) says you must tell your family of your desire to be a donor.

      a. In most states, drivers' licenses contain check-off boxes for those who desire to donate.

      b. Carrying an organ-donor card or writing a living will can accomplish the same purpose.

      c. Let your family know; most states and the District of Columbia have passed "required request" laws that mandate doctors to ask survivors about organ donation when appropriate.

   3. "This is something much deeper than an act of civic duty or the exchange of a commodity," says David Thomas, Director of Medical Humanities at Loyola University. "It is a profoundly spiritual act that recognizes that all human beings have an obligation to help another." (Maier, 1990, p. 110).

TRANSITION: If these are followed through, it will be possible to give someone with failing organs a second chance with minimal costs and multiple benefits.

    D. The solution is practical.

        1. Reassure your family that there is no financial cost and no disfigurement in case of an open-casket funeral (FAQ, 2005).

        2. Giving may even benefit the family.

            a. Transplant coordinators say the act of giving marks the first step in successful grieving.

            b. It helps many families find meaning in tragic death.

                1) "For me the decision brought comfort, not more pain," says Peggy Bishop whose three-year-old son died of a cerebral hemorrhage. "My son turned out to be a gift of life to five other families" (Maier, 1990, p. 111).

                2) Nine out of ten donor families would make the same decision again (Maier, 1990).

        3. Success rates are high in transplantation.

            a. 91% of kidney recipients, 86% of heart recipients, and 82% of liver transplant patients survive for at least a year after the donation (Transplant Statistics, 2005).

            b. Transplants give most recipients a second chance at life.

        4. More kidney transplants would cut high health care expenditures (News RX, 1999).

            a. According to the University of Maryland School of Medicine, kidney transplants are cheaper than staying on dialysis for more than 2 ½ years.

            b. "[N]ot only does a kidney transplant improve the quality of life for patients, it also saves money in the long run," said University of Maryland's Dr. Stephen T. Bartlett.

            c. Savings result from shortened hospital stays and elimination of expensive, hospital-administered intravenous anti-rejection drugs.

        5. People used to worry that donated organs would go only to important, wealthy, or well-connected people.

            a. In 1984, the National Organ Transplant Act set up a nationwide computerized system to which all transplant centers connect.

            b. Recipients of all ages get organs based on blood and tissue matching, urgency, organ size, and geographic location.

        6. As you can see, the cost is minimal; the savings are great.

III. Conclusion

    A. I hope you now realize what a desperate need there is for organs, why there is a shortage, what can be done to solve the problem, and the many benefits that come from donating.

    B. I want you all to get out your driver's licenses when you get home, look at the little box in the corner, and see if there is a "D" for DONOR.

        1. If not, go to the DMV and get a donor card.

2. More importantly, tell your family that you want to be a donor and encourage them and others to donate, too; although licenses are legal documents, doctors always discuss the issue of donation with family members (Myths and Facts, 2003).

C. Several weeks after his death, Kevin's parents received a letter telling them who had benefited from their generosity.

1. One kidney went to a 37-year-old woman; the other, to a 37-year-old man.

2. Kevin's liver saved the life of a Minnesota mother of two teenagers.

3. His heart went to a 14-year-old, dying of heart disease.

4. His lungs were used in research.

5. His skin and his bone helped an undetermined number of people.

6. His corneas restored the sight of two people.

D. I strongly urge you all to donate; what greater gift can you possibly give than the gift of life?

References

Frequently asked questions. (2005). HHS organ donor Web site. Retrieved September 29, 2005, from www.organdonor.gov/faq.html.

Gallup Survey (2000, May 11). American public's attitudes toward organ donation and transplantation. Retrieved March 11, 2003, from at www.transweb.org/reference.

Greve, F. (2005, July 31). Organ donation rates are rising nationwide as tiny federal effort pays off. *Knight Ridder Washington Bureau*. Retrieved September 29, 2005, from InfoTrac College Edition.

"Gift of Life" Donation Initiative. (2002, April 22). Department of Health and Human Services. Retrieved March 1, 2003, from www.hhs.gov/news/press/2002pres/20020422.html

Gupta, S. (2005, April 11). The gift of life. *Time, 165(5),* 65.

Facts about kidney disease. (2005). American Kidney Fund. Retrieved September 29, 2005, from www.akfinc.org/facts_kidney_disease.asp

Maier, F. (1990, March). A final gift. *Ladies Home Journal,* 107, 102, 110.

MOTTEP Facts and Figures. (2005). Organ donation. Retrieved September 29, 2005, from www.nationalmottep.org/statistics.shtml.

NewsRX. (1999, May 31). The "break-even" cost of kidney transplants is shrinking. *Transplant Weekly.* Retrieved September 29, 2005, from InfoTrac College Edition.

Palliative Care Council of South Australia Inc. (1999). Multicultural palliative care guidelines: Language groups—Chinese. Retrieved September 29, 2005, from www.pallcare.asn.au/mc/mcchinese.html

Office of Minority Health. (2005). Closing the health gap 2004. Retrieved September 29, 2005, from www.omhrc.gov/inetpub/wwwroot/healthgap2004/otdonation.htm

Organ Procurement and Transplantation Network. (2003). The critical shortage. Retrieved September 29, 2005, from www.optn.org/about/donation/criticalShortage.asp

PR Newswire. (2004, April 13). Team of transplant survivors and donors to "Ride Across America" as part of National Donate Life Month. Retrieved September 29, 2005, from InfoTrac College Edition.

Transplant Statistics. (2006). USTransplant.org: Scientific Registry of Transplant Recipients. Retrieved January 13, 2006, from www.ustransplant.org/csr_p507/nats.aspx

Danielle Schutz, Oregon State University (updated 2006)

Persuasive Speech Rubric

Remained within time limits (6 to 7 minutes)	Yes _____	No _____
Minimal use of note cards	Yes _____	No _____
Memory – obviously well rehearsed	Yes _____	No _____

Criteria	Exemplary	Satisfactory	Inadequate	Points Possible	Score
Purpose — To alter or reinforce attitudes, values, beliefs or actions.	Clearly fulfilled the purpose	Attempted to fulfill the purpose but missing some elements.	Failed to fulfill the purpose.	10	
Introduction — Gain attention, reveal your topic, relate to the audience, provide your qualifications for this topic, preview your main points.	Strong opening statement. Clearly fulfilled the purpose.	Somewhat strong opening. Attempted to fulfill the purpose but missing some elements.	Weak or insufficient opening. Failed to fulfill the purpose.	5	
Organization	Clear organizational pattern used.	Attempted to use organizational pattern but missing some elements.	Weak or insufficient organization.	10	
Topic Development — Ethos, Logos, Pathos.	Used appeals to logic, emotion, and your own credibility to convince the audience.	Attempted to use appeals to logic, emotion and own credibility to convince the audience but missing some elements.	Failed to use appeals to logic, emotion and own credibility to convince the audience.	25	
Topic Development — Develop the issue with evidence from several sources.	Offered statistics, examples, and testimony to support your main points. Cited sources.	Attempted to offer statistics, examples and testimony and to cite sources to support your main points but missing some elements.	Failed to offer to statistics, examples and testimony to support your main points. Failed to cite sources.	25	
Conclusion — Signal the end; review your main points; refer to the introduction; provide a memorable ending.	Strong closing. Clearly fulfilled the purpose.	Somewhat strong closing. Attempted to fulfill the purpose but missing some elements.	Weak or insufficient closing. Failed to fulfill the purpose.	10	
Delivery — Eye contact, gestures, extemporaneous.	Components are adequately addressed in the speech.	Components are somewhat addressed in the speech.	Components are not addressed in the speech.	15	

65

Comments:
EVALUATION FORM: Persuasive Speech (General Form)

Time: 6 to 7 minutes

NAME _____Time _____ Claim: _____

Invention and Disposition

_____ Topic Appropriate to Audience and Time
_____ Speech Purpose Clear

<u>Introduction</u>

_____ Attention gained
_____ Related to Audience
_____ Credibility Revealed
_____ Preview

<u>Body</u>

_____ Clearly organized points
_____ Proofs
      _____ Pathos: audience appeals
      _____ Ethos:
      _____ Rational proofs
      _____ Supporting evidence
_____ Adequacy of data/claims/warrants
_____ Evidence of research (sources)
_____ Ethics of argument
_____ Transition statements

<u>Conclusion</u>

_____ Signal of end
_____ Review of main points
_____ Tie to introduction
_____ Impact ending/call to action

Style

_____ Language appropriate
_____ Vivid language
_____ Clarity

Delivery

_____ Vocalics: rate, volume, variation, quality
_____ Pronunciation
_____ Body language: posture, gestures, eye contact
_____ Other: appearance, space, time

Memory

_____ Fluency of thought
_____ Minimal use of notes

Grade _____

Persuasive Speech Rubric: Monroe's Motivated Sequence

Remained within time limits (6 to 7 minutes)   Yes _____   No _____
Minimal use of note cards   Yes _____   No _____
Memory – obviously well rehearsed   Yes _____   No _____

Criteria	Exemplary	Satisfactory	Inadequate	Points Possible	Score
Attention Step (Introduction)	Gained attention, related to the audience, established credibility, previewed speech.	Attempted to gain attention, relate to audience, establish credibility & preview speech but missing some elements.	Failed to gain attention, relate to audience, establish credibility, preview speech.	20	
Need Step	Established problem, significance, support & need.	Attempted to establish problem, significance, support & need, but missing some elements.	Failed to establish problem, significance, support & need.	20	
Satisfaction Step	Described & explained solution, connected to need, practical, meet objections.	Attempted to describe & explain solution, connect to need, practical, meet objections.	Failed to describe & explain solution, connect to need; not practical, did not meet objections.	15	
Visualization Step	If yes, positive, if no, negative, contrast.	Attempted to show positive and negative results, and contrast, but missing some elements.	Failed to show positive and negative results, and contrast.	15	
Action Step	Summarized, call for response, stated personal intention, end with impact.	Attempted to summarize, call for response, personal intention, end with impact, but missing some elements.	Failed to summarize, call for response, state personal intention, end with impact.	15	
Delivery — Eye contact, gestures, extemporaneous.	Components are adequately addressed in the speech.	Components are somewhat addressed in the speech.	Components are not addressed in the speech.	15	

Comments:

EVALUATION FORM: Monroe's Motivated Sequence

Time: 6 to 7 minutes

Name _____Time_____

Claim: _____

Invention and Disposition

I.   Attention Step (Introduction)
_____ Attention
_____ Related to audience
_____ Credibility established
_____ Previewed

II. Need Step
_____ Problem demonstrated
_____ Ramifications given
_____ Use of sufficient support
_____ Pointing to audience need

III. Satisfaction Step
_____ Solution described
_____ Solution explained
_____ Need and solution logically connected
_____ Practicality of solution
_____ Objections met

IV. Visualization Step
_____ Hypothetical positive results
_____ Hypothetical negatives if not implemented
_____ Contrast

V.   Action Step
_____ Summarized
_____ Called for response
_____ Stated personal intention
_____ Ended with impact

Style

_____ Vivid language
_____ Clarity

Delivery/Memory

_____ Vocalics: rate, volume, tone, quality
_____ Body language: posture, gestures
_____ Other nonverbal: appearance, space, time
_____ Minimal use of notes
_____ Eye contact   Grade _____

SPEECH ASSIGNMENT: Panel Discussion: A Current Controversial or Problematic Issue

Time: 20 to 25 minutes

Description: You will work with a group to discuss a controversial or problematic topic in depth in an informal "fishbowl" setting with other members of the class observing.

Skills
- All of the abilities of invention, disposition, style, and delivery from previous speeches.
- Ability to cooperate with a group to discuss a problem in depth.

Guidelines
1. Choose an interesting topic that represents a problem on the campus, local, national, or international level.

2. Meet with a small group of people who share your interest in the topic, and divide up areas of the topic to research individually.

3. Gather information, using the worksheets that follow. In an "A" level discussion, each participant should find 5-7 items from newspapers, magazines, books, Internet sources, interviews, and the like.

4. Meet with your fellow panelists to discuss your information in depth.

5. Decide on the questions your group will discuss.

6. Select one person to act as emcee. She or he should do as much research as other panelists and prepare by sharing information with others. See the role description below.

Participants Should:
- Listen without interrupting (even if they violently disagree).
- Avoid a discussion between two people only; this is not a conversation.
- Make comments relatively brief.
- Ask fair, brief, and clear questions of other participants.
- Speak to the point of the issue being discussed at the moment.
- Be courteous to other participants.

The Emcee Should:
- Be familiar with the subject.
- Prepare a tentative outline to cover the main phases of the problem.
- Introduce the topic, relate it to the audience, and preview the discussion.
- Act as gatekeeper who invites all panelists to participate about equally, preventing one or two people from dominating the discussion.
- Keep the discussion on course.
- Summarize, when appropriate, the points on which discussants agree.
- Harmonize areas of disagreement.
- Conclude the discussion with a summary.

Topic Examples

      media violence
      rising cost of _____ (e.g. gasoline, insurance, college tuition, health costs)
      obesity
      grade inflation
      male-female differences
      distance learning
      the methamphetamine epidemic
      emerging technologies
      alternative medicine

A group of students discussed the problem of <u>campus parking</u>. They followed the problem solving method shown in the textbook, Appendix A. In a panel format, they:

      defined the problem
      analyzed related facts, causes, effects, values, and policies
      discussed criteria for a solution
      listed possible solutions
      and argued for construction of a new parking garage as the best possible solution

Another group did an investigative report on <u>immigration issues</u>, including the history of immigration, global immigration, political asylum, the positive effects of immigrants on the United States, and the cost of immigrants to taxpayers.

SPEECH ASSIGNMENT: Group Presentation: Movie Reality vs. Print Reality

Time: presentation to last approximately 20 minutes

Description: Historical narratives often make good movie plots. Consequently, you can find a number of films based on historical events or characters. Working with a group, watch a movie that's based on history, then do research to evaluate the movie's accuracy. Present your findings to your classmates in a panel or symposium format.

Skills
- All of the skills of invention, disposition, style, and delivery from previous speeches.
- Research into movie reviews, historical texts, and the like.
- Ability to compare and contrast movie reality and print reality.
- Ability to cooperate with a group to discuss a problem in depth.

Guidelines
1. Select a historical movie that interests you and make arrangements for your group to watch it—preferably together.

2. Locate three (for a "C"), five (for a "B") or seven (for an "A") related print sources *per group member*. Photocopy, take notes, make a mind map or otherwise record your findings.

3. Meet with your group and discuss your information thoroughly. Identify questions or gaps in your information that require further research. Plan additional library research and group meetings as needed.

4. Work with your group and plan a way to present your findings to the rest of the class. You may divide up the topic and have each member present one aspect of it. Or you may present your information in a panel format. Don't overlook the use of visual aids, including brief clips from the movie that illustrate your major points.

5. Participate in the group presentation.

6. Prepare a written summary of your findings, complete with a bibliography.

Topic Ideas:
Movies about people: *Evita* (starring Madonna and earlier Fay Dunaway as Evita Peron), *Samson and Delilah, Alexander the Great, Nixon, Patton,* John Nash (*A Beautiful Mind*), *Malcolm X, Gandhi,* Eric Liddell (*Chariots of Fire*), Navajo Code Talkers, (*Windtalkers*), William Wallace (*Braveheart*).

Movies about events: *All the President's Men* (Watergate), *Pearl Harbor, JFK* (the assassination plot), *Mississippi Burning* (civil rights workers murdered), the sinking of the Titanic, *Munich* (the Israeli response after Israel's athletes were killed at the Olympic games in 1972), *Thirteen Days* (JFK and the Bay of Pigs incident).

<u>NOTE</u>: Controversial movies work well.

JFK was released with enormous amounts of press coverage. Critics accused filmmaker Oliver Stone of everything from propaganda to paranoia. *Time* and *Newsweek* made the movie a cover issue. The *New York Times* presented a host of letters to the editor and related opinion pieces—including one from Oliver Stone. The *National Review* provided lengthy pieces by authors who participated in the actual events. To locate these materials, find out when the movie was released, then go to newspaper and magazine indexes from that date.

Another recommendation is *All the President's Men* because June 2002 marked the 30th anniversary of the Watergate break-in. This means that thousands of words were written during the middle of June, 2002, about the facts as well as the monumental impact of Watergate. Find a textbook or encyclopedia to get a basic overview of the events which stretched out over months. Go back to the original *Washington Post* stories—which you can discover from indexes. Do research in news magazines from the following months. Read Woodward and Bernstein, David Halberstam, and other media historians. Include conservative as well as more liberal sources.

2005 saw the release of *Munich*, another film based on a historical incident that includes fiction and questionable conclusions. Like the other two suggested movies, the history of the actual event is easy to locate in additional sources.

73

EVALUATION FORM: Panel Discussion or Group Presentation

Time: presentation to last approximately 20 minutes

Names _____

Group Topic _____

The Group as a Whole

_____ Introduction/Orientation to topic

_____ Purpose of presentation clear

_____ Evidence of group co-creation of meaning

_____ Transitions

_____ Conclusion

_____ Question and answer period

Group grade _____

Individual Participation

_____ Main points clear

_____ Adequate support for ideas

_____ Interesting (relevant)

_____ Appropriate language (clear, correct, etc.)

_____ Evidence of Research

_____ Sources Cited

_____ Extemporaneous delivery

_____ Conversational

_____ Eye contact

_____ Vocal variation   Individual grade _____

Part II

CHAPTER-BY-CHAPTER INSTRUCTIONAL RESOURCES

Each chapter includes the following resources:

Chapter Overview
Chapter Goals
Chapter Outline
Suggested Videos
Discussion Topics
Application and Critical Thinking Exercises
Supplemental Resources (some or all of these may be included)
- Teaching Ideas
- Research Notes
- Handouts

Chapter 1

INTRODUCTION TO PUBLIC SPEAKING AND CULTURE

This chapter lays out foundational themes you'll encounter throughout the text. Opening with a rationale for studying public speaking, it helps students realize the value of taking a course many say they'd like to avoid. The definition of culture and a diversity perspective emphasizes the impact culture has on public speaking and vice versa. Another major theme is the dialogical nature of communication that depends on the participation of listening speakers and responding listeners.

Chapter Goals

At the end of this chapter, your students should be able to:

- Explain the value of public speaking courses
- Define culture in the context of public speaking
- Give reasons for studying public speaking from a cultural perspective
- Explain how public speaking influences culture
- Identify three ways culture affects public speaking
- Understand aspects of the dialogical theory of communication
- Identify elements of the transactional model of communication

At the end of this chapter, you should be able to:

Say your students' names. (At Oregon State, I once said "Hi, Eric" to a student who'd been in my class a couple of years before. He went home and wrote me a note that said, "Out of all my years here, you're the only professor I've had who knows my name.") Here are some ideas for learning names:

- I often ask students to pronounce their names and tell their high school (and its mascot). Somehow this helps me place the student in my mind. With an unusual mascot (the Tillamook Cheesemakers, for example), I might ask a question such as, "You really said, 'Go Cheesemakers, go!' during football games?"

- Partly because my name is Clella (KLELL uh) Iles Jaffe, I applaud teachers who pronounce names correctly. I write out unusual names according to the way they sound. For instance, a Casi (Cassie? Casey?) pronounced her name as KAY-see. I jot it into my book that way.

- Never say to people with unusual names, "That's an unusual name." (Believe me, they know.) Just pronounce the name correctly and move on!

- I often go over the names again just after I call roll and before I dismiss the class. And I ask students to sit in approximately the same area the first few days of class until I have their names down.

- Have students fold over pieces of notebook paper with their names written large and place these nameplates on their desks until everyone knows one another's names.

- Have students learn four names on the first day--names of the people on both sides, in front, and behind them. In later class sessions, have them learn a few more names at a time.

- Assign a speech of introduction--either a self-introduction or the introduction of another student. Chapter 2 in the text refers you to several self-introduction speeches that you can assign students to watch on the CD-ROM included with the text. The teaching suggestions for Chapter 2 in this manual provide guidelines for a speech to introduce a classmate; pairs of students interview one another and draw pictures which they use as visual aids for their speeches.

Chapter Outline

I. Taking a **public speaking course** has many benefits.
  A. You can increase your critical thinking skills.
    1. **Critical thinking** is "the ability to engage in reasoned discourse with intellectual standards such as clarity, accuracy, precision, and logic, and to use analytic skills with a fundamental value orientation that emphasizes intellectual humility, intellectual integrity, and fair-mindedness."
    2. The ability to present ideas is valued today in our media rich culture as well as historically in cultures such as Greece, and Rome.
      a. Rhetoric refers to the art, practice and study of human communication.
      b. Rhetoric was one of the original seven liberal arts.
      c. The word 'rhetoric' is often viewed negatively.
      d. Most definitions associate rhetoric with some form of persuasion.
  B. You can improve your professional, civic, and personal skills.
    1. Employers want new hires who can listen well and communicate effectively, both verbally and nonverbally.
    2. You can use these skills to promote civil engagement regarding social issues you view as important.
    3. You'll find guidelines for speaking in social situations.
    4. Many students feel more competent and more confident about their skills after taking this course.
      Stop and Check: What Do I Hope to Gain from Taking this Course?
II. A cultural perspective is important because people from distinctly different cultures regularly interact.
  A. **Cultures** are integrated systems of learned beliefs, values, attitudes, and behaviors that include both visible and invisible elements.
  B. **Co-cultures** are groups who share many aspects of the dominant culture, but diverge in some way.
  C. Public speaking matters to cultures, and cultures matter to public speaking.
      Diversity in Practice: Public Speaking in Ancient Cultures
III. Public speaking affects culture in four distinct areas.
  A. Speakers *transmit* cultural beliefs, attitudes, values, and behaviors.
  B. Public speeches *reinforce* existing traditions and ideas we want to preserve.
  C. After threatening situations or tragedies, speakers try to *restore* order and community.
  D. Speakers speak out to *transform* dysfunctional elements within cultures.
      Stop and Check: How Has Public Speaking Affected your Campus Culture
IV. Culture influences public speaking in a number of ways.
  A. Cultures provide **core cultural resources** that influence public speaking.
    1. Beliefs are ideas we mentally accept as true or false.
    2. Values are underlying ideals of what's important, right, or ethical.
    3. Attitudes are predispositions to evaluate things positively or negatively.
    4. Behaviors are actions; cultures identify a range of actions considered normative.
  B. Cultures provide technological aids to communication.

1. An **oral culture** has no technology for recording, storing, or transmitting messages, and speakers in those cultures must memorize all that they know.
2. Most cultural groups globally have access to literacy or electronic devices that allow them to store their ideas and convey them to audiences separated by distance and time.
3. Technology also aids speakers in remembering ideas, projecting their voices, and presenting images and sounds that support their ideas.

C. Cultures provide expectations about speaking and listening.
   1. Cultures range along an individualistic-collectivist dimension.
      a. Members of **individualistic cultures** learn to depend on themselves and their families, and they are judged by personal merits; they speak out about problems.
      b. Members of **collectivist cultures** are integrated into an in-group that protects them throughout their lives; they may feel discomfort if they are singled out, and they hesitate to shame others.
      c. Members of individualistic cultures use more "I" and "my" pronouns; (English is the only language that capitalizes the word "I" but not "you.")
   2. Cultures vary in the level of expressiveness they value.
      a. **Non-expressive cultures** expect their members to guard their emotions and ideas rather than express them indiscriminately; they may be reluctant to speak publicly.
      b. **Expressive cultures** encourage members to give their opinion, speak out and let their feelings show.

Ethics in Practice: Vir Bonum, Dicendi Peritus

   3. Cultures influence who speaks and to whom.
      a. Some cultures limit speakers by age, sex, and perceived wisdom.
      b. Other cultures silence voices and opinions they find undesirable.
   4. The "how to" of speaking depends on a culture's preferred **communication style**.
      a. The U.S. uses a *problem orientation* communication style.
      b. Directness, rather than beating around the bush, is the norm.
      c. Precise words are preferred to indirect allusions or nonverbal messages.
      d. Informal, conversational delivery is common in the United States.
      e. *Personal involvement* leads speakers to establish common ground and share personal experiences.
   5. Cultures influence appropriate topics.
      a. The Polynesian word **tabu** or **taboo** refers to inappropriate topics in contrast to the word *nua*, which refers to discussable subjects; religion, sex, and death are taboo in many cultures.
      b. **Bicultural** individuals learn to speak in both the larger culture and a co-cultural group.

Stop and Check: Recognize Your Cultural Speaking Traditions

V. The dialogical theory and transactional model commonly depict communication.
   A. The **dialogical theory** argues that all communication is based on conversation.
      1. Like public speaking, conversation relies on nonverbal communication.
      2. Conversation and public speaking both require speakers and listeners to take *respons*-ibility for co-creating meaning.
      3. Both conversations and public speeches come in ready-made forms or **speech genres**.
      4. Meanings are based on who says what, where and when, why and for what, in what manner, with and for whom?
      5. However, public speeches are generally more formal than conversations.
   B. The transactional model depicts communication as a process wherein the communicators create mutual meanings.
      1. The sender-receiver encodes a message.
      2. The message is intentional or purposeful.
      3. Message is sent through a channel—in the classroom the channel is face-to-face, voice-to-ear, plus nonverbal elements.

4. The receiver-sender decodes the message and encodes feedback.
5. Feedback goes through a channel to the sender-receiver who adapts to it.
6. Noise (external and internal) can interfere with the message or its reception.
7. The communication takes place within a specific situation.
8. The larger cultural framework also creates expectations for what is and what is not acceptable.

<u>Practically Speaking: Bruce McQuakay, Native American Activist</u>

Suggested Videos

Book CourseMate. Show one of the speeches available on the website or from your personal or department files. Consider showing one or more examples so that your students have a positive model of what you look for in classroom speeches. (knowledge)

Professional Speeches<u>: Search for Majora Carter (pp. 1-2)</u> by name on www.ted.com. This site features several of her speeches, given in an effort to transform culture. President Obama's speech at the Pentagon on the anniversary of 9/11 is but one example of how public speaking affirms (restores) national values after a tragedy. It's available on www.youtube.com.

Your Library's Video Holdings. Check your campus library collection for videos about culture or co-cultural groups. Or look for a video about a social movement (such as suffrage or civil rights) that shows public speakers demanding change.

Feature Films. Short clips from movies such as ***Crash*** (2004), ***Freedom Writers*** (2007), or ***Sweet Home, Alabama*** (2002) show co-cultural differences within the United States. To highlight differences in cultural influences on public speaking, show the locker room pep talk clip from ***Mr. Baseball*** (1992). It illustrates the contrasting expectations of Japanese and American athletes.
- Review the section "Culture Affects Public Speaking."
- Show the clip; have students take notes on what they see.
- Discuss their observations of the ways Mr. Baseball violates the expectations of his Japanese coach and teammates. The term "Ugly American" is common overseas. How is Mr. Baseball an Ugly American? Would his behaviors be ugly in the United States, too? Why or why not? (comprehension, application, analysis, synthesis)

Discussion Topics

<u>The value of public speaking</u> (pp. 1-4). Many students have a negative attitude toward public speaking initially; it's a class they take to fulfill graduation requirements. Attitudes change incrementally, as Chapter 18 points out, but begin early to help students understand and appreciate the value of skills learned here. Most want to feel more confident; most want good jobs and successful careers. Some are interested in ideas; they enjoy knowing that the skills necessary for good speaking and listening are so important that they've been formally taught for millennia.

<u>Stop and Check: What Do I Hope to Gain From Taking This Course?</u> (p. 4). Have students answer the questions in writing, then stand up and share their answers with their class. Afterward, lead the students in discussion about the similarity and differences of answers. What common themes emerged?

<u>Diversity in Practice: Public Speaking in Ancient Cultures (p. 5).</u> Ask students to consider why writers in such varied cultures considered it important to write about public speaking. Which skills, if any, still apply? Why are they still appropriate?

81

Stop and Check: How Has Public Speaking Affected Your Campus Culture?. (p. 6) Use the questions in the box to discuss how public speaking is valued, created, and maintained at your institution.
- Then navigate to the main page on your school's website. How do the photographs and features illustrate your school's distinctive culture and values? How does the page work as a recruiting tool?
- Ask students how it presents the culture of the institution? The values of the institution? (Comprehension, application, analysis)

Core resources of belief, value, attitude, and behavior (pp. 6-7).The text repeatedly refers to these core resources; Chapters 6 and 18 discuss them in some detail. Research Note: Beliefs supplements this section.

Ethics in Practice: Vir Bonum, Dicendi Peritus (p. 8). Ask students to read the feature, and explain why this was considered good advice then, and good advice today.

Stop and Check: Recognize Your Cultural Speaking Traditions (p. 9). Students could use this feature as a journal entry or as material for small group classroom discussions.

Figure 1.2: The Communication Model (p. 11). Ask students to explore alternative ways of modeling communication. Have them work in small groups and do outside research on other models or variations on this model. Then, in class, give each group a transparency on which to draw their model. Have a spokesperson from each group explain the diagram to the entire class.

Practically Speaking: Bruce McQuakay, Native American Activist (p. 12). Ask students to read the feature, and, working in groups, to answer the discussion questions that follow.

Application and Critical Thinking Exercises

2. Brainstorm with the class to expand their view of public speakers. Examples: a scout leader giving how-to instructions for a project; a coach giving a pep talk at half time; a student giving an announcement; a recovering alcoholic narrating her story; a stand-up comic; a tour guide at a national park. Bring short clips from TV shows to provide ideas (Jerry Seinfeld's monologue, a lawyer summing up a case, a parent whose child was killed by gun violence testifying at a Congressional hearing on C-SPAN). (application)

3. Have interested students identify a city, regional, or campus event and prepare an announcement using guidelines in Appendix B. Give extra credit points, or use the assignment as an non-graded way for students to gain practical speaking experience. (application)

4. If your classroom has wireless access, have students bring computers to class (one computer for about three students works best). Direct them to a site such as www.youtube.com or www.google.com/news, or give them a specific URL for an item you'd like the entire class to consider. Then follow the questions in the exercise. (analysis, application)

4. This could be a homework assignment followed by a classroom discussion of their findings. (comprehension)

5. Watching for the use of the word "rhetoric" can become a term- or semester-long project. (application)

6. This exercise provides an opportunity for students to collect information in a face-to-face interview. (See Chapters 2 and 7 for interviewing tips.) Have them record their findings in a journal entry or present their information in small groups or in a whole class discussion format. (application)

7. President Obama's speech is available on YouTube. (analysis, evaluation)

8. For a variation, ask students to select an incident that involves social media. First, have them discuss how communication through social media and face-to-face communication differs. Then ask them to work in groups and compare and contrast the communication model when social media is the message channel and when and the channel is face-to-face interactions. Have students identify scenarios where each type of communication would be appropriate or inappropriate. (analysis, evaluation, synthesis)

Internet Activities

The CourseMate for Public Speaking, accessible through http://login.cengage.com, offers a broad range of resources that will help students better understand the material in the chapter, complete assignments, and succeed on tests. The CourseMate also features speech videos with critical viewing questions, speech outlines, and transcripts. It also offers interactive practice activities, self-quizzes, and a sample final exam.

Supplemental Resources

- Research Note 1.1: Beliefs
- Research Note 1.2: Communication Apprehension and Culture

Research Note 1.1: Beliefs (for use with pp. 6-7 in the text)

Milton Rokeach classifies beliefs into several categories, depending on their source and their relative importance to their adherents.

- Core beliefs (primitive beliefs) are the most fundamental. We learn them by direct encounters with objects, combined with social consensus. They have a taken-for-granted quality. Examples: An orange is round. The sky is blue.

- Authority beliefs are our assumptions regarding persons, reference groups, or traditions we should accept as authoritative. These are our beliefs about whom to trust or distrust, such as parents, teachers, and coaches. We also learn to accept or reject the authority of traditions, religious texts, scientists, political parties, and business leaders. Those who accept the *Bible* (or *Qur'an*) as authoritative and those who reject its authority differ profoundly. Whom we accept as authoritative determines whom we quote as experts and what quotations we use to influence other people--see Chapter 8.

- Derived beliefs come from the authorities we trust. Thus, we accept or reject ideas received from sources such as newspapers or television, books or scientific journals, professors and other scholars, parents and talk show hosts.

- Inconsequential beliefs are matters of taste that vary from individual to individual. For instance, some believe that broccoli is a waste of money or that stocks are a better investment than bonds, but we generally don't fight wars over these opinions!

We often speak to change people's beliefs (especially derived beliefs and inconsequential beliefs--see Ch. 17). It's far more difficult to change core beliefs and authority beliefs.

Source: Rokeach, M. (1968, 1972). *Beliefs, attitudes, and values: A theory of organization and change.* San Francisco: Jossey-Bass.

Research Note 1.2: Communication Anxiety and Culture (InfoTrac College Edition article) (for use with pp. 2 and 7-9 of the text)

Hsu, C-F. (2004). Sources of differences in communication apprehension between Chinese in Taiwan and Americans. *Communication Quarterly, 52(4),* 370-390.

Hsu examined cross-cultural differences in communication apprehension "from the cultural framework of independent and interdependent self-construals, temperaments of neuroticism and extroversion, and CA components--fear of negative evaluation and communication competence." Chinese students in Taiwan expressed significantly more CA than did their American counterparts.

Cultural factors. According to Geert Hofstedte, cultures range across a continuum of individualism-collectivism. People from more individualistic cultures like the U.S. strive to be unique, to express themselves directly, and to set goals and strive for them. In contrast, people from more collectivist or interdependent cultures strive to fit in harmoniously with others, to act appropriately and for the good of the group. They tend to fear and avoid negative evaluation and situations that would embarrass them, and they tend to avoid confronting and embarrassing others.

Temperament. Introversion is associated more closely with communication anxiety, and Chinese students in Taiwan tend to be more introverted than students in the United States.

CA components. CA components include speakers' motivations, their assessment of how others are responding to them, and their subjective appraisal of their competence in a given situation. Chinese students marked themselves lower on perceived competence, but this may be attributable to the fact that what's considered competent in Taiwan and in the U.S. are different. Further, Chinese culture emphasizes modesty, and students may have rated themselves lower on competency as an expression of personal modesty.

In summary, Hsu found that cross-cultural differences in CA appear to be attributable to understandable patterns grounded in cultures, temperaments and situations. For a variety of reasons, Taiwanese Chinese experience more CA than Americans in the U.S. do.

The article concludes, "As the world gradually becomes 'global village', such understanding is necessary for more effective intercultural communication."

Chapter 2

GIVING YOUR FIRST SPEECH: DEVELOPING CONFIDENCE

This chapter provides an overview of the speechmaking process. Because public speaking is almost always a humanities or liberal arts course, I introduce classical terminology relating to the canons of rhetoric. Because public speaking anxiety (PSA) is a major problem for many, even most, beginning speakers, specific strategies for dealing with nervousness come here.

Chapter Goals

At the end of this chapter, your students should be able to:

- Develop skills to overcome process anxiety
- Explain the five canons of rhetoric: invention, disposition, style, memory, and delivery
- Develop strategies to deal with performance anxiety
- Develop strategies to deal with physiological anxiety
- Develop strategies to deal with psychological anxiety
- Learn skills for effective rehearsal

At the end of this chapter, you should be able to:

Identify any student who has major anxiety that shows up on the PSA self-test. Consider setting up an individual or group conference with anxious students early in the term; in that meeting, plan strategies together for dealing with this anxiety.

Chapter Outline

I. People can have **communication apprehension (CA)** and/or **public speaking anxiety (PSA)** (usually either **process anxiety** or **performance anxiety**) when faced with the task of giving a speech.
  A. Developing skills will help overcome process anxiety.
    1. **Anticipatory speech anxiety** is highest right after a speech is announced and is a fear of the unknown.
    2. One way to lessen anxiety is to learn the process or "how-to" of speechmaking by understanding the standards or principles in five **canons of rhetoric**.
  B. Principles in the **canon of invention** help you choose a topic and purpose, do research, and develop supporting information for the content of the speech.
    1. Consider the audience and the setting.
      a. Consider the audience as a group and as individuals within the group.
      b. Consider situational factors such as room, lighting, noise, and time of day.
    2. Choose a topic.
      a. Understand the expectations of the assignment.
      b. Reveal something unusual.
      c. Select a significant subject.
      d. Consider telling a story.
      e. Do not violate listeners' sensibilities.
      f. Check it out on people you trust.

3. Identify a general purpose that indicates the desired audience response.
    a. The purpose "to inform" wants listeners to learn something.
    b. A speech "to persuade" targets listeners' behaviors or beliefs.
    c. The purpose "to entertain" wants listeners to laugh and have fun.
    d. A speech "to commemorate" highlights and reinforces a particular cultural ideal.
    e. Purposes often overlap.
4. The canon of invention provides principles for gathering speech materials.
    a. Consult a variety of outside resources.
    b. Self-introductions sometimes require little research.
    c. Conduct an interview when you introduce a classmate.
C. The **canon of disposition (arrangement)** contains standards for organizing speech materials.
    1. The introduction orients the audience toward the topic.
        a. First, draw audience attention to the subject.
        b. Motivate them to listen by relating the topic to their concerns.
        c. Demonstrate credibility to speak on the topic.
        d. Preview the major points or central idea of the speech.
    2. The body takes most of the speaking time; explain and develop major ideas here.
        a. Develop major ideas by using sufficient evidence for clarification and support.
        b. Organize by using a linear pattern such as topical or cause-effect.
        c. Alternative, less linear, patterns are common in other cultures.
    3. The conclusion summarizes and provides a sense of closure.
        a. Provides a transition.
        b. Summarizes major ideas.
        c. Gives a sense of psychological closure.
        d. Ends memorably.
    4. **Connectives** are words, phrases, and sentences that link ideas and help the speech flow smoothly.
D. Choose suitable language using principles from the **canon of style**.
    1. In rhetoric, **style** means language, not individuality expressed in someone's actions and taste.
    2. Guidelines include choosing appropriate language for the occasion and the audience.
    3. Omit offensive language.
    4. Choose understandable vocabulary.
    5. Use less slang than used in conversation.
E. Learn the speech using principles from the **canons of memory** and **delivery**.
    1. Romans used to memorize speeches; today the canon of memory is sometimes referred to as the "lost" canon.
    2. Avoid **memorized delivery**.
    3. Don't use **manuscript delivery** (reading the speech).
    4. Avoid **impromptu delivery** (minimal preparation) in classroom speeches.
    5. Use **extemporaneous delivery** (outlined, prepared, and rehearsed in advance with specific wording chosen during the speech).
    6. Use the **canon of delivery!** Be sure to rehearse your speech in front of family or friends—anyone that can act as an audience and provide feedback.
        a. Make eye contact.
        b. Use facial expressions.
        c. Avoid being monotone.
        d. Smile appropriately.
        e. Show confidence with posture.
        f. Use appropriate gestures.
        g. Be conversational.
        h. Respect time limits.

II. Overcome performance anxiety by developing rehearsal skills.
  A. Develop strategies to deal with **physiological anxiety** or bodily responses to stress.
    1. Bodily responses to anxiety include the ***fight-or-flight mechanism***.
      a. This burst of energy enables people to fight against or run from dangerous situations.
      b. The body doesn't distinguish between physically and psychologically threatening situations.
      c. The adrenaline rush can itself increase feelings of stress.
      d. Counteract this type of stress by getting a good night's sleep and engaging in some sort of physical exercise.
    2. **Systematic Desensitization** can help minimize the physical effects of PSA when you can't escape or avoid speaking.
      a. Order a list of frightening activities from least to most frightening.
      b. Learn principles of relaxation.
      c. Learn to relax as you think you way through your list.
  B. Plan to deal with psychological or mental anxiety.
    1. Control negative **internal monologue** (I-M) or self-talk through a process called **cognitive modification** (identify negative thoughts and replace them with positive ones).
      a. Think positively about the message.
      b. Think positively about the audience.
      c. Maintain a positive self-image.
      d. Think realistically about the assignment.
    2. Use visualization; imagine the speech proceeding successfully from beginning to end.
      a. Create vivid images.
      b. Control these images.
      c. Rehearse several times out loud or before an audience of friends.
      d. Anxiety lessens with **habituation**, which is repeating an experience time and again with fewer negative outcomes than expected.

Suggested Videos

Book CourseMate. Have students view one or more of the self-introduction speeches on the interactive video activities. The full text of Natasha Bevis's speech is included at the end of Chapter 2; Mona Bradsher's speech is located in Appendix C resources.

Elizabeth. (1998) A short clip from this feature film portrays Queen Elizabeth I rehearsing a speech. (She tries out various wording before she addresses rival clergy on the importance of a unified Church of England.)
  • Show the clip.
  • Have students contrast her extemporaneous delivery with impromptu or memorized delivery. (evaluation)
  • Discuss what Elizabeth did to overcome her apprehension. (comprehension, application)

The King's Speech. (2010) Use excerpts from this movie to show how King George VI of England worked diligently to overcome his stammer. The trailer is available on YouTube. Or you can search YouTube for "King George VI," where you'll find additional clips about his struggle to speak as well as the audio of him actually giving the speech.

Discussion Topics

Stop and Check: Assess Your Public Speaking Anxiety (p. 26) Have students take this test and develop specific strategies they can use to overcome the physiological and psychological symptoms that often accompany public speaking. (synthesis)

Public Speaking Anxiety (PSA) Use various scenarios for this topic. Divide the class into small groups and assign one of the following scenarios (or one you make up) to each group. They are counseling a friend who describes her or his fears (they list them), and the reasons for the fears (they list them). As "counselors," they then come up with at least one specific thing the subject can do to minimize her or his anxiety. (application, analysis, synthesis)

- Scenario 1: Tamara is extremely shy, especially around strangers. She has to take a public speaking class in order to graduate, and she's totally scared. During "Show and Tell" in second grade, she forgot her speech, and the other kids laughed at her; she's never spoken in front of a group since.
- Scenario 2: Ariko's first language is Japanese. She can read and write English quite well, but she's noticed that Americans often look puzzled when she talks, and they often say, "What?" or "Can you repeat that?" The few who take the time to talk with her sometimes exaggerate their words and talk louder. She feels like they think she's dumb. Now, horror of horrors, she must give a speech in English to people who've spoken the language from their first word on.
- Scenario 3: Bob is 39-years-old, married, with two teenaged children. He's returning to school to get a degree in hopes of getting a better job. He works as a nursing assistant in a nursing home (his manufacturing job was "downsized"). All but one other student in the class are in their early twenties and single; about half of them are in sororities or fraternities where the parking lots are filled with expensive cars. He thinks he has little or nothing in common with his classmates who largely ignore him in class.
- Scenario 4: John is dyslexic. He has heard that this class requires lots of research and several outlines. The prospect of that much reading and writing–in addition to all the other classes he's taking–is daunting.
- Scenario 5: Ellen was nearly killed in a car crash the night of her senior prom. She has a prominent scar on her right cheek and a permanent limp. She was once proud of her looks; now people either stare or quickly look away from her. The thought of having twenty people eyeing her during the several minutes she'll speak causes her distress.

The Canons of Rhetoric (pp. 17-23) Use **Teaching Idea 2.1**, "The Canons of Rhetoric," to help students classify the elements of speechmaking into the five canons of rhetoric. You'll find this explained in detail in the **Supplemental Resources** section of this chapter. If you need additional information on the canons, Brigham Young University presents many materials that define and explain the canons. The URL is http://humanities.byu.edu/rhetoric/Canons/Canons.htm.

Habituation (p. 27) Give students as much opportunity to speak on their feet in front of the audience as possible. Have them answer questions standing at their seat in the beginning of the class; as the class goes on, move students with answers to the front of the room. (application, analysis, synthesis)

Build Your Speech (p. 23) This exercise helps students apply the chapter principles in preparing their first speech. (application, analysis, synthesis)

Visualization (p. 27) Lead the whole class in a visualization scenario. Direct them to include specific vivid images and control those images. (application)

<u>Grading Criteria</u> Set up your grading standards early in the course. Part I in the IRM include a copy of criteria for grading speeches that's widely used by professors in the National Communication Association. (comprehension)

<u>Practically Speaking: Manfred Tschan, Health Professor and Soccer Coach.</u> (pp. 28-29)
Ask students to read the feature, and, working in groups, to answer the discussion questions that follow.

Application and Critical Thinking Exercises

1. This exercise would make a good journal entry. It asks students to consider the relationship between preparation, rehearsal, and competence and to strategize ways to use preparation to their advantage. (synthesis)

2. This activities can help students analyze their own area of difficulties in public speaking. Have students share their own strategies for improvement with the class. (analysis, synthesis)

3. This works well as an in-class group activity.

4. Divide the class by their majors or by occupational categories of interest. Have them do this exercise in small groups. This question is designed to help them identify transferable skills developed in public speaking class to everyday situations. (comprehension, application, analysis)

5. Chapter 5 deals with audience analysis in detail, but this exercise helps students be audience-centered from the start. Refer back to elements of diversity described in Chapter 1 that might make a difference in how various class members will speak or listen. (application, analysis, synthesis)

6. Delivery is commonly the most frightening aspect of speechmaking. Chapter 14 elaborates on these four methods of delivery, but introducing them here enables students to become more aware of each mode. As you show clips from movies and videos throughout the term, ask students to identify the mode of delivery and assess its appropriateness for the setting, the audience, and the topic. (For example, in the movie mentioned earlier, Queen Elizabeth delivers her speech extemporaneously. She knows her material, but she practices different wording and chooses her exact words the moment she speaks them, adjusting to audience feedback throughout.) (application, analysis, synthesis)

Internet Activities

The CourseMate for Public Speaking, accessible through http://login.cengage.com, offers a broad range of resources that will help students better understand the material in the chapter, complete assignments, and succeed on tests. The CourseMate also features speech videos with critical viewing questions, speech outlines, and transcripts. It also offers interactive practice activities, self-quizzes, and a sample final exam.

Supplemental Resources

- <u>Teaching Idea 2.1</u>: The Canons of Rhetoric
- <u>Teaching Idea 2.2</u>: Alternate Assignment: Drawing a Speech of Introduction
- <u>Research Note 2.1</u>: Treating Communication Apprehension
- <u>Research Note 2.2</u>: Behavioral Inhibition and the Perception of Anxiety

Teaching Idea 2.1: The Canons of Rhetoric (to go with the text, pp. 17-23)

Purpose: To help students classify the elements of speechmaking into the five canons of rhetoric.

Procedure
1. Begin by asking students the essentials of speechmaking–from beginning to end. Divide the blackboard or a blank transparency into five sections, but don't label them yet. As they give answers, categorize and list their responses according to one of the five canons.

    You'll typically get "eye contact," "get a topic," "find out about your topic," "introduction," "speak loudly enough to be heard," "remember the speech," "make it understandable," "gesture." (You may have to hint to get items related to the canon of style.)

2. On the board, place "eye contact" and "speak loudly" together (delivery). "Get a topic" and "find out about your topic" belong together in another category (invention). Place each response into one of the five sections.

3. After your five categories have several items in them, label each according to the name of the canon. That is, "Delivery" goes above the list that includes eye contact, speak loudly, etc. "Invention" goes above topic, research, etc. Label Style, Memory, and Disposition similarly.

    D. Define a <u>canon</u> as the body of principles, rules, standards, or norms that they can learn in order to speak more effectively.

Teaching Idea 2.2: Alternative Assignment: Drawing a Speech of Introduction

Bia Bernum, an instructor at the University of Central Arkansas, presented this creative idea at the Speech Communication Association convention, November 1996.

Description: A speech of introduction serves as both an icebreaker and an introduction to public speaking. If the purposes of this speech are to:
1) introduce students to one another,
2) introduce them to public speaking, and
3) allow the instructor to get to know students better,

an alternative "Drawing Speech" may help you accomplish your goals better. Students can spend ample time interviewing and conversing while reducing some speech anxiety associated with their first speech. This speech also encourages risk taking, and it gives you time to meet students on a more relaxed level. I use this exercise on the first day of class, just after I introduce the syllabus.

Total Time: About 75 minutes. If you do this in two class sessions, have students turn in their drawings after the first session.

Procedure
•   Pair students with someone they don't know, and give a list of questions to ask (name, major, interests, family, job, favorite things, hometown, something unique, etc.). You can work as a class to identify these questions which you write on a transparency or the board.

•   Give each student a sheet of newsprint and drawing materials (e.g., crayons or magic markers). Or give them a blank transparency and an erasable transparency pen. Instruct them to draw what they found out about their partner – a drawing that they'll use as a visual aid in their speech. Encourage creativity.

- One student drew a beehive on a tree branch to represent the other person's hometown of "Bee Branch."

- Another drew green hair on her partner whose last name was "Green."

- As students draw, they begin to interact by sharing markers and ideas. This also gives you an opportunity to walk around, speaking with students personally.

- When the drawings are completed, the pairs present their "works of art" to the class. The artists explain the drawing while their partners hold it or display it using the overhead projector.

- After the pair finishes speaking, invite classmates to comment.

Follow-Up: Ask how students felt after the first speech and why it seemed easier than they expected. Someone inevitably comments that s/he is not an artist, which is a good segue into the communication process, specifically, that we tend to think communication is simple when it is actually not as easy as we think. Explain that some may have experienced trouble drawing what they wanted because they lack artistic training to encode their messages and put them on paper. Similarly, we often have difficulty communicating what we want, because we lack the necessary speechmaking skills to be effective. This reinforces the main point of the chapter.

Research Note 2.1: Treating Communication Apprehension

Recent research affirms the value of combining a variety of methods to combat nervousness. Whitworth and Cochran report that nervous students reported less apprehension when they are presented with multiple treatments rather than a single method for reducing anxiety. Learning the process of speechmaking, combined with visualization and positive self talk worked together to lessen their anxiety and help students focus more on communicating their ideas than on simply "performing" their speeches.

Source: Whitworth, R. H. & Cochran, C. (1996). Evaluation of integrated versus unitary treatment for reducing public speaking anxiety. *Communication Education, 45*, 306-314.

Research Note 2.2: Behavioral Inhibition and the Perception of Anxiety (This article is available on InfoTrac College Edition)

Abstract: "Researchers studying the communication of public speaking anxiety have reported that audiences consistently underestimate the state anxiety of public speakers and that speaker behavior, rather than audience decoding skills, are primarily responsible for the discrepancy. In the present study, behavioral inhibition is advanced as explanation of this phenomenon. Analyses of variance for trends revealed an inverse linear relationship between state anxiety level and audience decoding efficiency. Behavioral assessments of speaker inhibition and rigidity, however, were positively related to state anxiety levels. These findings are consistent with the operation of behavioral inhibition within Buck's readout theory of emotion. Implications are advanced for future research and pedagogy."

Source: Sawyer, C. R. & Behnke, R. R. (2002). Behavioral inhibition and the communication of public speaking anxiety. *Western Journal of Communication, 66(4)*, 412-423.

Chapter 3

ETHICS IN A DIVERSE SOCIETY

Diversity often divides people whose core beliefs, values, attitudes, and cherished behaviors vary significantly; individuals and groups deal with diversity in both unproductive and productive ways. Fortunately, leading communication scholars offer several ethical responses that apply both to listening and speaking in a diverse culture. The chapter uses principles from both the dialogical and democratic approach to ethical speaking and listening. Although Chapter 3 emphasizes ethical issues, you'll find additional opportunities to discuss moral reasoning throughout the text.

Chapter Goals

<u>At the end of this chapter your students should be able to:</u>

- Define ethical communication
- Describe three responses to diversity
- Explain three democratic principles for public speaking
- Identify characteristics of dialogical speaking and listening
- Discuss ethical responsibilities of listeners
- Define two kinds of academic dishonesty: plagiarism and fabrication
- Explain three types of plagiarism
- Paraphrase and cite sources correctly

<u>At the end of this chapter you should be able to:</u>

Identify ways your campus encounters diversity, and help students see that dialogical and democratic principles can help them be actors in creating a more civil campus culture.

Chapter Outline

I. A range of differences among people calls for **ethical communication** in which we focus on both rights and responsibilities (**rightsabilities**) as we respond to diversity.
   A. **Assimilating** groups or individuals surrender some or most of their ways and adopt cultural patterns of another group.
   B. **Resisting** groups or individuals refuse to change and defend their positions, withdraw from situations, or attack the other.
   C. **Accommodating** people or groups listen and evaluate the views of others; both sides adapt, modify, and bargain to reach mutual agreements.
   D. A **multivocal society** actively seeks expression of a variety of voices or viewpoints. People who accommodate hear and evaluate diverse views open-mindedly.
   <u>Stop and Check: Your Responses to Diversity</u>
II. As a speaker, you have ethical responsibilities to your audience, your topic, and yourself.
   A. Speaking ethically is a democratic principle
      1. Practice democratic principles including free and responsible expression.
      2. Develop a habit of research.
      3. Be honest and fair.
      4. Practice **civility**, a social virtue that involves moderation instead of pride.

<u>Practically Speaking: NCA Credo for Ethical Communication</u>
B. Dialogical communication relies on a mindset that has three essential components.
    1. Dialogue theory has three essential components.
        a. Equality requires mutual respect between speaker and audience.
        b. Empathy means all participants try to see the others' perspectives.
        c. Examination requires all participants to be willing to look at theirs as well as the others' assumptions with an open mind.
    2. A dialogic perspective relies on three skills: the ability to respond to another's invitation, the ability to invite others into dialogue, and the ability to create contexts that facilitate dialogue.
    3. Amitai Etzioni suggests several rules of engagement.
        a. Don't demonize the other side.
        b. Don't offend the other side.
        c. Talk less about "rights" and more about negotiable needs, wants, and interests.
        d. Don't deal with every issue.
        e. Don't abandon your convictions, but balance them against the convictions of others.
    4. Dialogue has brought about international as well as local changes.
<u>Diversity in Practice: Does Facebook Encourage Civility?</u>
B. Democratic guidelines were formed out of tensions between free speech and responsible expression in a democracy.
    1. Ethical speakers develop a habit of research, realizing that they are the primary source of information for their audiences.
    2. Ethical speakers are honest and fair.
    3. Ethical speakers and listeners practice **civility**, a social virtue that involves self-control or moderation and leads to persuasion, consulting, and compromise, not coercion or manipulation.
<u>Diversity in Practice: Seeds of Peace</u>
III. Ethical listeners take a dialogical attitude.
    A. Listening empowers others by recognizing them as significant enough to be heard.
    B. In contrast, there are many ways to silence a speaker—walking away, ignoring, and heckling are among them.
        1. This indicates disrespect for the speaker and his or her ideas.
        2. It also disrespects other listeners who want to hear the speech.
    C. Ethical listeners encourage speakers to meet ethical standards.
    D. Open minded listeners expose themselves to various viewpoints.
<u>Stop and Check: Ethical Listening</u>
IV. Ethical speakers practice academic honesty.
    A. Ethical speakers avoid plagiarism.
        1. **Plagiarism** is presenting the ideas of others as if they were one's own.
        2. **Deliberate fraud** is intentional plagiarism.
        3. **Cut-and-paste plagiarism** involves copying entire sections from other people's work and pasting them together without quotation marks or citations.
        4. **Improper paraphrase** involves changing a few words but keeping the basic structure and ideas intact without citing the source.
        5. **Accidental plagiarists** innocently plagiarize because they don't know the rules.
        6. Plagiarism can result in severe penalties.
        7. **Sources** can be published or unpublished; either way, they should be cited using a standard format.
<u>Diversity in Practice: Plagiarism and Culture</u>
B. Ethical speakers avoid **fabrication**.
    1. They will not make up or guess at information and present it as factual.
    2. They double check information, staying alert for conflicting data.
<u>Stop and Check: Good Versus Bad Paraphrasing</u>
<u>Speech Video: Engaging the Mind and Spirit, Randy Smolla</u>

Suggested Videos or Audio Resources

Video, Audio, and Written Texts. Michael Eidenmuller, from the University of Texas at Tyler, has created a website, American Rhetoric (www.americanrhetoric.com), which provides scripts, audio, and video clips of thousands of contemporary and historical speeches, including movie speeches. (You may have to upgrade your plugins to access the videos.) YouTube is also a good source for videos on thousands of topics. (analysis)

- To illustrate dialogical speaking: Use Bono's commencement address (2001, Harvard University) on americanrhetoric.com or on YouTube (in two parts). Read the text and/or listen to the audio of Bono's speech and notice all the ways he invites his audience to think along with him about the problems that concern him.

- To illustrate civility in a democracy: Use the excerpt from President Barack Obama's speech at the Tucson Memorial Service (2011) that calls for civility. The excerpt cited on page 38 follows his acknowledgement of the people who died; it's about 16 ½ minutes into the speech. The speech video is available on YouTube. The text and an audio recording are also on www.americanrhetoric.com.

- To illustrate resistance to diversity: The Virginia Law Foundation and Virginia Holocaust Museum hosted the Law Day 2010 Conference on Civil Discourse. YouTube has many speeches from this conference (including one by Rod Smolla, whose address on civility comes at the end of this chapter). Use Part 2 from Rick Eaton's three-part series about digital terrorism and hate speech; he talks about the variety of hate websites, including game sites, conspiracy sites, anti-ethnic groups, anti-religious groups, and so on.

News Clips. Share news stories from broadcast news websites (such as www.cnn.com, www.pbs.org, or www.foxnews.com) or from www.google.com/news or YouTube that highlight the kinds of differences illustrated in Figure 3.1. (Use local, national, or global conflicts.)
- Discuss Figure 3.1 and the three responses to diversity explained in the text.
- Play the clip.
- Ask students to analyze the conflict. The comments that follow the report often highlight the divisive areas. Are basic beliefs at issue? Core values? Attitudes? Behaviors? (See Chapter 1.)
- Ask how a dialogical approach to communication, taken by both sides, could potentially change the problem. (application, analysis, synthesis)

Feature Films. Cultural differences provide the theme for many movies and television shows. Examples include ***Stand and Deliver*** (1988), ***The Kids Are All Right*** (2010), ***Smoke Signals*** (1998), and ***The Joy Luck Club*** (1993). Use clips from these movies or others like them to illustrate the section Encountering Diversity. Page 43 of the text directs students to the heckling example from ***O Brother, Where Art Thou?*** (comprehension)

Discussion Topics

Encountering Diversity. (pp. 34-36) Discuss current events or campus events that highlight resistance, assimilation, and accommodation. Use videos or news clips, or use Teaching Idea 3.1: Irreconcilable Differences located in the **Supplemental Resources** at the end of this chapter.

Diversity in Practice: Seeds of Peace (pp. 41-42) Consult the group's website for more information about this inspiring organization, which continues to expand the number of people it influences. (comprehension)

<u>Policy Positions of the National Communication Association (NCA)</u> (pp. 36-38) NCA scholars are concerned about ethics and communication in a diverse culture. *The Credo for Free and Responsible Communication in a Democratic Society* (1972) is printed in the **Supplemental Resources** at the end of this chapter in a form suitable for duplication and distribution. The text prints the 1999 version.

- Divide the class into six subgroups, and assign each group one section of the document to explain and illustrate with an example.
- After all the groups' spokespersons have finished, discuss with the entire class the questions that follow the Credo. (Refer back to Chapter 1 for a list of some core cultural resources that underlie the Credo's assertions.)
- Compare and contrast the 1972 Credo with the most recent *NCA Credo for Ethical Communication*, located on page 41 of the text. In which one is the dialogical perspective more evident? The democratic ethic? Ask students to account for the differences.
- A search on the NCA website www.natcom.org will also turn up the *Credo for Free and Responsible Use of Electronic Communication* (1994), *Policy on Political Communication* (1995), and *Policy on Diversity* (1995). Have students correlate these policy statements with current political and social events.

<u>Stop and Check: Ethical Listening</u> (p. 43-44). Ask students to read the feature, and, working in groups, to answer the discussion questions that follow.

<u>Academic Honesty</u> (pp. 44-47). Internet sources like School Sucks (www.schoolsucks.com) or Evil House of Cheats (www.cheathouse.com) make plagiarism--at least of papers--easy and common. Frat files are no longer necessary. Interestingly, professionals commonly use speechwriters, and www.buyaspeech.com is a successful enterprise.

- In class, log onto one of the Internet sites mentioned in the text. OR make a handout of your college's or university's plagiarism policy. Ask students to discuss the reasons students cheat, the upside, the downside, and the consequences of cheating. Then ask reasons that students do their own work, the upside, the downside, and the consequences of avoiding plagiarism.
- Discuss the use of professional speechwriters in politics and other professions. Is this plagiarism? Why does society consider this OK but penalize students for not doing their own work in their speech classes?
- Remind students that plagiarism has consequences. On October 20, 2005, Wal-Mart heir, Paige Laurie, surrendered her University of California degree in communication after her roommate's *20/20* confession that Laurie paid her $20,000 for writing term papers and doing other assignments over a period of 3 ½ years. (The roommate dropped out for lack of funds, but she said she learned a lot!)

<u>Diversity in Practice: Plagiarism and Culture</u> (p. 47). Ask students to discuss the challenges of developing ethical standards or criteria regarding plagiarism in our global age.

<u>Stop and Check: Good Versus Bad Plagiarism</u> (pp. 48-49). Ask students to write an appropriate paraphrase of a paragraph. Use the example on p. 50 or bring in a variety of paragraphs from other sources.

Application and Critical Thinking Exercises

1. Lead the class in a discussion on their findings of the examples of "hate speech." Where does the right of the individual to free speech end in the discussion of hate speech?

2. Drawing a minimum-maximum scale representing campus, community, and regional differences helps students analyze the diversity of "home." Ask students to work in small groups in the class; then report their work back to the group as a whole. Refer back to Chapter 1 and discuss ways that speakers in their community transmit, support, restore, change, or improve your specific campus, city, state, or region. (application, analysis, synthesis)

3. Use the diagram from exercise #1 as the basis for the class discussion. (application, synthesis, evaluation)

4. Divide students into groups and have them choose a controversy that pits one belief, value, or behavioral system against another. Ask them to list principles or tips that people from each side could use to communicate dialogically. This question builds on work done in Questions #1 and #2. Have students identify areas of common ground among diverse groups. For example, some pro-life and pro-choice groups sat down and agreed that both groups wanted to help women facing unplanned, unwanted pregnancies. Both cared about children and families. They set up some projects they could jointly support. And they stopped demonizing one another. (synthesis)

4. This exercise is similar to the one above, but it asks students to discuss their *personal* ideas and to listen to others with different opinions. You might add that listening empowers people who might otherwise be silenced. We can actually "listen into speech . . . voices that ordinarily would not be heard" (Wang & Burris, 1994, quoted in Helge Folkestad, 2000, Getting the picture: Photo- assisted conversations as interviews. SJDR, 2(2). Retrieved October 25, 2005, from http://home.hib.no/ansatte/hfo/getting%20 the%20picture%20-%20photo-assisted%20conversations%20as%20interviews.pdf.) (application)

5. Here, students apply chapter concepts to real life situations by identifying ethical and unethical speakers. Have them work in small groups to identify two types of speakers: bad people who are good speakers; good people who are bad speakers. Have them then post their lists on the board and discuss the implications of both types of speakers. (analysis, evaluation)

6. Lead students in a debate on a subject that has been controversial on campus. Divide class into teams, both for and against the controversy. Have each team prepare arguments either for or against the controversy, then have students begin informal debates in class. (analysis, application)

7. Assign students to read JFK's speech outside of class and discuss the core U.S. values he affirms. (application, analysis)

8. Assign this question as a journal entry or short thought paper. Direct students to the www.natcom.org site described "Discussion Topics" for samples. (synthesis)

9. This, too, could be a thought paper or journal entry. Students might enjoy "The Ten Commandments of Heckling," written to guide hecklers at sporting events. (www.techhecklers.com/ 10_commandments. htm). Have students rewrite the principles so that they apply to public speaking. (application, analysis, evaluation)

10. Use the course catalog to discuss specific plagiarism policies on your campus. (application, analysis, evaluation)

11. Combine this assignment with a trip to the library. I'm always amazed at the number of students who get to be in upper classes and have never been to the college library. If your school has a library liaison for your department, ask them to prepare a lecture on research resources available at your institution.

Internet Activities

The CourseMate for Public Speaking, accessible through http://login.cengage.com, offers a broad range of resources that will help students better understand the material in the chapter, complete assignments, and succeed on tests. The CourseMate also features speech videos with critical viewing questions, speech outlines, and transcripts. It also offers interactive practice activities, self-quizzes, and a sample final exam.

Supplemental Resources

- <u>Teaching Idea 3.1</u>: Irreconcilable Differences
- <u>Teaching Idea 3.2</u>: Ethical Research
- Credo for Free and Responsible Communication in a Democratic Society

Teaching Idea 3.1: Irreconcilable Differences (for use with "Diversity in Practice: Seeds of Peace" on pp. 41-42.)

Purpose: To have students examine underlying core beliefs and values that create irreconcilable differences between people and groups. To help students listen to both sides of such an argument.

Procedure: Choose one or more of the following activities, then discuss the two sides' differing core beliefs, values, and attitudes. Explore shared beliefs, values, and attitudes that might allow both groups to construct civil interactions with one another. (For example, neither pro- or anti-war advocates want innocent civilians to be slaughtered):

- Invite representatives of two opposing sides of a controversial national topic to come to class and share their views.

- Show videotapes of student speeches about both sides of a controversial topic and then ask students to discuss the underlying core beliefs, values, attitudes, and behaviors that are in dispute. Analyze how the dispute has typically been handled, and suggest ways to respond more ethically. (For example, educational reformers typically value education highly; they also tend to see a role for public education. However, they disagree on traditional means of educating and on the role of nonpublic sources in education.)

- Use written materials from the National Issues Forum (NIF). These publications present many perspectives on controversial issues. Write National Issues Forums, 100 Commons Road, Dayton, Ohio 45459-2777. Phone 1-800-433-7834. Or look at their website, www.nifi.org, for topic suggestions. The NIF Forums emphasize deliberation, not debate.

- Have students explore an issue of interest that's covered in the *Congressional Digest: The Pro and Con Monthly.*

Teaching Idea 3.2: Academic Honesty (pp. 44-47)

Purpose: To help students identify deliberate fraud.

Procedure: Have students examine plagiarized outlines from your files, but <u>be sure</u> that all identifying features are omitted in order to protect the plagiarizers' privacy.

1. Divide the students into groups of two or three.

2. Give each group an outline. I give a "culture shock" outline (copied exact words) to one group, another just like it to a second group. I similarly give three groups three separate outlines on "fat in our diet" (copied idea for idea). Two groups get a "phobias" outline, and so on until every small group has an outline.

3. Have them examine their outline, noting the opening, the central idea, the main points, and the conclusion.

4. After a few minutes, have them trade outlines with the other pair with the matching outline. They usually read for a few seconds and look up, quizzically, saying, "This is the same outline." Some are identical, and others are rephrased, which leads to a discussion of deliberate fraud and plagiarism of ideas.

5. Explain your campus's policies for dealing with plagiarism. Discuss the effects of plagiarism on the students who cheat and on those who don't.

Credo for Free and Responsible Communication in a Democratic Society

Recognizing the essential place of free and responsible communication in a democratic society, and recognizing the distinction between the freedoms our legal system should respect and the responsibilities our education system should cultivate, we members of the Speech Communication Association endorse the following statements of principles:

WE BELIEVE that freedom of speech and assembly must hold a central position among American constitutional principles, and we express our determined support for the right of peaceful expression by any communicative means available to humans.

WE SUPPORT the proposition that a free society can absorb with equanimity speech which exceeds the boundaries of generally accepted beliefs and mores; that much good and little harm can ensue if we err on the side of freedom, whereas, much harm and little good may follow if we err on the side of suppression.

WE CRITICIZE as misguided those who believe that the justice of their cause confers license to interfere physically and coercively with the speech of others, and we condemn intimidation, whether by powerful majorities or strident minorities, which attempts to restrict free expression.

WE ACCEPT the responsibility of cultivating by precept and example, in our classrooms and in our communities, enlightened uses of communication; of developing in our students a respect for precision and accuracy in communication, and for reasoning based upon evidence and a judicious discrimination among values.

WE ENCOURAGE our students to accept the role of well-intentioned and articulate citizens, to defend the communication rights of those with whom they may disagree, and to expose abuses of the communication process.

WE DEDICATE ourselves fully to these principles, confident in the belief that reason will ultimately prevail in a free marketplace of ideas.

Endorsed by the Speech Communication Association, December 1972. Reprinted by permission of the Speech Communication Association.

1. This *credo* (Latin for "I believe") was endorsed in 1972. What happenings in the USA in the late 1960s and early 1970s might have led members of the Speech Communication Association to endorse this statement of beliefs?

2. Some of these ideas are encoded into law. What laws are you aware of that support these principles?

3. Discuss the balance between freedom and responsibility in this document.

Chapter 4

EFFECTIVE LISTENING

To participate in dialogical communication, students must be savvy, yet responsible listeners as well as speakers. Let's face it; we spend infinitely more time listening than we do giving speeches. The chapter opens with a discussion of the importance of listening followed by a section describing the barriers to listening-- linguistic, cultural, and personal. Next are strategies to improve comprehensive and critical listening. The final section describes verbal and nonverbal behaviors students can use to be more dialogical listeners.

Chapter Goals

<u>At the end of this chapter, your students should be able to:</u>

- Distinguish listening from hearing
- Appreciate the importance of listening skills
- Describe the linguistic, cultural, and personal barriers that affect your listening
- Draw and explain four thought patterns that are common during listening
- Use cultural schema to improve their listening
- Discuss diverse cultural listening styles
- Identify strategies to improve your comprehensive listening
- Improve your critical listening skills
- Practice dialogical listening through nonverbal feedback
- Give appropriate verbal feedback, using the D-R-E Method

<u>At the end of this chapter, you should be able to:</u>

Know which, if any, students say they need better listening skills, and help those students devise a strategy to improve their listening.

Chapter Outline

I. Listening skills are valuable
    A. **Hearing** (a physical process) and **listening** (an active mental process) are different.
    B. We use listening more than any other communication skill.
    C. Good listening skills are good job skills.
    D. Good listening skills are good academic skills.
    E. You have an investment in the listening situation.

II. Barriers to listening come from linguistic, cultural, and personal factors.
    A. There are two major linguistic barriers.
        1. People must share a language; accents and dialects can hinder understanding.
        2. Vocabulary differences can hinder comprehension.
    B. Cultural barriers may mean that an audience doesn't understand a speaker's **cultural allusions**.
    C. Personal barriers can obstruct listening.
        1. Physical factors such as hearing loss or sleepiness hinder listening.
        2. Psychological factors such as stress or worry divert attention.
        3. **Stereotyping** and **prejudices** interfere with listening.

4. Attention wanders, partly because of the **speech-thought differential** (also known as **leftover thinking space**).
5. Four thought patterns characterize listening.
    a. Small departures from the communication line can help or hinder.
    b. Going off on a tangent means the listeners depart into their own worlds.
    c. Engaging in private argument is one way to close one's mind.
    d. Taking large departures means that listeners' minds wander to unrelated topics, return, wander, and return.
        <u>Stop and Check: Listening Skills Self-Assessment</u>

III. Several strategies can improve listening.
   A. Use cultural **schemas**.
      1. Schemas are mental plans or models used to perceive, interpret, store, and recall information.
      2. We develop schemas for many types of speeches.
   B. Have a listening purpose.
      1. **Comprehensive listening**, listening for information, is an important skill.
         a. Prepare in advance by finding some information on the topic.
         b. During the speech, direct attention by taking notes.
         c. Enhance the meaning by elaborating mentally on the speaker's ideas.
         d. Look for organizational patterns that can aid comprehension and retention.
         e. Use strategies that complement one's personal learning style.
         f. Pay attention to the speaker's manner--whether confident or tentative.
             <u>Diversity in Practice: Cultural Listening Styles</u>
      2. **Critical listening** requires reflection and weighing the merits of various appeals.
         a. Critical listening builds on the skills of comprehensive listening.
         b. It also questions the speaker's goals, reasoning, sources, appeals, and so on.
         c. Use it on topics you agree with as well as those you oppose.
             <u>Ethics in Practice: Laptops in Lectures</u>
             <u>Stop and Check: Develop Strategies to Listen More Effectively</u>

IV. Dialogical listening involves nonverbal, verbal, and written feedback.
   A. Nonverbal messages are communicated through posture, movements, and distance.
      1. A posture of involvement can help focus attention.
      2. Eye contact helps focus attention.
      3. Shorter distances between speakers and listeners can increase involvement.
      4. Avoid disruptive movements and make supportive movements that help the speaker.
   B. Appropriate verbal feedback includes both questions and comments.
      1. **Clarification questions** ask for information to clear up confusion about the message.
      2. **Closed questions** ask for brief, specific answers.
      3. **Open questions** invite more lengthy responses.
      4. **Loaded questions** have implicit assumptions that put the speaker on the defensive.
      5. **Requests for elaboration** ask speakers to expand on their ideas.
      6. **Comments** provide information that supplements the speech.
          <u>Diversity in Practice: Saving Face</u>
   C. Provide written feedback using the **D-R-E Method** (describe-respond-evaluate).
      1. Describe what you heard.
      2. Respond with a personal interpretation or reaction.
      3. Evaluate by critiquing what was effective and what could improve.
          <u>Stop and Check: Write a Critique</u>
          <u>Practically Speaking: Receiver Apprehension</u>

Suggested Videos

Malcolm X. (1992) Show a clip from this film (www.americanrhetoric.com has several excerpts) or from another film that shows a speaker and audience in a "call and response" interaction. (knowledge, comprehension)

- Before the clip, review the pattern and emphasize that some cultures place great value on the co-creation of meaning.
- After the clip, discuss specific words and phrases the audience used to respond.
- Analyze the function of the responses. That is, what effect do they have on the speaker? On the listener personally? On the rest of the audience? (analysis, synthesis)
- Why isn't the call and response form common in board meetings or committee meetings? Or is it there, but less obvious? Do you think a board made up of African Americans would use more dialogical forms in meetings? Why or why not? (synthesis, analysis)

Informative Student Speech. Choose a video from your files or from the interactive video activities on the book CourseMate. ("Cyber-Bullying" in Chapter 17's resources or "The *Dun Dun* Drum" in Chapter 16's resources are two possibilities.)

- Before the speech, announce the topic and give students about three minutes to jot down their knowledge about it, their interest in it, and its significance to them personally, and what they must do to pay attention and learn from the speech.
- Direct them to write a few questions they'd ask the speaker and then show the speech.
- Afterwards have them evaluate their listening. Did they comprehend? Did their attention wander? Where? What did they do to refocus? Did they encounter biases? What did they do to overcome them? Was something about the speaker distracting? What did they do to overcome that? (application, evaluation)

Book CourseMate. Choose a persuasive speech, such as "Fat Discrimination" in Chapter 18's interactive Video Resources or "You Have My Deepest Sympathy: You Just Won the Lottery" (Chapter 10).

- Beforehand, announce the topic and ask the students to assess their general attitude about it, ranging from highly positive--positive--neutral--negative--highly negative.
- Play the video.
- Have them write an in-class response--first, describing their emotional response to the speech and then analyzing how their emotions affected their listening. Have them relate their responses to their original attitude.
- What was the speaker's bias? What were listeners asked to believe? To do? Was enough evidence presented? What was the speaker's source of information? Was the speaker believable?

There is no speech in the end of chapter materials. Students are directed to view their choice of videos on the book CourseMate that supplements the text.

Speech Illustrating a Schema. To help students understand the concept of schemas, play President Reagan's eulogy or tribute to the *Challenger* crew, Tiger Woods' apology, or William Faulkner's acceptance of the Nobel Prize for Literature, available on www.americanrhetoric.com or on YouTube. Each was given because each speaker needed to "say something" about the situation he addresses.

- Before the clip, describe the context in which the speech occurred.
- In a whole group discussion, elicit the elements expected in an eulogy, apology or acceptance speech.
- Play the video clip, directing students to listen for the expected elements.
- After the video, ask what it was about the speech that met or exceeded the expectations that people had in their schemas? (comprehension, application, analysis)

Discussion Topics

The Value of Listening (p. 55) Have students rank their communication behaviors in the order they think they use them. Emphasize that listening takes up most people's time. Then bring along a page from your school's catalogue that shows the course offerings and search for a course on listening skills. (If your department offers a listening course, pat yourself on the back and read the course description aloud; if not, discuss why not.)

- Discuss the specific skills they need to listen in various contexts--with family and friends, in the classroom, on the job, to radio or television programs.
- Give them ten or so minutes of in-class writing. Have them divide their waking time into hour-long segments, then log their communication activities during a typical day. Ask them to figure a rough percentage of how much time they spend in reading, writing, listening, and speaking. Collect their papers and skim them, making appropriate comments. (comprehension, application, evaluation)

Figure 4.1: The Chinese Character for Listening (p. 56) Use question #1 in the **Application and Critical Thinking Exercises** to reinforce this concept.

Barriers to Listening (pp. 56-58 Discuss the listening barriers described in the text and then follow up by having them diagnose and suggest a plan for William and for Gail, who describe their listening problems on page 57. Divide the class into four groups; have two groups come up with an "Ann Landers" type of advice letter for William and two groups prepare advice for Gail. Debrief by comparing and contrasting the advice each group gave. (application, synthesis, synthesis)

Figure 4.2: Four Thought Patterns (p. 58) Elicit examples that illustrate each pattern. (application)

Stop and Check: Listening Skills Self-Assessment (p. 59) Have students take the test in their text and tell you their results. Do a needs assessment of your class and plan specific lessons or activities to address the most common listening problems. (analysis)

Figure 4.3 Schemas (p. 60) Use the suggested videos on www.americanrhetoric.com to identify elements of specific speech schemas.

Diversity in Practice: Cultural Listening Styles (p. 62) Use one of the **Suggested Videos** that illustrates cultural listening styles. Or ask students to contribute examples from their cultural traditions. (application)

Listening Purposes (pp. 60-62) Use Teaching Idea 4.1 in **Supplemental Resources** to illustrate a variety of listening purposes. (comprehension, application)

Improving Comprehensive Listening (pp. 58-62) Use one or more of the **Suggested Videos** of informative speeches.

Improving Critical Listening (pp. 62-63) Use one or more of the **Suggested Videos** to show and discuss a persuasive student speech.

Ethics in Practice: Laptops in Lectures (pp. 63-64). Ask students to read the feature, and, working in groups, to answer the discussion questions that follow.

Co-creation of Meaning (Dialogical Listening) (pp. 64-65) Review the concept of co-creation of meaning and ask how the student listeners can create meaning in a variety of contexts—examples include: a protest rally, a lecture, a dispute with a parent, a religious service. (application, synthesis)

Nonverbal Feedback (p. 64-65). Have students listen to a classroom speech using the suggestions for #5 **Application and Critical Thinking Exercises**. Alternatively, direct students to an article on InfoTrac College Edition (search for Shut AND already AND surefire) about a student who decided not to speak for a year; in the process, he learned many things about the value of listening. Silence did not keep him from communicating, however, and you can use his story to review the communication model in Chapter 1. When Brett no longer used speech as a channel, he turned to the Internet and communicated via a Web page. Assign students to read the article and then work with them to design an experiment that will help them listen more effectively. (comprehension, analysis) (application)

Give Verbal Feedback. (pp. 65-66) Discuss the types of questions and comments listed on page 64 and ask students to keep them in mind as they listen to you lecture on a short section of the chapter. After you finish, assign them to small groups and have them construct at least two types of questions. After a few minutes, reassemble the entire class and elicit their questions, identifying each type. Answer appropriately. Discuss how this process co-creates meaning.

Provide Written Feedback. (pp. 66-67) Have students watch a videotaped speech or listen to a classmate's speech and then use the D-R-E Method for writing comments. Discuss how this process is one way to co-create meaning.

Diversity in Practice: Saving Face (p. 66) Link the notion of saving face to ethics, as discussed in Chapter 3. How is helping someone else save face arguably ethical? When is public shaming ever called for? (Discuss specific incidents in American politics and public life in which people's embarrassing mistakes were publicized through extensive media coverage. Assess the positive and/or negative results of the incident.) (synthesis, evaluation)

Practically Speaking: Receiver Apprehension (pp. 67-68). Ask students to read the feature, and, working in groups, to answer the discussion questions that follow.

Application and Critical Thinking Exercises

1. Use this question as a journal article. Have students write about what they could hear in their thirty seconds of listening. (analysis)

2. Use this question as an in-class written response on the day you discuss the Chinese symbol for listening (Figure 4.1), or assign it as a journal entry. Alternatively, discuss typical responses to a speaker who presents unwelcome or diverse ideas. Many people turn away their eyes (or they hide in their book or look at their neighbor). What do they do with their ears? With their heart? Consider using this question as a basis for a guided imagery experience that summarizes the concepts in Figure 4.1. For instance, have students close their eyes and think of a recent lecture they enjoyed. Ask them to focus their mental attention on what they were seeing. Second, focus on what they were hearing. Next, ask them to focus on their heart involvement. Change the scenario to a boring lecture and guide them through what they saw, heard, and felt. You can also have them envision a speaker they agreed with and one whose views totally upset them. Debrief by discussing the "heart" aspect of the Chinese character--especially as it affects their listening to a boring or an upsetting speaker. (application, analysis)

3. Students can complete this in a journal entry, or you can have them discuss their typical listening habits in the situations depicted in this exercise. (analysis)

4. Assign students to actually DO this exercise during a class period. Have them discuss how listening in a lecture setting is different than listening in a bar setting talking to a best friend. (application)

5. Have students create their Listening Skills Development Plans, using guidelines from the Utah State University's Academic Resource Center. They can link to idea sheets and find three sheets for Note Taking and Listening: (1) listening skills for lectures; (2) effective note taking strategies; and (3) note taking: Cornell method. Assign one-half of the class to follow the "active listening skills" link and the other half to read the material in the "listening skills for lectures." Have them summarize their findings in a one page paper and discuss those findings in class.

6. Assign one or two specific students to write out at least two questions as they listen to another classmate's speech. After the speech, have a question and answer period. (application)

7. Give some examples of description, response, and evaluation remarks and then assign students to do a D-R-E analysis of one of their classmate's speeches.

8. Use a controversial public figure to begin a discussion of listening obstacles. Perhaps bring a radio to class and listen to a talk radio program that airs during your class period. (Rush Limbaugh, Dr. Laura, Don Imus, Tom Leykis, Michael Medved . . . all these hosts are opinionated and controversial.) Or use a speech from www.americanrhetoric.com that your class would find controversial. Examples Louis Farrakhan, Patrick Buchanan, Michael Moore, Rush Limbaugh, and the like. (application, analysis)

Internet Activities

The CourseMate for Public Speaking, accessible through http://login.cengage.com, offers a broad range of resources that will help students better understand the material in the chapter, complete assignments, and succeed on tests. The CourseMate also features speech videos with critical viewing questions, speech outlines, and transcripts. It also offers interactive practice activities, self-quizzes, and a sample final exam.

Supplemental Resources

- Teaching Idea 4.1: Listening to Various Types of Material
- Teaching Idea 4.2: Lecture Option--The Process of Listening

Teaching Idea 4.1: Listening to Various Types of Material

Purpose: To have students understand various listening purposes.

Procedure: Make three tapes with excerpts (about 3 minutes long) from three very different types of speeches. Examples: a biology class lecture, an opinion piece taped off the radio such as a commentary from National Public Radio, and an excerpt from an inspirational narrative like Dave Dravecky's life story. I've used a clip from a news program that is arguably more persuasive than informative.
　　Construct a handout with 4-5 questions that ask specific information about each speech. For example (from an anatomy and physiology lecture):

1. How does the speaker support his claim that muscles are important?
2. What does "masticate" mean?
3. What is his point (his claim) in the butterfly example?
4. What is his general purpose?
5. What do you remember most about the lecture?

Have students listen to all three tapes without taking notes. Then, divide the class into groups, give each group a set of questions, and have a recorder write the group's answers. Go over their answers together.

Throughout, refer to the material in the text and the supplementary lecture, if you used it. Did vocabulary words hinder comprehension? Were there any unknown cultural allusions? What listening schema, if any, did they activate to help them interpret the various speeches? Where did their attention wander? Which material do they remember best? Why?

Teaching Idea 4:2: Lecture Option--The Process of Listening

Listening is part of the total process of cognition or thinking that includes five stages: receiving, discriminating, attending, assigning meaning, and remembering. (You'll find a list of the stages, suitable for transfer to a transparency, in the materials at the end of this chapter.)

Receiving If our ears function normally, we hear sounds continually. However, if there are problems in our anatomy or in the sound itself, we cannot receive the sensory data basic to good listening.

- Some people have anatomical impairments that prevent reception and processing of sounds.

- Problems can also exist in the sound source. Speakers' voices may be too soft to carry. Competing sounds, such as static in the microphone or noise in the hall during the speech, may also make it difficult to receive sounds.

Discriminating Not only must we hear, we must distinguish among the sounds we hear and make out meaningful words and phrases. Many factors can hinder this. A speaker's accent might make the discrimination of sounds difficult, or static in the microphone may distort the sound. Furthermore, acoustics can be so poor that resulting echoes distort the sounds.

Attending If there are no problems in the reception or discrimination of sounds, we must then focus our perception by paying attention--which is not always easy. There are three important things to know about attention:

- Attention is selective. Our interests, beliefs, and experiences predispose us to listen through *filters* by which we focus on some sounds and not others.
  - ➤ Example: You're driving a car and talking to your friend as the radio plays, your attention is on the conversation--not the road noise or the radio sounds. When a traffic bulletin warns of an accident in your area, your attention shifts to the bulletin. Your friend continues to speak, but you are not hearing her; your focus is on the radio message.
  - ➤ Example from public speaking: Some people pay close attention to physics lectures but find a discussion of the economy difficult to follow. We often listen differently to a speaker who supports our ideas on capital punishment than one whose ideas differ radically from ours. We may also pay more attention to certain parts of speeches, ignoring the statistics but paying attention to stories about real people.

- Attention fluctuates. Our attention can shift due to external causes--there's a noise outside, then the microphone static attracts our attention, finally, our focus returns to the speaker. However, instead of paying attention to her words, we notice a distracting mannerism or hear the noise her bracelet makes as it hits the podium.
  - ➤ We also have internal reasons for fluctuating attention. We think at the rate of about 500 words per minute, but the normal speaking rate is about 150 words a minute. The difference in the speed of thinking and the speed of speaking is termed the *speech-thought differential*.

- ➤ It is common for a speaker's words to trigger related thoughts in our minds, and we may find that we have "wandered" off on a tangent where we remain in our own mental world until something-- perhaps audience laughter or a teacher's question--returns our focus to the speaker. Although we continue to receive sounds the whole time, we do not attend to them.

- <u>Attention requires energy</u>. Because we often listen quietly, it may seem that we are doing nothing; however, listening is an active process. Our minds busily receive and sort ideas, relating them to what we already know, checking them against our beliefs, sifting the important and significant from the less important, and searching for categories to classify the information. During the speech-thought differential, we form images in our minds, predict what will be said next, or predict consequences.

<u>Assigning meaning</u>. Listening is more than simply hearing or even focusing on sounds, it requires that we assign meaning to the sounds we hear by thinking about the literal and figurative meaning of the words and ideas presented.

We also assign meaning to the way in which speakers present their ideas. If they speak confidently from conviction, their intense involvement with the topics becomes part of the total message such as, "This is important, pay attention," or "I care about this topic and so should you." If, however, they are tentative and apologetic or appear apathetic about the subject, we may get an entirely different message, concluding, "This does not matter a great deal."

<u>Remembering</u>. A test of listening skill is our ability to understand and remember what we hear, for ideas are of no long term value unless we can recall them. The common saying, "In one ear and out the other," reflects the fact that we forget much of what we hear. Many people tend to overestimate how well they listen-- thinking they remember 75-80% of what they hear, when, in fact, average listeners recall only about 25%.*

Example: Think about a lecture you heard last week in any class. Can you remember the main points? What arguments or evidence did the instructor use? Would you feel confident taking a detailed test on the information today? What if your term grade depended on that test?

Remembering involves a deep level of mental processing in which we put the ideas into our long term memories. This process is aided by mentally repeating and translating the speaker's ideas into our own words, making extensive connections to related ideas, and taking notes and reviewing them after the speech or lecture.

*Roach, C. A. & Wyatt, N. J. (1990). Listening and the rhetorical process. In J. Stewart (Ed.) *Bridges not walls: A book about interpersonal communication* (5th ed., pp. 169-173). New York: McGraw Hill.

The Listening Process

1. ## Receiving

2. ## Discriminating

3. ## Attending

    o **Attention is selective.**

    o **Attention fluctuates.**

    o **Attention requires energy.**

4. ## Assigning meaning

5. ## Remembering

Chapter 5

SELECTING YOUR TOPIC AND PURPOSE

This chapter is devoted to the skills of identifying an appropriate topic and deciding on a specific purpose and central idea. Additional materials in Chapter 17 provide more guidance on topic selection--one of the biggest problems students identify. Many find the mind map method of topic identification useful for generating a list of usable subjects.

Chapter Goals

At the end of this chapter, your students should be able to:

- Choose your speech subject
- Narrow your topic to fit the situation
- Identify a general purpose and a specific purpose for your speech
- Write a thesis statement that states your subject and its importance to the audience
- Write a preview that summarizes your main points

At the end of this chapter, you should be able to:

Have some idea of topics your students will choose. Knowing my student's interests allows me to be on the lookout for information they might be able to use in their speeches. For example, if I know a student is interested in the topic of "extreme sports" and I see a teaser for a *20/20* segment devoted to the topic of ice climbing, I might send the student an email or videotape the segment for her.

Chapter Outline

I. Choose a topic.
   A. Assess the audience's need to know.
      1. The topic should be significant.
      2. It should have an element of novelty.
                    <u>Ethics in Practice: Are Any Topics Taboo?</u>
   B. Consider your personal interests.
      1. Draw from personal interests.
      2. Use unique life experiences to find topics.
   C. Develop topics from other courses; this also helps the speaker learn course concepts.
        <u>Practically Speaking: Brad Lau, University Administrator, Student Life</u>
        <u>Diversity in Practice: Does Requiring One Speech</u>
        <u>on "Communication and Culture" Increase Students' Empathy?</u>
   D. Investigate current issues and events.
      1. Source material is commonly available in media coverage.
      2. The topic addresses a societal interest or need; thus, it passes the significance test.
   E. Consider international and cultural subjects that can be connected to listeners' lives.

II. Narrow the topic to fit time constraints.
<u>Stop and Check: Identify Several Usable Topics</u>

III. Choose the purpose and focus.
  A. Identify a **general purpose**, keeping in mind that purposes often overlap.
     1. Speeches that explain, teach, announce, describe, introduce or increase understanding have the purpose "to inform."
     2. The intention to convince, nominate, reinforce cultural ideals, or motivate an audience to action has the general purpose "to persuade."
     3. Humorous speeches hope "to entertain."
     4. Speeches "to commemorate" highlight and reinforce cultural ideals.
<u>Stop and Check: Narrow Your Purpose</u>
  B. Identify a **specific purpose**, a summary of the desired audience response.
     1. Purposes relating to thinking or beliefs aim for **cognitive effects**.
     2. Hoping to influence the audience's feelings targets **affective** or emotional **effects**.
     3. Moving the audience to act hopes for **behavioral effects**.
  C. Write a **thesis statement** or **central idea** that summarizes the main ideas of the speech.
     1. Phrase the thesis statement as a single declarative sentence that states the topic and summarizes the speech's contents as simply and precisely as needed to guide the speaker and the audience.
     2. Begin to formulate the thesis statement early, but revise it if necessary.
     3. State the thesis in the speech, generally in the introduction.
     4. Also include a **preview** or short summary of the major points developed in the speech.
<u>Build Your Speech: General Purpose, Specific Purpose, and Thesis Statement</u>
<u>Study and Review</u>

Suggested Videos

Book CourseMate. "Males in Nursing," which is outlined at the end of the chapter, was created out of the speaker's career goals and his interest in men's history in nursing. The topic supplements the illustrations and the general topic example used throughout the chapter. It's available on the interactive video activities for the chapter. (application, analysis)

Excerpts from a televised news broadcast During the week you teach this chapter, collect excerpts (perhaps 30 seconds from several stories) of news items.
  • Before you show the clips, ask students to look for broad and for specific topics in the news.
  • After the clip, elicit broad topics covered in the news (e.g., crime, education, music) and specific topics (let's say the news story was about new neighborhood crime prevention measures, a new charter school, and an up and coming rap artist).
  • Ask students to use the clip to spin off at least three more specific topics within the broader subject. (application, analysis)

Discussion Topics

Need to Know. (pp. 72-73) Emphasize audience analysis by discussing the questions at the end of the first paragraph under "Assess Your Audience's Need to Know." Give examples of topics with a questionable need-to-know such as the dangers of drinking and driving, the importance of wearing seatbelts, why everyone should join a sorority or fraternity, how to make chocolate chip cookies, how to carve a jack-o-lantern. Ask students to decide if they would make good topics. Why or why not? (analysis, evaluation)

Ethics in Practice: Are Any Topics Taboo? (p. 73). Ask students to read the feature, and, working in groups, to answer the discussion questions that follow.

Choosing Your Topic. (pp. 72-76) Use news clips described in **Suggested Videos** to help students find topics, or use a suggestion from <u>Teaching Idea 5.1 "Identifying Topics"</u> in the **Supplemental Resources** section. (application, synthesis)

General Purposes. (pp. 77-81) Select several broad topics and divide the class into groups. Have each group select a topic and make a diagram similar to <u>Figure 6.3</u>. (application)

Narrowing the Topic, Purpose, and Focus. (pp. 79-82) Develop this skill by selecting a topic, such as developing good study skills, and having students identify a cognitive, an affective, and a behavioral purpose that relates to it. (application, synthesis)

Build Your Speech: General Purpose, Specific Purpose, and Thesis Statement. (p. 82) This would make a good in-class small group activity. Divide students into groups and assign each one to select two general topics from the list and decide together on a general purpose, specific purpose statement, thesis statement, and preview for an impromptu speech on the subject. Have a spokesperson from each group summarize their work. Then, invite volunteers to actually give a one-minute speech on one of the topics. (application, synthesis)

Application and Critical Thinking Exercises

1. and 2.   These two exercises work well as small group activities. See additional mind map ideas in <u>Teaching Idea 6.1: "Identifying Topics"</u> in **Supplemental Resources**. (application)

3.   Divide the class into small groups and ask them to work with the topics listed in this question.

4.   This question ties into the long liberal arts tradition that underlies public speaking courses. For centuries, thousands of rhetoric students have read Augustine's writings. (Remind your students that St. Augustine was a bishop, so his advice is given within the context of his religion. However, the principles in these chapters have wide application.) Rhetoric has often been disparaged as a tool for unscrupulous speakers to use to trick and manipulate unsuspecting audiences. In Chapter 2, Augustine argues that, if teachers of falsehood know how to make their speeches interesting and their listeners interested, should not those who teach the good and the true master rhetorical principles in order to persuade their audiences? In Chapter 11, Augustine argues for clarity, style, and a bit of flavor "to meet the tastes of the majority." Chapter 12 lays out three general purposes, and argues that teaching (informing) is the most essential. Have your students discuss why he thinks this is so. Chapter 13 stresses the importance of moving or motivating the listener to put noble ideas into practice.

5. and 6.   Have students use this list or suggest topics of their own that they could develop into informative, persuasive, or entertaining speeches. Then ask them to decide whether or not they could develop a commemorative speech around the topic. If so, how? If not, why not?

Internet Activities

The CourseMate for Public Speaking, accessible through http://login.cengage.com, offers a broad range of resources that will help students better understand the material in the chapter, complete assignments, and succeed on tests. The CourseMate also features speech videos with critical viewing questions, speech outlines, and transcripts. It also offers interactive practice activities, self-quizzes, and a sample final exam.

Supplemental Resources

- Teaching Idea 5.1: Identifying Topics
- Research Note 5.1: Accountants and Classroom Presentations

Teaching Idea 5.1: Identifying Topics

Purpose: To generate a number of speech topics that students can use throughout the term.

Procedure: Use one or more of the following ideas:

- On the board put a variety of broad categories such as people, places, issues, events, processes, controversial issues, international topics, concepts or ideas. Suggest a couple of topics within each category (people: musicians, politicians) then have small groups of students identify additional narrowed subjects within the category. Collect their work. After class type up the suggested topics and make a handout that you distribute during the next class session. Or have a recorder from each group put their group's list in the course's email folder.

- Instead of using the board, write broad categories onto separate transparencies. Give each small group a transparency and have them make a mind map on it. Save the transparencies and use them throughout the chapter and throughout the term whenever students need to choose speech topics.

- Bring 6-7 sheets of newsprint and felt pens to class. Divide the class into groups of 3 or 4. Assign a category to each group and have the members come up with a list of topics within each category. Tape or pin these sheets around the room and discuss them. After class, roll up the lists and store them for use with Chapters 16 (Informative Speaking) and 17 (Persuasive Speaking).

- Use excerpts from TV news, as described in **Suggested Videos**, to identify significant topics of interest or significance to the broad audience that views television. Stop after each story and identify possible informative and persuasive purposes you might develop for the broader topic.

  ➢ For instance, hurricanes recently battered the eastern seaboard. Topic possibilities: hurricane staging (informative), different types of hurricanes (informative), destructive hurricanes in history (informative), buying special hurricane/flood insurance (persuasive), emergency preparedness measures to take before a hurricane (persuasive).

- Bring in a number of current magazines. Lead a group discussion of topic possibilities from the cover page of just one magazine. (Magazines such as *Time* or *Newsweek* work best.)

> Example: a *Time* with a cover headline that read, "The Hottest Jobs of the Future." Topic possibilities—What jobs are up and coming? What will our offices look like? Will good service become more valued? Which careers will flourish? Which careers will vanish? Etc. After students get the idea, divide the class into pairs or groups of three and give each a current magazine. Ask them to identify five good topics from their magazine cover and write their list on the board.

Research Note 5.1. Accountants and Classroom Presentations

Source: InfoTrac College Edition Article A11583351

Lucinda Van Alst & James Schmitte. (1991, October). Practitioner's guide to making student presentations. (Management of an accounting practice). *The CPA Journal, 61(10),* 74-78.

The authors are practicing accountants who give advice to professional who are invited to make presentations to college students, either in classroom presentations or for groups such as Beta Alpha Psi, the financial information honorary for students and professionals. Their article provides information about timing, topic selection, and so on that you could use with Chapter 5 (audience analysis) and Chapter 6 (selecting your topic and purpose). They also discuss visual aids which you could use with Chapter 12.

Abstract: "Presentations aimed at introducing students to the professional world of accounting offer accounting firms the opportunity to enhance on-campus recruiting activities. Small firms, in particular, should take advantage of this chance to display the financial attractiveness of non-national firms, as compared to the much larger national firms, through a show of their viability and professionalism. Crucial to a presentation is the **selection** of a suitable **topic** or theme with the assistance of the school's faculty, the use of sufficient lead time in the preparation of the presentation, and the development of a detailed and logical outline of the presentation. Other useful tips in enhancing student presentations are presented."

Chapter 6

AUDIENCE ANALYSIS

To maintain the dialogical theme of the text, this chapter emphasizes the speaker's view of the audience and the audience's view of the speaker. Effective speakers understand what motivates audiences and adapt their messages accordingly. This chapter begins by identifying different motivations that audiences bring to a speaking situation. Demographic analysis is discussed as one tool for identifying those motivations. Next students learn how to develop a questionnaire that can be used to generate an audience's psychological profile. The effects of environmental variables, such as time and environment, are then discussed. The chapter ends with the audience's perception of the speaker and the perception of speaker credibility.

Chapter Goals

At the end of this chapter, your students should be able to:

*   Describe various audience motivations
*   Tell how demographic audience analysis helps you adapt your topic to a particular audience
*   Develop a questionnaire to assess the listeners' psychological profile
*   Explain how the situation, including time and place, affect your audience
*   Analyze your audience's perception of your credibility

Chapter Outline

I.   This chapter focuses on the audience's motivations and perspectives on you and your topic.
    A.   Knowing the audience's motivations helps speakers adapt their strategies.
        1.   **Unmotivated audiences** do not have a purposeful listening goal and are **random**.
        2.   **Passive audiences** listen in order to accomplish other goals; speakers should select interesting topics and relate them to listeners' lives.
        3.   **Motivated audiences** voluntarily and intentionally seek out an opportunity to hear a particular speech.
        4.   **Homogeneous** audiences share an attitude--either positive or negative; with positive audiences, speakers must develop their ideas clearly. **Hostile** audiences have negative attitudes toward the speaker or the topic (see Chapter 17).
               Ethics in Practice: Pandering: Telling Audiences What they Want to Hear
    B.   **Demographic audience analysis** analyzes listeners according to the populations or groups they represent; however, demographic factors are **salient** in different situations, and demographic elements function together rather than separately.
        1.   **Ethnicity** refers to one's cultural tradition and heritage stemming from national and religious origins.
        2.   **Race** or racial categories are culturally constructed.
          a.   Racial categories are not distinct and they are not genetically significant.
          b.   Being **racist** assumes that people behave in certain ways because of racial categories.
        3.   Religious beliefs can be held loosely or intensely; wise speakers consider the range and intensity of religious commitments in every speech.
        4.   **Gender**, not biological sex, is a cluster of traits culturally labeled as masculine, feminine, or androgynous.

   a. **Sexism** assumes that someone will act a certain way because of one's sex or gender.

   b. Gender is salient at gender-exclusive events but is less important in other contexts.

  5. Marital status and sexual expression influence audience responses, and students often make unwarranted assumptions about sexual orientation and sexual activity.

  6. Age influences listeners' motivations and concerns.

   a. Mature Americans have adapted to enormous social and technological changes.

   b. The large group of baby boomers experienced the turbulent 1960s and the technological developments of the last few decades.

   c. The racially and culturally diverse Generation Xers are the first latchkey generation who grew up with a great deal of media and a lot of cultural changes.

   d. The millennium generation, born around 1980, inherited social and environmental problems that tend to make them civic minded; they have always lived in a fast-moving, high tech world.

  7. Group affiliation, affiliating with people that share their interests, experiences, or hobbies, often matters; group identity is highly salient.

  8. Education, occupation or socioeconomic status must be taken into consideration in particular speaking situations.

  9. Regional differences in the United States can influence audience interests, language, political affiliation and perspectives.

Stop and Check: Analyze Yourself Using Demographic Categories

 C. Analyzing the audience's **psychological profile,** their beliefs, attitudes, values and behaviors related to your subject helps speakers adapt to specific listeners.

  1. Using **direct methods,** including interviews, focus groups, or questionnaires, helps speakers know what information the audience needs.

  2. **Indirect methods** include personal observations, and secondary sources.

  3. **Questionnaires** are one type of **direct method** to help you learn the audience's disposition to the topic. Knowing audience attitudes, the tendencies to have negative or positive feelings about a topic, helps the speaker adapt.

   a. **Scaled questions** measure attitudes along a range or continuum from highly positive to highly negative.

   b. Attitudes are made up of feelings, beliefs, and predispositions to act.

   c. A single audience generally includes people with a variety of attitudes.

  3. **Values** are standards used to judge good or bad, moral or immoral, beautiful or ugly, and so on; they are measured across a range.

  4. Beliefs, values, actions, and attitudes are always interrelated.

Stop and Check: Construct a Questionnaire

 D. Speakers also need to assess the specific situation in which they speak.

  1. The time can affect the audience.

   a. The time of day the speech is scheduled has physical effects on the audience.

   b. The cultural time system makes some people watch the clock while others are more relaxed about the length of the message.

   c. Timeliness also affects the audience response to a topic.

  2. The environment--things like the size and color of the room, the temperature, outside conditions, and noisy equipment--can all affect audience attention.

Stop and Check: Do a Situational Analysis

II. The audience forms a perception of the speaker known as **credibility,** or believability.

 A. **Prior credibility** is what the speaker brings to the speech.

  1. This is the reputation or expertise the speaker brings with him- or herself.

  2. Most students lack prior credibility; they must find ways to develop credibility.

Diversity in Practice: Prior Credibility in Other Cultures

 B. **Demonstrated** or **intrinsic credibility** comes in the speech itself.

116

1. The speaker shows her knowledge and understanding of the topic.
2. Poise and self-control are components of demonstrated credibility.

C. **Terminal credibility**, the balance between the speaker's prior reputation and her demonstrated expertise, is flexible and open to change.

Practically Speaking: What Audiences Do Nurses Address?
Speech Video: Kelsey Bennett "Advergaming: The Future of Advertising"

Suggested Videos

Book CourseMate. "Advergaming: The Future of Advertising" by Kelsey Bennett is outlined at the end of the chapter and available on the interactive speech activities for Chapter 6. This speech has many interesting features. Her topic is unfamiliar to many of her listeners, but she does a good job of defining new terms throughout her speech. In addition, she uses survey findings to support her points and she creatively uses visual aids.

1999 AFA-NIET After Dinner Speech. The "N-Word Speech." (Available from the AFA-NIET Tournament; the forensics coach at your school may have a copy.) In this award winning presentation, Marlita Hill works masterfully with an audience that includes people who are uncomfortable with her topic. Here's an example where race or ethnicity is highly salient. Ask students to note the specific ways she confronts listeners with their anxiety. How does the audience react? How does the ethnicity of the listener matter? How does the ethnicity of the speaker matter? Discuss their observations in class. (comprehension, application, analysis)

Discussion Topics

Audience Motivations (pp. 88-90) Introduce the subject by using Teaching Idea 6.1: "Kinds of Audiences" in **Supplemental Resources**. (analysis)

Demographic Analysis (pp. 90-93) Use magazine ads as described in Teaching Idea 6.2 (**Supplemental Resources**) to help students articulate aspects of demographic analysis that ad makers routinely use. (analysis, synthesis)

Salience (p. 92) Refer also to **Figures 6.2**. (comprehension)

Psychological Profiles (p. 98) Demonstrate how to do a psychological profile by creating a combination questionnaire of your own on a topic of particular interest to you. Ask students to complete the questionnaires in class and then discuss the variety of responses. Ask how speakers should use the information gained to guide their speech purpose and preparation. (comprehension, application, synthesis)

Time and Public Speaking (p. 97) One of my personal research emphases is chronemics, the nonverbal time system. Consequently, I'm very interested in the cultural uses of time. Consider presenting ideas from Research Note 6.1 in **Supplemental Resources** below. The case is reprinted here:

Professor Brain consistently violates time norms. Sometimes she continues her lecture up to six minutes after the class is scheduled to end. At other times, she's late to class, then she shuffles papers and talks to students so that she doesn't actually start until about twenty minutes into the class period. On occasion, she skips class entirely--with no note on the classroom door and no explanation.

- *Would you stay when Prof Brain is late? Why or why not? How often would you stay? How long? How would you feel?*

- *How would you signal Professor Brain that her time is up and she should quit talking so that you can get to your next class which is across campus?*

- *What's your response if you come to class (it's your only class that day, and you made a real effort to get there) and there's no Brain and no message?*

- *Would it make a difference if you found out later that she had a doctor's appointment that she'd scheduled two weeks ago? What if she had an emergency flat tire on the way to work? Would it make a difference if it were a sunny day and some students saw her out for a drive in the country?*

- *Are any of her behaviors grounds for some kind of administrative discipline? If so, what? Why?*

- *What end-of-the-course evaluation would you give her?*

- *What can you learn from this that applies to time limits on classroom speeches? To speaking on your scheduled day? To expectations in your future occupation?*

<u>Prior, Demonstrated or Intrinsic, and Terminal Credibility</u> (pp. 98-100) Ask students to give actual examples of each type of credibility.
- Prior credibility: have students name speakers who visit your city with prior credibility. Discuss what gives the speaker prior credibility.
- Demonstrated credibility: show a clip from C-SPAN and from a popular cooking show. How is credibility demonstrated differently in each setting?
- Terminal credibility: Use current and historical examples of people whose credibility was hurt when the truth was discovered. For example, Rep. Anthony Weiner denied sending inappropriate pictures to women via social media, which later proved to be untrue. South Carolina Governor Mark Sanford claimed to be hiking the Appalachian Trail when in fact he was in Argentina with his mistress. (comprehension, application)

Application and Critical Thinking Exercises

1. If you do not use <u>Teaching Idea 6.1</u>, "Identify Types of Audiences," let this question act as a review of the material on audience motivations. This can be an in-class writing assignment to apply the textual concepts. (application)

2. This question is designed for students who like to know that their courses are relevant and that the skills they are (sometimes painfully) learning will pay off eventually. Ask students to identify their major, future occupation, political and religious commitments, strong views on issues that might make them speak out publicly, and so on. If possible, form groups on the basis of a shared characteristic--their major, for instance. On the board, list the six types of audiences, and have each group record the possibilities for speaking to each type in the future. Debrief by having a spokesperson report to the whole class. (application, analysis)

3. Divide the class into four or six small groups. Assign Topic A to half the groups and Topic B to the other half. Give the groups plenty of time to identify adaptations needed for the varied audiences, then return to a whole group discussion time in which they share their conclusions with the entire class. Compare and contrast the strategies that the different Topic A and Topic B groups came up with. (application, synthesis)

4. Have students answer this question in a journal entry or an in-class written response that identifies their credibility in relationship to their next speech topic. (analysis)

5. Go through the two topics in class. Have students divide into groups to discuss how demographic factors would influence different topics.

6. This exercise lets students understand that audience analysis skills are useful in a wide variety of situations and occupations.

7. The first two editions of the text included the map of the Nine Nations of North America. Ask students to research the Nine Nations. Go to Google and do a search for "nine nations north America Joel Garreau." Discuss the information found regarding Garreau's theory. Is it still relevant today?

8. Have students compare your current classroom to other classrooms they've been in. How would the class be different if it were held in a prison? How about in a local bar?

9. Try this as a blog or journal entry for students. What do they personally check for when giving a speech?

10. After viewing Reba McIntire's song, as the students for suggestions of other audiences served by other music artists. How is audience of an Eminem video different than the McIntire audience? What specifically in the videos indicate that difference?

11. Having students conduct this discussion in class will help them to apply the material found in this chapter.

Internet Activities

The CourseMate for Public Speaking, accessible through http://login.cengage.com, offers a broad range of resources that will help students better understand the material in the chapter, complete assignments, and succeed on tests. The CourseMate also features speech videos with critical viewing questions, speech outlines, and transcripts. It also offers interactive practice activities, self-quizzes, and a sample final exam.

Supplemental Resources

- Teaching Idea 6.1: Kinds of Audiences
- Teaching Idea 6.2: Demographic Audience Analysis
- Research Note 6.1: Relevance and Student Motivation
- Research Note 6.2: Cultural Time Differences

Teaching Idea 6.1. Audience Motivations

Purpose: To understand the motivations of various audiences.

Procedure: Begin by having students describe a specific audience they've been part of. Elicit responses until you have several examples for each category found in the text. List these on the board as they are given. (You may have to provide hints for pedestrian audiences or absent audiences.) After students have named several audiences, display a list of the six audience types. Then, use one of the ideas listed below:

- In a whole group discussion, have students match the list of audiences on the board to the list on the transparency. Throughout, teach the characteristics of each type of audience.

- Divide the class into six small groups, have class members use their text to identify characteristics of the audience they have been assigned, then match audiences listed on the board to their category. (If there are only a few in a given category, have students add to the list.) Have a spokesperson from each group share information with the rest of the class.

Teaching Idea 6.2 Demographic Audience Analysis

Purpose: To help students identify demographic considerations that affect the way a message is presented.

Procedure: Begin the lesson by displaying two different ads for a similar product. (Example: dog food ads-- one from *Better Homes and Gardens* and one from *Field and Stream*.) Ask students to identify the magazines in which the ads appeared. Lead them to see that the demographic characteristics of the target audience resulted in two very different ads with essentially the same message--"buy dog food."

Then have them work in pairs to complete the following task:

- Before class, mount ads from 14-17 magazines on construction paper or some other backing. Choose ads targeted to a specific audience from a wide variety of magazines--those targeted to bodybuilders, families, dog fanciers, music lovers, artists, Christians, nurses, etc. Include magazines such as *Time*, *Discover* (science), *Working Woman*, *Modern Maturity*, *Ebony*, and *Psychology Today*. For example, a Hitachi ad in *Discover* magazine shows a robot; the same product in *Rolling Stone* might feature a sophisticated piece of playback equipment.

- Number the ads, and place them in various locations throughout the room.

- List the titles of the magazines on a separate handout. Provide a blank beside each name for students to match the number on the ad to the correct periodical.

- Give one handout to every two persons requiring them to work in pairs to do the matching.

- Direct them to discuss between themselves how the topic and details in the ad have been chosen specifically for the target audience.

- Have them get out of their seats, walk around the room, and fill in all the blanks. They do not have to work in order.

- Then go over the ads together. Discuss how audience interests help determine what ad goes into each magazine. Link this to topic selection in public speaking. Speakers choose topics that are linked to the interests of their audiences.

- Discuss how marketers specifically design details in their ads to account for demographic variables. For instance, an airline ad in *Modern Maturity* shows senior citizens; one in *Ebony* features African Americans. Help them see that, even with the same topic, ads differ in details. Relate this to public speaking in which speakers select specific details depending on their audience's beliefs and values.

Research Note 6.1. Relevance and Student Motivation

According to the classifications in the text, students are mostly passive audience members. A few may be in the course because of your reputation as a terrific teacher or because they love public speaking, and they're anxious to learn more about the subject. Most, however, take the course to meet other goals—to get the credit, to graduate. The major challenge with passive audiences is to make the material interesting and relevant.

Focusing on the student question, "What's in it for me?" Frymier & Shulman (1995) explored the link between relevance and motivation to study. They found a moderate, positive correlation. Instructors whose examples came from student experiences, personal experiences, and current events increased relevance for students. Other strategies that helped maintain student attention and resulted in greater overall course satisfaction included links to other content areas, career-related assignments, and explicit statements that helped students understand the importance of the content and recognize how public speaking related to their career goals.

Source: Frymier, A. B. & Shulman, G. M. (1995). "What's in it for me?": Increasing relevance to enhance motivation. *Communication Education, 44,* 40-50.

Research Note 6.2. Cultural Time Differences

Robert Levine's recent book, *A Geography of Time: The Temporal Misadventures of a Social Psychologist, or How Every Culture Keeps Time Just a Little Bit Differently,* describes temporal variations among cultural groups globally. Researchers in cities worldwide measured the accuracy of clocks, the time it took pedestrians to walk 60 feet downtown, and the length of time a postal worker took to sell a stamp.

Faster paced U.S. cities included Boston, Buffalo, and New York; the slowest were Shreveport, Sacramento, and Los Angeles. The four fastest moving countries were Switzerland, Ireland, Germany, and Japan with El Salvador, Brazil, Indonesia, and Mexico the slowest paced.

Levine says that much of the world lives on "event time" illustrated by Burundi where people agree to meet when the cows return from the watering hole. A Madagascar resident might tell you that you can walk to the nearest market in "the time it takes to cook rice."

In contrast, people who plan their lives around the clock often seem obsessed with or addicted to temporal precision. In the West, for instance, we've developed an atomic clock that is predicted to be accurate, almost to the second, a million years from now.

The world seems to be moving toward clock time, although a culture's temporal rhythms are deeply embedded. For instance, revolutionaries have tried to change cultural time norms—usually unsuccessfully. French Revolutionists imposed a rational, secular calendar, based on the number ten and stripped of religious significance such as saints' days. They reorganized time into three ten-day weeks per month and divided the day into just ten periods rather than the traditional twenty-four. This reform lasted thirteen years.

121

Calendars are another way to keep time, and a commitment to diversity means we are aware that some students are straddling two calendar systems. For example, when I lived in New York City, my Muslim neighbors fasted during the month of Ramadan; some Jewish residents built temporary shelters outside their homes to celebrate *Sukkot* (Tabernacles) in the month of *Tishri* (roughly mid-September-October). In Oregon, Russian Old Believers immigrants use the Julian calendar that differs from the Gregorian calendar by thirteen days.

Chapter 7

RESEARCHING YOUR SPEECH IN THE DIGITAL AGE

In the years since the first edition came out, we've witnessed an explosion of information available electronically. (The first manuscript went to the editor in December of 1993; this means that I finished the original research chapter a year before pictures went onto the Internet in 1994.) The rapid expansion of technology for recording and storing information means that I must continuously update this chapter.

Chapter Goals

At the end of this chapter, your students should be able to:

- Plan your research
- Distinguish between primary and secondary sources
- Locate and gather materials from a variety of sources
- Include diverse perspectives in your research
- Critically evaluate your sources
- Record information in a way that suits your learning style and avoids plagiarism

At the end of this chapter, you should be able to:

Understand and assist more effectively with students who may have difficulty doing research. (See Research Note 7.1 in **Supplemental Resources**.)

Chapter Outline

I. Gather appropriate materials.
   A. Developing a research plan using tips from a **research librarian**.
      1. Budget enough time.
      2. Include a librarian in the research plan; **subject librarians** have an advanced degree in a discipline as well as a library degree.
                    Diversity in Practice: Research in Kenya
      3. Identify key terms to use in a search of computerized catalogs, databases, or the Internet.
      4. Identify known experts in the field.
      5. Include critical evaluation into the plan from the very outset.
      6. Keep a running list of all sources during the search.
      7. Make critical evaluation a part of your plan.
                    Stop and Check: Begin Your Research Plan
   B. Distinguish between primary and secondary sources.
      1. **Primary sources** are created by individuals and groups who are directly involved in events at the time they take place; they include **original documents**, **creative works**, and **relics** or **artifacts**.
      2. **Secondary sources** are produced by non-participants who summarize and interpret original source materials and include biographies, movie reviews, and textbooks.
   C. Personal experiences can provide usable material and make the speaker more credible.
   D. Interviews with experts or laypeople (peers) are helpful for clarifying confusing ideas.
      1. **Experts** know about a subject though study, experience, or occupation.

2. **Laypeople** or **peers** gained insights and opinions from ordinary living and personal experiences with a topic.
3. Several tips help make an interview more satisfying to both participants.
   a. Prepare in advance.
   b. Give the interviewee an idea of the topic and the desired information in advance of the interview.
   c. Take careful notes, and have the interviewee add or correct the information.
   d. Take the interviewee's perspective.
   e. Ask to tape the interview and place the recorder in full view throughout.
   f. Be conscious of the time when setting the appointment and during the discussion.

E. Lectures and oral performances, live or mediated, can also provide information.

Stop and Check: Revisit Your Research Plan

F. The library and online sources provide an enormous variety of materials.
2. Books are a good source of information if they are not outdated.
   a. Many classics and other full text books are now online.
   b. **Scholarly books** are written by experts and based on research.
   c. **Trade books** are aimed at a general audience and include bestselling novels.
4. Periodicals are issued once during a time period--weekly, monthly, quarterly, or yearly.
   a. Popular or general-interest magazines have a wide audience.
   b. **Trade** and **academic journals** target specific occupations or people who share a research interest.
   c. Most major magazines and many scholarly journals are on the Internet and InfoTrac College Edition.
5. Newspapers are valuable for in-depth coverage and opinion pieces about current issues.
   a. Newspapers come daily, weekly, or monthly and vary widely in circulation.
   b. Elite newspapers, like the *Washington Post* and the *New York Times,* have detailed coverage of stories that smaller papers often use.
   d. Many newspapers are available on InfoTrac College Edition.

Diversity in Practice: International and Ethnic Presses

6. Reference materials provide a quick source for specific information.
   a. Encyclopedias collect and summarize information.
      1) **General encyclopedias** summarize thousands of topics; many are available online.
      2) **Specialized encyclopedias** provide information on specific subject areas.
   b. A **dictionary** defines and provides information about words and specialized subjects.
   c. Sources for statistics store numerical information on a variety of topics including population, education, government finance, and crime.
   d. Indexes help researchers locate articles from both scholarly and popular periodicals.

CourseMate: Reference Materials on the Internet
Practically Speaking: Wikipedia

II. Internet research strategies overlap with traditional research strategies with some differences.
1. Search tools fall into three general categories.
   1. **Search engines**, including Google and Yahoo! are built by spiders and list webpages that contain your search terms.
   2. In contrast, **subject directories** are hand-picked by humans, classified by subject, and often annotated.
   3. Most Web documents lie in **specialized databases**, including the **Academic Invisible Web** (**AIW**)
2. It is important to evaluate critical judgment about Web sources and content.
   1. Begin by examining the source. The URL (uniform resource locator) provides a domain suffix (e.g., .gov or .edu or .org) that indicates the sites primary purpose and tax status.
   2. Content should be evaluated based on the following tips:

  a. *What's its purpose?*
  b. *Is it biased?*
  c. *Is it up-to-date?*
  d. *Is it accurate?*
  e. *Is it original?*
  f. *Is it organized well?*

Stop and Check: Critical Thinking and the Internet

III. A method of recording information is vital.
 A. Note cards have several advantages, especially in avoiding cut-and-paste plagiarism.
  1. **Source cards** are written in standard bibliographic format.
   a. They tell where the material came from--its author, date, URL, and the like.
   b. **Annotate** the bibliography by including brief descriptions of the information found in the source.
  2. **Information cards** each contain a different idea.
   a. Having a separate topic on each card makes it easy to sort the cards into piles by topic.
   b. Supporting material can then be arranged and rearranged under the points.

Practically Speaking: Students and Research

 B. Some people like to photocopy materials or download and print them from computer sites.
  1. They then write directly onto the copy.
  2. It is important to be sure the entire reference is on each copy.
  3. The **Fair Use provision** of the federal Copyright Act allows for printing and using information for non-profit educational purposes.
 C. Some researchers prefer a more holistic method of recording such as a mind map.
  1. The subject is in the center of the map; there are branching lines to each subtopic and its supporting materials.
  2. It is important to create a bibliography alongside the mind map.
 D. Using a standard format like those from the American Psychological Association (APA) or Modern Language Association (MLA) is important for source citation.
  1. Use the style your instructor recommends.
  2. Use the style consistently.

Stop and Check: Complete Your Research Plan
Student Speech: Applications of Neuroimaging, Jennifer Salame

Suggested Videos

Book CourseMate. "Neuroimaging" by Jennifer Salame integrates sources throughout. It is available in the interactive video activities for the chapter. The text is at the end of the chapter. Students should find the topic interesting as well.

Clip of a recorded interview. Show a segment of an interview by someone like *Charlie Rose* (PBS), one of the interviewers on *The PBS NewsHour,* or a host on MSNBC, CNN, or Fox News. YouTube also has thousands of interviews with historical characters such as ex-presidents, civil rights leaders, and even John Lennon's assassin.

- Refer to the textual discussion of interviews (pp. 111-112), noting that valuable information can be gained from recorded interviews.
- Play the interview, and have students take notes on what's said, especially noting what the interviewer asked, and how he or she asked the questions.
- Have them compare and contrast their notes within small groups. How hard was it to get the information down?

- What are the advantages and disadvantages of live interviews compared to mediated interviews? (evaluation)
- Teach the source citation for a mediated interview, using the bibliographical style manual of your choice. (knowledge)

Professional Speakers. TED has thousands of speeches that illustrate how good speakers integrate research into their speeches. In "Battling Bad Science" (14:20), Ben Goldacre humorously talks about ways to evaluate the credibility of sources.

Discussion Topics

<u>Stop and Check</u>: <u>Begin Your Research Plan</u> (p. 110) Emphasize the importance of having a plan throughout the chapter. Stop at various points throughout the chapter and have students fill in the seven step plan on page 110. Occasionally ask them to share their plan with a small group. (application, synthesis)

<u>Interviewing</u> (pp. 111-112) Show a video of a skilled interviewer as described above. Analyze the interviewer's verbal and nonverbal behaviors, using the guidelines found in the text on p. 111-112 and the suggestions provided in **Suggested Videos**. (application)

<u>Key Terms</u> (p.110) For an interesting experience, have students look up a single word or key term on different domains. For example, the Catholic Church worldwide has millions of adherents and millions of websites devoted to Catholic topics. Have students compare and contrast information at various domains, including www.catholic.org; www.catholic.com; www.catholic.net; www.catholic.edu; www.catholic.jp; www.catholic.ca. (comprehension)

<u>International and Ethnic Presses</u> (p. 114) Application and Critical Thinking Exercise #7 asks students to explore diverse materials in their library. You can also direct them to do exercise #8 and specifically look for a variety of materials there. (application)

<u>Stop and Check: **Critical Thinking and the Internet**</u> (p. 118) The Internet contains everything from complete novels by Kate Chopin to today's weather report--with kiddie porn chat rooms lurking in the shadows. What to do with this overwhelming mass of information? Discuss the difference in trustworthiness between a Wikipedia version of President Obama's biography and that put out by the White House. (analysis)

<u>Crediting Sources</u> (pp. 124-125) Many, even most, of my students do not know how to cite sources correctly. Teach the style you (or your department) prefers. Most instructors use either APA (American Psychological Association) or MLA (Modern Language Association). Use a style manual in class to demonstrate how to cite sources. Direct students to the outline in Chapter 11 in this text (APA style) so they can see a completed bibliography.

Application and Critical Thinking Exercises

1. Students can purchase, read a library copy, or access an online copy of many current newsmagazines. Have them bring their lists to class and discuss the types of people who are quoted in their articles. Compare it with an academic journal written on a similar topic. What is similar about the two? What's different?

2. Lead a class discussion that compares and contrasts information about the Internet. Before class, have students read material about the history of the Internet on the Internet Society (ISoC), www.isoc.org, and

www.wikipedia.com. Which has the most detailed information? Which seems more credible? Why? What generalization, if any, can they make about .org and .com materials? (comprehension, evaluation)

3. Many sites provide online tutorials. The University of California Berkeley site, mentioned in the text, is located at www.lib.berkeley.edu/TeachingLib/Guides/Internet/FindInfo.html. Other good tutorials include The BBC www.bbc.co.uk/webwise/course/, and Rutgers University http://aresty.rutgers.edu/researchtools.htm. (application)

4. Consider doing this exercise as a whole group. Have the entire class visit the library, and use one of the suggestions in Teaching Idea 7.1 while they are there. (application)

5. Many of these materials are probably on your library's website. Students can download them and print them off for inclusion in a reference notebook.

6. Have students look through the periodicals and newspapers in the library and bring to class a list of five diverse publications in each category. Put their lists on the board and discuss them. (application)

7. This is an interesting exercise. As of this writing a google search for "dictionary of" turned up more than 36 million hits. Of course, many are duplicates, but students will probably be surprised to find an online "Dictionary of Difficult Words" or a "Dictionary of Botanical Epithets" or a "Dictionary of Livestock Management." Similarly, "encyclopedia of" turns up more than 28 million hits, including one for Chicago, another for Cajun culture, a third for Arda.

8. Discuss in class students' insights about the future of newspapers and magazines. Will there ever be a time when online access is more popular than print? (analysis, evaluation)

9. Have students keep a blog for one week, using either your school's course management system or one of the free blogging services on the Internet. After the week, discuss the experience with students. Will they continue blogging? Why or why not? What, if any, responsibility do they feel for the material they share with the blogosphere?

10. Have your students cooperate to find information on a single, controversial topic of your choice. Send some to the *Congressional Digest*, and have others go to newspapers and newsmagazines (hard copy and on-line). Refer some to recorded library resources and others to knowledgeable people they might interview. Assign some to consult diverse perspectives. On the day they bring this material to class, have them work in small groups (with several types of sources represented in each) where they'll compare, contrast, and evaluate the information.

11. Try this activity as a class to provide practical instruction. The variety of data available is sometimes overwhelming to new researchers. Helping students evaluate material to use in their research projects grows their information literacy skills.

12. Ask students to think about their preferred method of recording data; then discuss their preferences with others to reinforce the importance of methodical recording.

Internet Activities

The CourseMate for Public Speaking, accessible through http://login.cengage.com, offers a broad range of resources that will help students better understand the material in the chapter, complete assignments, and succeed on tests. The CourseMate also features speech videos with critical viewing questions, speech outlines, and transcripts. It also offers interactive practice activities, self-quizzes, and a sample final exam.

Supplemental Resources

- <u>Teaching Idea 7.1</u> Expanding Your Students' Library Skills
- <u>Research Note 7.1</u> Students with Physical Disabilities

Teaching Idea 7.1. Expanding Your Students' Library Skills (for use with pages 112-115).

Purpose: To increase students' skill in using the college or university library.

Procedure: Do one or more of these activities:

- Schedule an instructional session with a librarian who will present specific information that will help them use their college or university library effectively.

- Share some of the materials your school librarians have created to assist students in using the library effectively. Provide a printout of different guidelines for every two students. Have these pairs examine one set of guidelines for one minute only before passing it on to the next couple--until all students have skimmed all the materials. Discuss the variety of guidelines and how they can use information in them in their own research.

- Visit the library. Instead of working with a librarian, give pairs of students a handout with a list of items to find. (A SILENT scavenger hunt.) Have them find:
  - ➤ dictionary
  - ➤ encyclopedia title
  - ➤ index
  - ➤ article title on educational reform (from the *Reader's Guide*)
  - ➤ newspaper from another country
  - ➤ scholarly journal in their major(s)
  - ➤ ethnic periodical
  - ➤ item from a media library such as a CD of the work of an Italian composer or a videotape of JFK's inaugural address

Research Note 7.1: Students with Physical Disabilities

A trip to the library often makes a physical disability salient. Most students easily walk into the building and perch on stools at computer terminals; a blind student or a student in a wheelchair approaches the research task differently. An able-bodied instructor must take these physical challenges into account.

Hart and Williams (1995) studied the interactions between able-bodied instructors and students with physical disabilities. They found that instructors tended to respond in one of four ways when their classroom includes a wheelchair, a seeing eye dog, or an interpreter.

- <u>Avoiders</u> are nervous; they avoid interaction and don't mention the disability. Able-bodied students notice this, and they may think it's OK to similarly avoid interacting.

- <u>Guardians</u> are overly protective, so much so that they lower their standards to protect the student emotionally, physically, or intellectually. Guardians feel sorry for the students, and they often believe them to be less capable. This response is detrimental both to the students, who may come to feel they should get special favors, and to the rest of the class, who resent the unequal treatment.

- <u>Rejectors</u> destroy the student's confidence in his or her ability to be a productive class participant. Rejectors withdraw emotionally and academically. For instance, a rejector might address the student's interpreter, but never the student. The rest of the class may feel anger and contempt for this type of behavior from an instructor.

- <u>Nurturers</u> instruct physically challenged students as persons with capable minds, and they give them opportunities to learn as capable students. Nurturers are patient, self-assured, and concerned. They focus on commonalities, not differences.

What causes negative responses to students with physical challenges? Hart and Williams suggest that instructors experience the communication apprehension that typically accompanies uncertainty. To reduce uncertainty, they suggest more verbal interactions and more nonverbal expressiveness toward students with physical disabilities.

<u>Source</u>. Hart, R. D. & Williams, D. E. (1995). Able-bodied instructors and students with physical disabilities: A relationship handicapped by communication. *Communication Education, 44*, 140-154.

Chapter 8

CHOOSING SUPPORTING MATERIALS

This chapter is so closely linked to the previous one that it's hard to separate them. In fact, when I initially outlined the first edition, I considered and reconsidered whether to rearrange the order of presentation. I eventually decided to identify research tools before I described the objective of the search -- to find a variety of appropriate, trustworthy evidence. This is a skills chapter that helps students identify and evaluate various types of evidence they can use to support their ideas.

Chapter Goals

At the end of this chapter, your students should be able to:

- Identify types of facts and learn how to test factual data
- Use examples effectively
- Select appropriate visual evidence
- Quote authoritative sources
- Select numerical data carefully
- Use comparison and contrast

Chapter Outline

I. Factual information provides the basis for most speeches.
   A. **Empirical facts** are defined as data that can be verified by observation; **established facts** are consistently validated by many observers.
   B. Generally accepted **definitions** are also considered facts.
      1. Dictionary definitions give the generally accepted or common usage.
      2. It is easy to interject personal **opinion** into definitions.
   C. Providing vivid **descriptions** is another way to provide factual information.
   D. Speakers should take care not to pass on unverified or inaccurate information.
      Stop and Check: Think Critically About Facts

II. **Examples** attract listeners' attention, involve them emotionally, and let them know the speaker understands the implications of theories and ideas.
   A. **Real examples** actually happened.
      1. Examples can be experiences and events.
      2. Personal examples can bolster the speaker's credibility.
      3. Kenyans rate personal stories as the most convincing type.
   B. **Hypothetical examples** are useful for discussing sensitive topics.
      1. The incident didn't happen, but something like it did or could occur.
      2. Sometimes hypothetical examples are woven together from elements of real people's stories.
      3. When discussing private, confidential matters, hypothetical examples may be more appropriate than real ones.
      4. Imaginary scenes get listeners emotionally involved in the subject.
      5. In general, hypothetical examples are better for informative than for persuasive speeches.
         Ethics in Practice: Hypothetical Example or Fabrication?

C. Developing details of a story in an extended example creates points of emotional connection.
    1. Additional details provide additional points of identification.
    2. Extended examples clarify, explain in depth, and motivate listeners.
D. Combining two or three brief examples is useful in the introduction to gain people's attention.

Stop and Check: Think Critically About Examples

E. Use visual evidence.
    1. Literal images show the actual subject under discussion.
    2. Metaphorical images can evoke an emotional response.

Stop and Check: Think Critically About Visual Evidence

III. A **direct quotation** or **paraphrase** of the words of culturally accepted authorities is a type of support.
A. Culturally accepted **experts** include scholars, elected officials, practitioners, and so on.
    1. Provide information about the expert's credentials.
    2. Quoting people whose opinions are different than might be expected can be powerful.
B. Credible **peers** or **laypeople** are credible because they have a participant's perspective.

Diversity in Practice: Proverbs in a West African Culture

C. Sayings, proverbs, and words of wisdom are another source of quotations.
    1. Each culture has a store of proverbs and sayings that encapsulate important ideas, beliefs, and values.
    2. Quote parents or other personal figures whom the audience would respect.
    3. Religious texts provide quotations for religious adherents.

Stop and Check: Think Critically About Quoting Authorities

IV. Use statistics carefully.
A. Providing a count (**enumeration**) can be useful if two guidelines are followed.
    1. Round the numbers up or down.
    2. Enliven numbers by comparing them to something in the listener's experiences.
B. Choose statistics critically.
    1. The **mean** is the average of a group of numbers, but extreme figures at either end of the range will skew the mean.
    2. The **median** is the middle number in a set of numbers that are arranged in a ranked order; half lie above and half lie below.
    3. The **mode** is the most commonly appearing number.
    4. **Percentages** show the relationship of a part to the whole, represented by the number 100.
        a. **Rates of increase** or **decrease** compare growth or decline to an earlier baseline figure.
        b. These numbers are relatively meaningless unless the baseline number is known.
    5. **Ratios** often replace percentages when the percentage is very small.

Practically Speaking: Engineers and Evidence

C. Visual aids can clarify numerical data that might otherwise confuse an audience.

Stop and Check: Critically Analyze Numerical Data

V. Compelling comparisons show how new information compares or contrasts with the known.
A. **Literal analogies** compare things that are similar in important ways.
B. Vivid **figurative analogies** highlight similarities between otherwise dissimilar things.
    1. The audience must apply their imaginations and make the comparisons.
    2. Analogies are effective only if the comparison makes sense to the audience.
C. **Contrasts** point out differences between new concepts and a more familiar one.

Stop and Check: Think Critically About Analogies
Student Speech: America's Infrastructure Problem, Rob Sepich

Suggested Videos

Book CourseMate. Show one or more examples of student speeches with a variety of types of evidence for student analysis.

- Beforehand, divide the class into five groups, and ask each one to look for a different kind of evidence (facts, examples, quotations, statistics, and comparison/contrast).
- As they watch, each group jots down specific instances when the speaker uses the type of support they're assigned.
- Give them a few minutes afterwards to evaluate the evidence they heard, using the tests given in the text.
- Then ask volunteers to discuss the speaker's use of evidence. (application, evaluation)

Feature Film. In *A Time to Kill* (1996), the defense's closing arguments include a hypothetical example. Play the clip and discuss with students whether or not it is effective and why.

Educational videos. Show a professionally prepared video on a health related topic, paying attention to the type of support used. Search your campus media library or a local public library for usable informative videos on health related topics. Or use a speech from TED such as Elliot Krane's "The Mystery of Chronic Pain" or Elizabeth Pisani's "Sex, drugs, and HIV." (You can choose specific sections by clicking on the interactive transcript.)

- Ask students what kind of evidence they'd expect in a speech about the topic you choose.
- Watch the video, taking notes on the kind of evidence that's presented.
- Afterwards, evaluate the quantity and quality of the supporting material. (application, evaluation)
- Compare and contrast the type of support expected and used on the health video with that used on another educational video about history, literature, geography, communication, etc.

The Public Mind with Bill Moyers: Leading Questions. This video explores the power of professional pollsters in "virtually every facet of American culture." Show clips when you teach the section on statistical support. (Films for the Humanities & Sciences)

1. Explain that many factors affect poll results, and they should exercise caution when using statistical information.
2. The order in which the answers are presented may influence results. If asked, "How will you likely vote: Republican? Democrat? Independent?" a person may answer differently than if he were asked, "How will you likely vote: Democrat? Independent? Republican?"
3. The wording of the question can influence results. Asking "Should the U.S. give more money to welfare mothers?" may give more NO responses than "Should the U.S. give more money to women who are the sole support of young children?"
4. Show the clip.
5. Give the students five to ten minutes of in-class writing time. Ask them to summarize how they should treat poll data they find during their research. Collect, read, and comment on their responses. (knowledge, analysis)

C-SPAN. Show a clip from a recent speech on C-SPAN (www.c-span.org) that would be of interest to your class. Ask students to evaluate the evidence provided in the speech, using tests for evidence found in the text. (application, evaluation)

Discussion Topics

Finding and Evaluating Evidence Use one or both of the suggested procedures in <u>Teaching Idea 8.1</u> (**Supplemental Resources**). (application, analysis, evaluation)

Testing Evidence The best way to teach this chapter is to use actual supporting materials. Have students go over Rob Sepich's speech at the end of the chapter. Rob uses facts, explanations, statistics, examples, and testimony. Use any or all of the <u>Stop and Check</u> features as guides for testing evidence. (analysis, evaluation)

Ethics in Practice: Hypothetical Example or Fabrication? (p. 135). Ask students to read the feature, and, working in groups, to answer the discussion questions that follow.

Stop and Check: Thinking Crically about Facts (p. 133) Students must learn to evaluate evidence critically—especially quantified evidence, which is often repeated as factual when it is derived from dubious sources or is inflated for "political" reasons. Begin your own file of distorted statistics to use as classroom examples. They're surprisingly easy to find. Look for public opinion polls and then examine the way questions were phrased. For example, the public may resent "welfare" but overwhelmingly support "helping needy children." Excerpts from Bill Moyers' *Leading Questions* may be helpful. Christina Hoff Sommers's controversial book, *Who Stole Feminism,* contains a number of examples of dubious numbers that made their way into print and then got a life of their own as subsequent writers and speakers repeated them. Continue the emphasis on ethical speaking that's developed throughout the text. (analysis, evaluation)

Practically Speaking: Engineers and Evidence (pp. 142-143). Ask students to read the feature, and, working in groups, to answer the discussion questions that follow.

Application and Critical Thinking Exercises

1. Use student responses as an in-class activity and discussion. Alternatively, modify this exercise for an email discussion. Have students identify a specific issue and post examples, statistics, quotations, analogies, and other supporting materials on the class's email discussion site. Set it up so that each respondent first evaluates at least one preceding message, then contributes her or his piece of evidence.

2. Have students develop their hypothetical examples in class. Use the examples as a quick impromptu speaking exercise. Have students develop their examples, then trade them with a classmate. Have each student share the hypothetical examples in front of the class, allowing them to read the material if necessary. (application)

3. Bring a variety of print magazines to class. Have each student choose one advertisement, then, working in pairs, have them describe the ad without allowing their partner to see it or revealing the name of the product. Lead students in discussion—how important is visual evidence in advertising? What is missing from the verbal representation of the ad? What do radio advertisers have to do differently than print advertisers when promoting a product?

4. Make a list of your students' expertise to share with the class. Everyone has some area of expertise whether they realize it or not, from being an award-winning cheerleader to the person in their family who makes the best Rice Krispie Treats. Sometimes students are too shy to 'brag' about themselves, so you might have to use your own expertise as a conversation starter.

5. Divide the class into two groups. On the same topic, have one group develop only examples to support ideas. Have the other group only use statistics (this is sometimes difficult without supporting examples, keep students on task!). Is it possible to use one without the other? What kinds of topics are more appropriate for statistical support? Evidential support?

6. Try this in class as a way to support lecture and text material.

7. Have students use this activity as a journal or online blog entry. Have students give support to show the type of evidence they used in their writing.

8. These examples came from real student speeches.
   - Is the source cited reliable? Could it be biased?
   - Killer bees? Are they like sharks or rattlesnakes? Which would be a better analogy for a Texas audience? Why mix the two?
   - The quotation could be effective if we trust the congressman. Is New Jersey a state known for its amusement parks? Would a quotation from a California or Florida representative (e.g., Disney) be better? Does region matter? (Would an Oregonian view the congressman's credibility differently than a New Yorker might?)
   - The chopsticks excerpt has facts, comparisons, and numerical information. Is it credible?
   - The speaker is paraphrasing a peer or lay person who actually has the disease and actually had the operation. How credible is this?

Internet Activities

The CourseMate for Public Speaking, accessible through http://login.cengage.com, offers a broad range of resources that will help students better understand the material in the chapter, complete assignments, and succeed on tests. The CourseMate also features speech videos with critical viewing questions, speech outlines, and transcripts. It also offers interactive practice activities, self-quizzes, and a sample final exam.

Supplemental Resources

- Teaching Idea 8.1: Finding and Evaluating Evidence.

Teaching Idea 8.1: Finding and Evaluating Evidence

Purpose: To enable students to find the information they need on a specific topic, then evaluate the quality and the appropriateness of that evidence.

Procedures: (do one or both of the following)

- Ask volunteers to bring examples of electronically stored supporting evidence. (If you offer extra credit, consider offering a few extra points for this.) Tape segments of programs such as *Animal Kingdom, Crossfire, 60 Minutes* or the nightly news. Or use educational videos from your campus media library, or even home videos. Show the piece, then discuss the supporting materials in it. Use programs that mostly emphasize opinion (*Crossfire*) and more factual shows (an excerpt from a Discovery channel program).

- As a group, walk students through the process of finding and evaluating evidence. Have the entire class select a popular topic (the latest recording of a popular musician, the latest political scandal, etc.), then have them each bring a piece of evidence relating to the topic for the next class period. Then, working in small groups, and have them share their evidence. Once they have shared, have them evaluate the evidence using the criteria discussed in this chapter, weeding out material that doesn't make the cut. Which criteria was most salient? Why?

Chapter 9

ORGANIZING YOUR MAIN POINTS

If you've gone through the chapters in order, your students are now sitting at their desks, topics firmly in mind, various bits of evidence scattered in front of them. They're about half way through the process of speech construction. What's left is to pull these disparate materials into some sort of coherent order, plan a way to introduce, conclude, and polish the language of their speech. They'll probably welcome this chapter and the next, which provide the basic organizational skills they need to create a meaningful speech.

Chapter Goals

At the end of this chapter, your students should be able to:

- Organize their main points
- Identify and use a number of linear patterns, including chronological, spatial, causal, problem-solution, pro-con, and topical
- Link the parts of the speech to one another through skillful use of connectives such as signposts and transitions, internal previews and internal summaries
- Identify and use alternative patterns -- including the wave, the spiral, and the star – when appropriate

Chapter Outline

I. Three guidelines help organize the main points of a speech.
   A. Limit the number of points.
      1. Our brains best learn material that's chunked into 2-5 major units.
      2. Return to your thesis statement developed in Ch. 5 to get an idea of how to cover the material in your speech.
         <u>Practically Speaking: Career Advice</u>

   B. Consider traditional organizational patters
      1. The **chronological pattern** is used for points that relate in an ordered sequence.
         a. Chronological patterns are good for biographical or historical subjects.
         b. **Process speeches** have a sequence of steps or stages.
         c. Events must occur sequentially in a "first, second, third . . . " order to be considered a chronological speech.
      2. A **spatial pattern** is good for describing places or objects with several parts.
         a. It is good for describing places.
         b. It can be used for subjects that are described from top to bottom, east to west, or side to side.
         c. The ordering of main points can be somewhat flexible.
      3. **Causal organization** (cause-effect patterns) reflects Euro-American thought patterns that look for reasons that explain a phenomenon.
         a. Cause-to-effect is one causal pattern.
         b. Effect to cause is the second.
      4. A **problem-solution pattern** examines a problem and explains proposed solutions.
         a. The pattern works for global, national, and personal topics.
         b. Informative speeches explain a variety of potential solutions.

c. Persuasive speeches often propose several solutions and then focus on the best one.
5. **Pro-con arrangement** summarizes both sides of an issue
    a. It works well to present controversial issues.
    b. It works best for informative speeches aimed to enlighten the audience on the scope of the issue.
6. **Topical arrangement**, the most commonly used pattern, organizes main points into topics or subdivisions
    a. Each part contributes to the whole.
    b. The parts don't have to occur in a specific order.
C. Choose the best pattern: Because speeches can be developed in a number of ways, speakers must decide the best pattern, given the specific purpose and available supporting materials.

<u>Build Your Speech: Developing Your Main Points</u>

II. Develop your main points.
A. Each point should be **distinct** and separate from one another.
B. Points should be **parallel**, similar in kind and length.
C. Support points with evidence that prove your point.

<u>Diversity in Practice: Some African Organizational Patterns</u>

D. Link your ideas with **connectives**, words, phrases, and sentences that unify your speech.
    1. **Signposts** help you know where you are, and include words such as *first*, or *next*, etc.
    2 **Transitions** summarize where you have been and where you are going in the speech.
E. **Internal previews** briefly summarize subpoints you will develop under a major point.
F. **Internal summaries** summarize subpoints after you have made them.

III. Because of cultural backgrounds or personal preferences, some speakers choose alternative, more organic organizational patterns.
A. The **wave pattern** consists of repetitions of themes and ideas.
    1. Major points come at the crests of the waves.
    2. A series of examples follows, then builds to the next wave.
    3. The conclusion can wind down or end on a dramatic peak.
    4. It is common in ceremonial speaking.
B. The **spiral pattern** is a useful way to conceptualize the organization of speeches that build in intensity.
    1. This pattern is good for a series of narratives that build in drama.
    2. Each loop can represent increasing tension.
C. The **star pattern** is a variation of the topical pattern; points are tied together by a theme.
    1. It is useful for speakers who give the same speech to different audiences.
    2. One way to develop the points is to first state them, then support them.
    3. Speakers may also want to develop the point fully, stating the purpose near the end.
    4. A thematic circle binds all the points together.
    5. This pattern is common in political speeches.

<u>Stop and Check: Develop Your Speech Using an Alternative Pattern</u>
<u>Speech Video and Outline: E-waste, Jordan Keagle</u>

Suggested Videos

Book CourseMate. Jordan Keagle created "E-Waste" as part of a civic engagement speech assignment. Students were asked to describe a problem and find an organization that was set up to help solve the problem. Have students outline the major points. (Organizational pattern: problem-solution).
- Before showing the speech, direct students to watch and outline the *body* of the speech (which begins when he says, "First, let's look at the problem . . ." (application)
- After the speech, discuss their outlines. Were his main points easy to detect? Why or why not? (application)
- Ask if Jordan follows the guidelines for organizing main points (pp. 155-160 in the text)--limited number of points, supported effectively, ordered effectively. Ask what they suggest he do differently. (evaluation, synthesis)

Wave Pattern Speech. Show a clip from a speech that illustrates the wave pattern. Martin Luther King, Jr.'s "I've Been to the Mountaintop" is another examples of a speech that uses the wave pattern. (See www.americanrhetoric.com or search for it on YouTube.) Nikki Giovanni's short "Closing Remarks at the Convocation for the Virginia Tech Shooting Victims" is included in the interactive speech activities for Appendix C on the book CourseMate.
- Before the clip, review the wave pattern. Alert students to the wave crests in the speech.
- During the speech, have students take notes on wave crests they hear.
- After the speech, identify the crests they noted.
- Sketch a diagram of several waves on the board or onto a transparency; write out the repetitive phrases at the top of each crest. Develop one or two complete waves by listing the examples the speaker used as supporting material. (application)

Discussion Topics

Principles for Organizing Points (p. 151) Students often want to start from the top down--introduction, body, then conclusion. You may need to convince them of the value of starting with the body of the speech, then formulating an introduction and conclusion that lead into and out of the main section. Return to Chapter 7 and demonstrate how they can use their mind maps, note cards, or photocopied materials to formulate three to five major points. For example, have them turn to the mind map (Figure 7.2) and identify several main points in the material. Write these points on the board. (application)

Traditional Patterns (pp. 151-155) Students can typically identify the chronological pattern but not the spatial pattern. Present each pattern, then discuss "Choosing the Best Traditional Pattern" here (p. 155). The following materials are appropriate here (application, synthesis):
- Build Your Speech: Developing Your Main Points (pp. 155-156)
- **Application and Critical Thinking Exercise #2**
- Teaching Ideas 9.1: Organizational Patterns (**Supplemental Resources**)
- Teaching Idea 9.2: Visuals and Organizational Patterns (**Supplemental Resources**)

Looking at Diversity: Some African Organizational Patterns (p. 158) The introduction-body-conclusion pattern that is so typical of Euro-American speeches is not universal. Organizational patterns follow cultural norms as this feature demonstrates.

- To extend your class discussion, look up Susan Hazen-Hammond's article, "Navajo Culture: Stories Grandmother Told," in the September, 1996, issue of *Arizona Highways*. The author describes a family storytelling session--a time when an older Navajo wise woman sits in her hogan and passes on family lore to her grandchildren. Hazen-Hammond was allowed to hear spring stories; she was not privileged to hear the winter stories which were too sacred for non-Navajos. Unfortunately, many authors have ignored the cultural significance of the tales and have written about some of these tales involving Coyote and other sacred characters.

Hazen-Hammond relates that the storyteller sat in the place of honor in her hogan, the wall facing the door. Her story of corn and of Holy People moved from point to point in a nonlinear manner. Hazen-Hammond's friend whispered, "Navajo stories don't have a beginning, a middle, and an end. They're like a circle, like a hogan, like the Earth, with a lot of different things inside" (p. 34).

- Invite students who have listened to or given speeches using alternative patterns to share them with the class.

Practically Speaking: Career Advice (p. 152). Ask students to read the feature, and, working in groups, to answer the discussion questions that follow.

Practically Speaking: Career Advice (p. 152). Ask students to read the feature. Then, ask them to think carefully about the career they intend to pursue. In small groups, ask them to discuss the following questions:
- When and how will public speaking be necessary in that career?
- What other interactions (e.g. staff meetings, employee coaching, client meetings) indirectly use principles of public speaking?
- How can the principles of organizing a speech be applied to the day-to-day activities of their desired careers?

Alternative Pattern: the Wave (pp. 160-161) This text (1/e) was the first to publish Professor Jorgensen-Earp's organizational patterns. The recognition of alternative patterns validates the speaking traditions of women, African-Americans, and Native Americans who often find that their cultural ways of organizing speeches don't really "fit" into the common patterns. Students should become familiar with the wave organizational pattern, because many great speeches by African Americans are organized this way. Teach this pattern by using the guidelines in **Suggested Videos**.

Alternative Pattern: the Spiral and the Star (pp. 161-162) Emphasize that some visually oriented speakers like more alternative models for their speeches. Note: Figure 11. 3 in Chapter 11 shows a speech outlined using this pattern. Question #6 in **Application and Critical Thinking Exercises** deals with alternative patterns, as does the **Stop and Check: Develop Your Speech Using an Alternative Pattern** feature (p. 163).

Application and Critical Thinking Exercises

1. Here's another opportunity for students to work together to think of several ways to organize a single topic.

2. I require my students to do a lot of outlining. You can also use speeches in the **Suggested Videos** to do this exercise.

3. Or refer students to www.americanrhetoric.com (Top 100 Speeches). There they will find Jesse Jackson's 1984 and 1988 speeches to the Democratic National Convention and Martin Luther King, Jr.'s, speech, "I've Been to the Mountaintop," delivered the night before he was assassinated.

4. Have students work in dyads and share their outlines. Instruct students to provide their partner's with constructive criticism, being sure to offer insight that is positive before anything negative.

5. This exercise can be done as a homework assignment. Have students bring their outlines to class to share with partners to gain critical evaluation practice.

6. Do this exercise as a classroom activity. Compare and contrast a speech by Martin Luther King, Jr., with one by Adolf Hitler. What is similar about the patterns of organization? What is different? (analysis)

7. Today, I got 2,640,000 hits for the exact phrase "I Have a Dream." I had 84,500 hits for "Ain't I a Woman?" The sheer number of sites shows how effective a repetitive phrase can be.

8. Our classes tend to emphasize linear forms of organization, because the types of speaking common in business, education, and politics tend to be organized more linearly. This exercise allows students to work in small groups to try out alternative forms of organization.

9. Contrast King's speech with one by George W. Bush. Do the patterns of organization vary? Lead students in a discussion: How does one's culture influence their public speaking aptitude?

Internet Activities

The CourseMate for Public Speaking, accessible through http://login.cengage.com, offers a broad range of resources that will help students better understand the material in the chapter, complete assignments, and succeed on tests. The CourseMate also features speech videos with critical viewing questions, speech outlines, and transcripts. It also offers interactive practice activities, self-quizzes, and a sample final exam.

Supplemental Resources

- Teaching Idea 9.1: Organizational Patterns
- Teaching Idea 9.2: Visuals and Organizational Patterns

Teaching Idea 9.1: Organizational Patterns (for use with pp. 151-156)

Purpose: To have students identify organizational patterns of a speech, given the preview of the speech.

Procedure: Using outlines from previous terms or sample outlines found in the text, read the preview of a number of student speeches, and ask class members to identify the organizational pattern of each speech. Or use the following central idea statements:

- I will describe the myths surrounding the Chupacabra and explain the truth about these animals. [Topical: 1) myths; 2) truth]

- Today, I will explain why texting while driving accidents are increasing and describe the effect this has on those involved. [Causal]

- I would now like to explain both sides of the controversy over condom distribution in the public schools. [Pro-con: 1) arguments for; 2) arguments against]

- I will explain who the Amish are, describe a few of their basic beliefs, and summarize two problems that confront the group's way of life. [Topical: 1) the people; 2) their beliefs; 3) their problems]

- Breast cancer is classified in five stages. [Chronological: 1) Stage One; 2) Stage Two, etc.]

- It is easy to remember the five Great Lakes using the HOMES acronym: Huron, Ontario, Michigan, Erie, and Superior. [Spatial]

Teaching Idea 9.2: Visuals and Organizational Patterns

Purpose: To have students recognize the organizational pattern when they're given the main points of a speech.

Procedure: Display transparencies that list the major points of student speeches and ask students to identify the organizational pattern the student used.

1. Make a collection of student-created transparencies or posters. Find visuals that outline the main ideas of the speeches. For example, many students have spoken on conflict. One gave steps involved in conflict resolution, another identified types of conflict, a third listed stages of conflict escalation. Each student made a transparency that outlined the major points of the speech.

2. Display transparencies or posters one at a time and ask students to identify the speaker's organizational pattern.

Chapter 10

INTRODUCTIONS AND CONCLUSIONS

This is another in the "how to" series of chapters that provide students with fundamental skills for speech construction. I like to think of the audience as being in a mental world that's removed from the "world" of the speech. A good introduction functions to take listeners from their world and move them mentally and emotionally into the speech's world. The conclusion delivers them back to their personal world . . . but more knowledgeable now, more convinced, more determined to act. I think the best way to teach a chapter such as this is to use lots of examples, both positive and negative.

Chapter Goals

At the end of this chapter, your students should be able to:

- Develop an introduction to your speech that gains attention, motivates the audience to listen, establishes credibility, and previews the speech
- Develop a conclusion that signals the end, summarizes, provides psychological closure, and ends with impact

Chapter Outline

I. Good introductions have four major purposes.
    A. Introductions gain the attention of the audience.
        1. Asking a question invites listeners to answer either mentally or out loud.
            a. **Rhetorical questions** are those that listeners answer in their minds.
            b. **Participatory questions** invite an overt response such as a show of hands.
            c. A good question is intriguing enough to engage the audience.
            d. Asking a question helps establish a speaker-audience dialogue.
        2. Vivid descriptions invite the audience to visualize a scene mentally.
                 Diversity in Practice: A Navajo (Diné) Speech of Introduction
        3. Using a quotation or a cultural proverb is another effective opening strategy.
            a. Quotations can be about or by the subject (in a biographical speech).
            b. Good quotations encapsulate the speech's theme.
            c. Song lyrics, poems, and family sayings can also be effective quotations.
        4. Audio or visual aids draw attention to the topic.
        5. An example attracts attention and involves listeners emotionally.
        6. Startling numbers can capture attention if they are unusual or if they are put into a relevant context.
        7. Refer to a current event to establish common-ground.
        8. Reference to a current event helps establish common ground with an audience that is familiar with the happening.
        9. Using humor is another attention-gaining strategy.
            a. Speakers should test jokes and funny stories with friends to ensure it is funny and appropriate
            b. The joke should relate to the topic and direct attention to the topic.

142

B. Give the audience a reason to listen; relate the topic to their interests.
   1. Answer the listener question, "Why should I listen to this speech?"
   2. Point out the relevance of the topic, especially if it might seem unclear.
   3. Frame the topic within a larger issue.
   4. Appeal to curiosity and the desire to learn new things.
   5. Show the economic impact of the issue if it seems otherwise too distant or unrelated to the listener.
C. Establish your credibility to speak on the topic and show why the audience should listen to you.
   1. Share topic-related experiences, interest, and research.
   2. Establishing credibility is optional when the speaker is introduced or when the link to the topic is already well known.
D. Preview the main points of the speech as a way to alert the audience to the organizational pattern of the speech.
   1. Be straightforward but clear.
   2. Use alliteration when appropriate.
   3. Use a metaphor when appropriate.
      Stop and Check: Create an Interesting Introduction

II. The conclusion should be planned for impact.
   A. Begin with a signal or transition.
      1. Use verbal phrases or sentences that alert the audience to the end.
      2. Nonverbal pauses or movements can work, alone or with words, to signal the end.
   B. Review the major points in the summary.
   C. Provide psychological closure by looping back or echoing an element from the introduction.
   D. End memorably in a way that leaves a positive impression by using the type of material used to gain attention.
      1. Echo attention-getting device from introduction, such as a rhetorical question or a quotation or example.
      2. Use parallel construction.
      3. Call people to action in a persuasive speech.
      4. Close by reinforcing a larger cultural theme or value.
         Stop and Check: Evaluating Introductions and Conclusions
         Speech Video by Bonita Persons, "Driving While Drowsy"

Suggested Videos

Book CourseMate. First, show just the introduction to Hillary Carter-Liggett's "Shakespeare" (Chapter 10 videos) or Maria DiMaggio's "You Have My Deepest Sympathy: You Just Won the Lottery" (Chapter 9 videos) in the interactive speech activities.
- Have students list each element of the introduction down the left side of their paper.
- As they watch, have them identify and jot down each element of the introduction.
- Afterwards, discuss the speaker's opening strategy, how he or she relates to her audience, his/her credibility, and the preview. (knowledge, application)

"Driving Drowsy," the speech at the end of the chapter is on the interactive speech activities for Chapter 10. Show this entire speech. When Bonita Person gave this speech in the classroom, students almost gasped at the end.

Introductions and Conclusions (pp. 168-178). Show a video of actual classroom speeches (from the text website or from your own collection) and ask students to outline the introduction and the conclusion. Then discuss the effectiveness of these parts of the speech. Or use Teaching Idea 10.2 (**Supplemental Resources**); it asks students to evaluate introductions and conclusions on actual student outlines. (knowledge, application, synthesis, evaluation)

Gaining Attention (pp. 169-173) Teaching Idea 10.1 (**Supplemental Resources**) gives several ideas you can use to teach this material. (application, analysis, evaluation)

Diversity in Practice: Considering Organizational Culture (pp. 172-173) Chapter 1 pointed out that smaller cultures exist within the macro culture of the United States. Chapter 2 introduced the concept of a classroom culture; this chapter presents organizations as cultures. (Appendix B extends this idea.) *Vital Speeches* provides excellent materials for comparing and contrasting introductions given in different organizations. (application, synthesis, evaluation)

Diversity in Practice: A Navajo (Diné) Speech Introduction (p. 170) Here is another reminder that the patterns presented in the text are commonly used in the United States, but they are not the only way to create and organize speeches.

Stop and Check: Create an Interesting Introduction (p. 175) Direct students to Figure 10.1, then have them work in pairs to create a four part introduction, given the central ideas given here. (This activity is on the book CourseMate.) (application)

Stop and Check: Evaluating Introductions and Conclusions (pp. 178-179) Given two conclusions, students evaluate each and compare and contrast the two. (evaluation)

Student Speech with Commentary: "Driving While Drowsy" by Bonita Persons (pp. 181-182) Ask students to read and/or watch Bonita's speech about driving while tired. In groups orally or individually in written form, ask them to answer the questions in the commentary. Additionally, ask them to suggest an alternative way that Bonita could have gained her audience's attention at the beginning of the speech.

Application and Critical Thinking Exercises

1. Writing instructors commonly use peers to comment on various drafts of a manuscript. This technique helps both originator of the outline and the one who reads and evaluates it. (application, evaluation)

2. This exercise also helps the student who outlines the speech as well as the student speaker; the outliner must listen closely and analytically; the speaker gets to see if his or her organizational pattern was clear and if all the elements of the speech were identifiable. This exercise also invites students to make judgments about a classmate's introduction and conclusion. (comprehension, application, evaluation)

3. Review prior, demonstrated, and terminal credibility from Chapter 5. Have students write responses to the questions, or use them as a basis for a class discussion. (synthesis)

4. There are thousands of speeches on www.americanrhetoric.com. Students are asked to make evaluative judgments, using the criteria established in the chapter. (evaluation)

5. Many excellent online websites provide additional information on introductions and conclusions. Students are asked to consider the differences between introductions in written essays and in speeches. (analysis)

Internet Activities

The CourseMate for Public Speaking, accessible through http://login.cengage.com, offers a broad range of resources that will help students better understand the material in the chapter, complete assignments, and succeed on tests. The CourseMate also features speech videos with critical viewing questions, speech outlines, and transcripts. It also offers interactive practice activities, self-quizzes, and a sample final exam.

Supplemental Resources

- Teaching Idea 10.1: Gaining Attention
- Teaching Idea 10.2: Using Outlines as Models

Teaching Idea 10.1: Gaining Attention (for use with pp. 169-172)

Purpose: To have students identify ways of gaining attention at the outset of the speech.

Procedure: Use one or more of the following methods:

- At the outset of the discussion, ask students what they've seen speakers do that was effective in gaining attention at the outset of the speech. Write their suggestions on the board. [My experience is that they are able to identify most of the means of gaining attention presented in the chapter.] After they have run out of suggestions, add any textual strategies they might have missed, such as reference to a current event. Then highlight any means of gaining attention you want to discuss in more detail; for example, review the pros and cons of telling a joke.

- Distribute student outlines with all identifying marks are removed. Ask class members what technique the speaker used to draw attention to the topic. Write the techniques on the board. Add any idea included in the text that they might have missed. Ask students to evaluate the effectiveness of the opening.

- Instead of using student outlines, use articles from newsmagazines or newspapers. Have students identify the writer's method of gaining attention. Develop the lesson as you did in option #2 above.

Teaching Idea 10.2: Using Outlines as Models

Purpose: To provide students with actual examples of student speeches that show both positive and negative models.

Procedure: Find online sample student outlines from different schools to protect your own students' confidentiality. Distribute an outline to each student or to a pair of students and then use these for the basis of a discussion.

- For example, if I were teaching the elements of a good introduction, I might ask, "Tom, what's the topic of your outline?" Then, I'll select a particular element such as establishing credibility and ask, "How did your speaker establish credibility to speak on that topic?" Tom reads that part of the outline, and I open the discussion to other class members. What do they think? Is credibility established well? Could it be improved? If so, how? etc.

Chapter 11

OUTLINING YOUR SPEECH

This is the final installment in the nuts-and-bolts series of skills chapters. Some students drag their feet when confronted with the task of crafting a written outline that represents their speech's structure. However, students like the one featured at the beginning of the chapter, keep me teaching these skills. During the first week of class she sat and glared; she refused to give her first speech. (Her advisor made her take my speech class--much against her will.) But Nadia didn't drop the class, and at the end of the semester she came into my office to personally thank me for the course. She said she'd learned to organize her thoughts coherently, and she knew she would transfer her newfound skills to many other classes. I wish for you a Nadia!

Chapter Goals

At the end of this chapter, your students should be able to:

- Outline the contents of your speech in a linear form
- Create a heading that summarizes what you plan to accomplish in your speech
- Use standard outlining features including, coordination, subordination, indentation, alternation, and full sentences.
- Prepare note cards or a speaking outline
- Know how to record your ideas using an alternative pattern

At the end of this chapter, you should be able to:

- Diagnose and correct student weaknesses in outlining.

Chapter Outline

I.   A **content outline** usually shows a speech's **structural elements** (the introduction, body and conclusion) and shows the speech's **logical elements** (a record of the speech's materials and their relationship to one another).
   A.   Write out points in complete sentences, but do not write the entire **script** of the speech.
   B.   Begin with a heading that tells the title, general purpose, specific purpose, and central idea, preview, and the organizational pattern.
   C.   Use a standard format.
      1.   **Alternation** and **indentation** show the levels of support and interrelationships.
      2.   **Coordination** of each level of points gives them the same basic value or weight; **subordination** indicates which information is more or less important.
                     Practically Speaking: Outines and Speaking Notes
                     Sample student outline with marginal annotations
            and a bibliography using the American Psychological Association (APA) style:
                     Biliary Atresia by Emily Smith

II. **Speaking notes**, the outlines taken to the podium, use **key words** to jog the speaker's memory and only use full sentences for transitions.

<u>Stop and Check: Evaluate Your Content Outline</u>

    A. Note cards offer advantages because of their convenient size.
       1. Use index cards (3" x 5" or 4" x 6").
       2. Write legibly.
       3. Number the cards.
       4. Use only one side.
       5. Delete nonessential words.
       6. Use only 5 or 6 lines per card and space words so they're easy to locate quickly.
       7. Highlight points to emphasize.
       8. Cite sources as you speak.
       9. Include delivery reminders.
       10. Practice with cards and revise them if they're not helpful.
       11. Use cards unobtrusively,
       12. Don't read from your cards, except when quoting long quotations or complex statistics.
    B. A speaking outline is created on standard sized paper.
       1. Use spacing to distinguish the sections of the speech.
       2. Use highlighter pens to distinguish sections.
       3. Vary font sizes and formatting features to direct the eyes to key points.
       4. Spread sheets out over the lectern in a way that page turns are unobtrusive.
       5. Use a dark-colored notebook or folder if a lectern is unavailable.

<u>Stop and Check: Evaluate Your Speaking Notes</u>
<u>Diversity in Practice: Individual Cognitive Preferences</u>

III. Alternative patterns can be useful to people whose cognitive styles are more visual or imagistic.
    A. Decide on the pattern and sketch it out.
    B. Write out the main points.
    C. Subordinate the developmental material.
    D. Plan the introduction, conclusion, and transition statements.
    E. Use standard indentation and numbering if it's helpful.

Suggested Videos

Book CourseMate. "Overconsumption of Sugar" by Hans Erian (briefly outlined on page 186 in the text) is available in the interactive speech activities for this chapter.

- Have students outline his speech. (application)
- After he finishes, evaluate the development of each element of the speech: introduction, speech body, and conclusion. Does he develop the points adequately? Where might he include more information? Is irrelevant material included? If so, where? Evaluate the overall effectiveness of the speech. (evaluation, synthesis)
- Ask students to work in pairs to create a heading: title, general purpose, specific purpose, and central idea for the speech.

"Biliary Atresia" by Emily Smith is also available in the chapter's interactive speech activities.

- Before you show it, have students work in pairs and study the speaking notes on page 191.
- Then ask them to create additional speaker note cards she could use to deliver the speech.

Discussion Topics

Linear Outlines Give students a scrambled outline and have them work in small groups to put the ideas in order. A handout is provided at the end of this chapter's materials. (analysis, application)

How Writing Helps Speakers For students who are staggering through the process of creating an outline, now would be a good time to review or present Quintilian's four emphases on the importance of reading, writing, listening, and speaking. Why is writing important to good speechmaking? How can computers assist in the creation of outlines? (analysis)

Key Word Outlines Give pairs of students a content outline of a student speech. Have them create a speaking outline to accompany it. Encourage them to create a usable memory aid . . . which may be a note card, a mini mind map, a series of drawings, or . . . (application)

Practically Speaking: Outlines and Speaking Notes (pp. 186-187) Ask students to read the feature, and, working in groups, to answer the discussion questions that follow.

Outlining with an Alternative Pattern Have students try their hand at representing a speech or outline (from Appendix C or at the end of a chapter) using a spiral, star, or wave pattern. (application)

Cognitive Styles Learning styles is an interesting topic. Most speech classrooms, even those with minimal visible diversity, have quite a bit of cognitive diversity. You might assign students to do an online learning styles test and discuss their results in class. (application)

Stop and Check: Evaluate Your Content Outline (p. 190) Ask students to bring their content outlines to class. Provide each student with 3-4 copies of the content outline evaluation checklist in this Stop and Check section. In groups of 4, ask students to pass around their outlines and have each student score the other outlines based on the checklist. If any item was checked "no," encourage the groups to work together to help improve that part of the outline. Lead a discussion of the

Stop and Check: Evaluate Your Speaking Notes (pp. 192-193) Ask students to bring their speaking notes to class. Provide each student with 3-4 copies of the speaking notes evaluation checklist in this Stop and Check section. In groups of 4, ask students to pass around their speaking notes and have each student score the other notes based on the checklist. If any item was checked "no," encourage the groups to work together to help improve that part of the speaking notes.

Application and Critical Thinking Exercises

1 - 4. All these exercises provide class members with an opportunity to create outlines of actual speeches. However, if you're like me, you tend to dig your way out of a pile of papers mid-term, and you'd welcome some help in reading and commenting on non-graded student work. Using students to evaluate one another's assignments eliminates some work for you while it reaps benefits to the student readers. In short, each reader must remember the criteria for a good outline and then apply that criteria to the outline in hand.

5. Several speeches in Appendix C came from this website.

6. If you cover 'how to interview,' use this exercise as an interview practice activity

Internet Activities

The CourseMate for Public Speaking, accessible through http://login.cengage.com, offers a broad range of resources that will help students better understand the material in the chapter, complete assignments, and succeed on tests. The CourseMate also features speech videos with critical viewing questions, speech outlines, and transcripts. It also offers interactive practice activities, self-quizzes, and a sample final exam.

Supplemental Resources

- <u>Handout</u>: A scrambled outline to use with the discussion topic, linear outlines

The entire outline of this informative process speech appears in Part I of this manual.

Unscramble the outline below. Then discuss with your classmates the cues you used to decide what material went into the introduction, the main points, the supporting materials, and the conclusion.

Specific Purpose: To inform my audience how to gather, report, and assess information on the 1040 tax form.

Group your expenses into appropriate categories.

Would your 1040 hold up during an audit?

The first step, collecting and classifying your tax data, is probably the most difficult.

The most important piece of information is the W-2 Wage Statement that your employer mails in January.

You also need a 1040 form which you'll find in the tax packet that the IRS mails out.

Information reported on the 1040 form must have back-up support, in case of future audit.

Report all income in the income section—even trivial amounts.

Many people dread it as the deadline for filing tax returns; however, everyone who receives a W-2 wage must file, and most people want to save money on the process.

Don't skip any lines; this may cause miscalculation.

Today, I will show you how to fill out the 1040 form by collecting data, disclosing information, and assessing the aftereffects of the process.

False information may lead to a fine, even imprisonment.

The second step is to disclose all relevant information on the 1040 form.

Fill in the sections reporting any accumulated interest.

I am majoring in finance, and I learned through my courses and my experiences that filing a return is not as hard as others make it seem.

Be sure to sign your return; it is void with no signature.

Finally, determine the aftereffects of turning in a false or dishonest return.

Collect receipts of additional income and taxable expenses.

If you expect a refund, it may take up to twelve weeks to get a check in the mail.

In short, the 1040 is a standard form each American worker must file.

Were you completely truthful?

It is simple enough that you can fill it out yourself by collecting and classifying important material, filling in every applicable section, and taking seriously the consequences of false returns.

April 15—what does that date mean to you?

April 15—don't forget this date—it will never change; it's a date the IRS looks forward to!

Adapted from an outline by Nila Sheth, St. John's University

Chapter 12

CHOOSING EFFECTIVE LANGUAGE

This chapter provides a blend of theory and application in a way that most students enjoy. I like socio-linguistics and was fascinated with Raymond Gozzi's book *New Words and a Changing American Culture;* I believe that language is a perfect diversity topic. Language has ethical implications because of its potential to include or exclude, to clarify or confuse, to insult or affirm. One way I address linguistic diversity is to ask a bilingual student to prepare and deliver a speech in her or his native language with an interpreter translating into English.

Chapter Goals

At the end of this chapter your students should be able to:

- Explain how words are linked to culture and meaning
- Understand the denotative meaning of words
- Define connotative meanings of words including epithets and euphemisms
- List six guidelines for effective language in public speaking
- Give guidelines for listening and speaking in linguistically diverse contexts

At the end of this chapter you should be able to:

- Better understand nonnative speakers of English, if you're not already familiar with language issues. Research Note 12.2: "Students Who Aren't Native English Speakers" in **Supplemental Resources** provides explanations and suggestions for dealing with linguistic issues.

Chapter Outline

I. **Languages**, the verbal codes made up of symbols that a community of language speakers use to share their ideas, reflect culture.
    A. **Words** are the names we give cultural memories or things significant enough to name.
        1. Our vocabularies form our interpretations of the world, creating our social realities.
        2. We create names for tangible and less tangible things.
        3. Languages change as cultures are transformed, and the enormous cultural changes of the last half-century have produced thousands of new words.
            <u>Diversity in Practice: Dialects</u>
        4. **Denotative meanings** are what the word names or identifies.
            a. **Ambiguous** words stand for more than one idea; their meaning depends on the context.
            b. Be sure to use the correct word for the context.
            c. **Jargon** denotes specialized or technical words that serve special groups or cultures of people.
        5. **Connotative meanings** are the emotional overtones that groups or persons associate with a word.
            a. **Epithets** describe some quality of a person or group, often with negative connotations.
            b. **Euphemisms** substitute an inoffensive term for an offensive or embarrassing term.
                <u>Stop and Check: Think Critically about Denotative and Connotative Words</u>

II. Effective language falls under the realm of the canon of style.
   A. Adopt an oral style.
   C. Be concise.
       1. Eliminate **verbiage** in the U.S., which values directness.
       2. Other cultural groups may value flowery words and language.
   F. Use Familiar Words.
   G. Choose specific **concrete words** instead of abstract **vague words**.

Stop and Check: Choosing More Precise Wording

   H. Build in **repetition**.
   I. Be interesting by using colorful, vivid language.
       1. **Alliteration** uses words beginning with the same sound.
       2. **Rhymes** are words that end in the same sounds; use rhymes throughout the speech.
       3. **Metaphors** are implied comparisons that speak of one thing as being another; **mixed metaphors** begin with one comparison and end with another.
       4. **Similes** also compare things that are alike in at least one essential detail; however, they explicitly state the connection in the word *like* or *as*; **archetypal symbols** emerge again and again.
       5. **Personification** gives human characteristics to nonhuman entities.

Practically Speaking: Speechwriters

   J. Use appropriate forms for the culture of your audience.
       1. Dialect may be appropriate for some audiences, out of line for others.
       2. The situation of influences your linguistic choices.

II. Using **inclusive language** is a way to use words ethically.
   A. Chose inclusive terminology.
       1. **Racist** language privileges one racial or ethnic group over others.
       2. **Ageist** language demeans or devalues age and privileges youth.
       3. **Sexist** language privileges men over women.
       4. **Nonparallel language** does not treat men and women the same; it privileges men.
   B. Present people and groups positively.
       1. Avoid using **dismissive language**.
       2. Mention differences only when they matter.

III. In pluralistic audiences, students enter classrooms with many types of linguistic diversity, including *monolingual, didialectical, multidialectical, bilingual*, and/or *multilingual*.

Ethics in Practice: The Interplay of Legal Rights and Human Rights

   A. Speakers should adapt to multilingual situations.
       1. A speaker must adapt by using several strategies.
           a. Analyze the words and jargon a nonnative speaker of English might find confusing.
           b. Choose simple words without talking down.
           c. Write potentially confusing words on visual aids.
           d. Define difficult and jargon terms throughout.
           e. Build in redundancy or repetition by repeating strategic information.
       2. Listeners should have patience and **perspective taking**.
           a. Be positive; expect to understand the speech.
           b. Listen all the way through; take notes to help wandering attention.
           c. Assume responsibility in co-creating meaning by giving nonverbal feedback.
           d. Control negative emotional responses.
           e. Don't laugh, even if the speaker does.
   B. Adapting to an interpreter involves a number of techniques or skills.
       1. Use simple, common words.
       2. Provide the interpreter with an outline in advance of the speech.

3. Speak in short units, allow the interpreter to speak after a sentence or two.
3. Look at the interpreter when she or he is speaking.
4. Shorten a speech that's being translated into another language.
   <u>Professional Speech with Commentary: I Have a Dream, by Martin Luther King, Jr.</u>

Suggested Videos

Abraham Lincoln's Gettysburg Address. This speech is available in several versions on YouTube including renditions by Johnny Cash, Colin Powell, and Gregory Peck. Listen to one of the versions, and discuss some of the vivid language (especially repetition) that makes people recite it almost 150 years after it was given.

Inaugural Address: John Kennedy. The text of this speech is at the end of the chapter, and it is available on *Great Speeches Collections* videos, americanrhetoric.com, the archives of The American Presidency Project [online], or on YouTube. January 2011 was the 50th anniversary of the speech, and an Internet search will turn up many articles, opinion pieces, and essays assessing its worth. It is especially famous for the use of antimetabole . . . "Ask not."
- Identify the element of vividness you want to emphasize.
- Show the clip, asking students to focus on the language in it.
- Discuss their observations.   (comprehension, application)

Discussion Topics

<u>Words and meanings</u> (pp. 198-199) Gozzi says that we name the things in our culture that we notice and consider important enough to label. Several years ago a book called *Sniglets* came out. The authors argued that some important things weren't named, but they should be, and they set out to label them. Three that I can remember are "furnidents" -- those little indentations in the carpet that remain long after you remove the chair; "rov-alert," the system that all dogs (Rover) use to join the chain of barking that usually starts about 1:00 a.m.; and "kawashocki," the startled response you have when you pull into a parking place and realize that a motorcycle is already there. Use www.google.com and search for the word "sniglets." You'll get over 107,000 hits with lots of funny words; one good site is http://bertc.com/sniglets.htm

Introduce your students to these sniglets or others you create or find online, and invite them to label objects or events that they've noticed that don't have names. Here's a starter list:
- The phenomenon that whenever you get into a check-out line behind only one person, that person will inevitably take five times as long as normal.
- The generation born after Generation X. (This group is still being named.)
- The feeling you have after you work hard on a paper and get two grades lower than you expect. (synthesis)

<u>Diversity in Practice: Dialects</u> (p. 199) Dialects like ebonics, "Spanglish" and Creole are well known, but fewer people think of differences in slang terms from city to city or region to region. (My New York students laughed when I talked about a "can of pop;" in contrast, Oregonians rarely ask for a "soda.") The suggested Internet sites in this box make for fascinating reading. Visit the site sponsored by the American Dialect Association when you prepare for teaching this chapter. Refer students to Exercise 2 in the **Application and Critical Thinking Exercises** (p. 213 in the text) for more about ebonics. (comprehension, application)

<u>Diversity and Language</u> You'll find many interesting topics relating to diversity in this chapter--among them are jargon, epithets, inclusive language, and language and pluralistic audiences. Seriously

consider asking at least one bilingual student to deliver a speech using an interpreter. (comprehension, application)

Stop and Check: Think Critically about Denotative and Connotative Words (p. 201) Do one of the exercises provided in this feature or have students list the names for popular brands of perfume. (Identify both "male" and "female" perfume names.) Then, in groups or as a whole group identify connotations for various brands. For example, to me, "Brut" (for men) connotes roughness, an untamed quality; in contrast, "Obsession" (for women) connotes clinging, passion, need, single minded devotion.

- Explore the subtle way that connotations can create unrealistic images of men or women. For instance, which, if any, fragrances for men appeal to their nurturing side? Do any suggest that they would cling to a woman?
- In contrast, which, if any, women's fragrances suggest that women are in control and strong?
- Refer to the section, "Use Language Ethically: Inclusive Language," and ask what qualifies as sexist language. Are perfume ads sexist? (comprehension, application, analysis)

Ethics in Practice: The Interplay of Human Rights and Human Rights (p. 210) Ask students to read the feature, and, working in groups, to answer the discussion questions that follow.

Vivid Language (pp. 205-207) Several strategies or exercises work well with this content:
- Use one or more of the speeches in the Great Speeches series (see **Suggested Videos**) to highlight vivid imagery and memorable language.
- With the class choose one paragraph of an article from the *New York Times* or a magazine such as the *New Yorker* or *Time* for instances of colorful language choices.
- Activity 13.2: "Use of Imagery" and Activity 13.3: "Eliminate Clutter" are appropriate with this section. (comprehension, analysis)

Stop and Check: Choosing More Precise Wording (p. 204) Our language choices are often imprecise, as this exercise demonstrates. Do this in pairs or as a whole group. (application)

Practically Speaking: Speechwriters (p. 207) Ask students to read the feature, and, working in groups, to answer the discussion questions that follow.

Adapt to Multilingual Situations (p. 210) Exercises #5 and #6 in **Application and Critical Thinking Exercises** supplement this section.

Application and Critical Thinking Exercises

1. To introduce this exercise, ask the class what word they think has the most meanings. Tell them the site provided here says "set" is the word. There are about 35 meanings for this word; see how many students can identify, e.g., a *set* of dishes, *set* the table, a tennis *set*, a math *set*, and *set* a stone into a ring. Ask them to search for other words with multiple meanings and bring to class a list of ten words that have more than ten meanings each.

2. This exercise supports the Diversity in Practice box on page 208. Note that the topic of ebonics can be emotionally loaded; my most recent google search resulted in 455,000 hits! Direct students to sites that present historical and academic information (from .org and .edu sources) – not to the humorous ones.

3. Have students try this exercise as a journal or blog entry.

4. Here's another opportunity for students to practice interviewing skills--this time to identify the jargon associated with specific occupations. Have students post their jargon terms on email and conduct the suggested discussion electronically. (application)

5. Try making the list as a small group exercise in class, then have small groups break up into triads to determine the elements of style they would use. Have students present their lists 'on their feet' (by their chairs, if necessary) to increase their public speaking opportunities. (application)

6. Play one of these speeches in class, having students list the language choices that they find most effective. Does the age or culture of the listener influence effectiveness of the speaker? (analysis)

7. Direct students to Appendix C where they'll find an extensive excerpt from a speech by Chief Joseph or have them find a speech on www.americanrhetoric.com. (application, analysis)

8. More students will probably listen to interpreted speeches than will give speeches through an interpreter. But who knows what the future will hold as we wire our board rooms and make other electronic links with international groups and individuals? If your classroom is linguistically diverse, your students will experience speaking and/or listening to someone who presents a speech in a second language as a matter of course. (analysis)

9. I've had students give classroom speeches in Italian, Romanian, and Spanish which were then translated into English. A speech given in ebonics or Spanglish and translated into standard English might be interesting! Refer students to Appendix C and the speech video for Uriel's entire speech which Kelly Bilinski interpreted into English. (application, synthesis)

Internet Activities

The CourseMate for Public Speaking, accessible through http://login.cengage.com, offers a broad range of resources that will help students better understand the material in the chapter, complete assignments, and succeed on tests. The CourseMate also features speech videos with critical viewing questions, speech outlines, and transcripts. It also offers interactive practice activities, self-quizzes, and a sample final exam.

Supplemental Resources

- Research Note 12.1: Women and Language
- Research Note 12.2: Students Who Aren't Native English Speakers
- Teaching Idea 12.1: Gender Differences in Speaking
- Handout Material: Japanese Women's Speech

Research Note 12.1: Women and Language (for use with Teaching Idea 12.1)

Background Information: Writer Ursula Le Guin[1] describes the "mother tongue" as the language used in private settings to discuss personal, everyday, down-to-earth matters. She contrasts this to the "father tongue"--the language of institutions, of the public world of work.

Other researchers have explored the relationship of language usage to the speaker's credibility. In a U.S. courtroom[2] researchers examined kinds of language that jurors judged as credible, competent, intelligent, and influential on their judgments. This they termed *powerful language.* In contrast, jurors judged *powerless language* negatively. In general, powerful language is direct, while powerless language includes elements that take away from its forcefulness. Hedges, tag questions, intensifiers, and use of hyperbole characterize it.

Women tend to use more "powerless" techniques.[3] Some scholars argue that they seek to maintain relationships in their communication. "Powerless" techniques, rather than being a liability, are thus an asset that allows women to keep conversations open and to include others.[4] However, in contexts such as public speaking, speakers should be aware of potential negative response to language choices.

Hedges Instead of using direct declarative sentences, speakers soften their assertions by adding words that make them appear less certain. For instance, instead of saying, "This product is good," the speaker adds a hedge, "This product is *sort of* good." Or instead of, "The University of Texas won the national championship in their 2006 Rose Bowl win," there is a hedge, "The University of Texas won the national championship . . . , *if I remember correctly.*" In the first sentences, the speaker sounds confident; in the second sentences he or she appears tentative and unsure.

It is common for student speakers to hedge on pronunciations of words, "The man was diagnosed with vilitigo, *or however you pronounce it.*" These hedges take away credibility, making them appear unprepared.

[1] U. Le Guin. (1989). *Dancing at the edge of the world: Thoughts on words, women, places.* New York: Grove Press.

[2] W. O'Barr. (1982). *Linguistic evidence: Language, power, and strategy in the courtroom.* New York: Academic Press.

[3] See R. Lakoff. (1975). *Language and woman's place.* New York: Harper and Row; M. R. Key. (1975). *Male/female language.* Metuchen, NJ: The Scarecrow Press; D. Spender. (1980). *Man made language.* (1980). London: Routledge & Kegan Paul; L. A. Hosman. (1989). The evaluative consequences of hedges, hesitations, and intensifiers. *Human Communication Research, 15,* 383-406.

[4] For a good summary of women's speech patterns, see J. T. Wood. (2001). *Gendered lives: Communication, gender, and culture, 4th ed.* Belmont, CA: Wadsworth.

Tag questions Speakers soften their words by attaching or tagging a question onto the end of their assertion, as if asking, for audience agreement. Polish sociolinguist Anna Wierzbicka says that tags are typical of Polish speech, and they reflect a "deep-rooted habit of acknowledging possible differences between individual points of view."[5]

Tag questions are easy to spot in interpersonal communication, in statements such as this: "It's a beautiful day, *isn't it?*" Or, "This is the best proposal, *don't you think?*" One tag question commonly heard in classroom speeches is, *"OK?"*

Intensifiers Intensifiers are additions of words such as "really," "very," and "totally" that intensify the emotion expressed in the sentence. "She is a candidate worthy of your vote" is more emotionally intense when you add two words, "She is an *awesome* candidate who is *truly* worthy of your vote." Women tend to use more intensifiers than men.

Hyperbole The text discusses the use--and possible misuse--of hyperbole.

Research Note 12.2. Students Who Aren't Native English Speakers

Four dimensions of language pose problems for nonstandard speakers of English: phonetics, semantics, syntax, and pragmatics.

Phonetics Phonemes are the basic units of sound of a spoken language. Students substitute, distort, and omit phonemes. For example, they say <u>d</u>is for <u>th</u>is, b<u>ea</u>rd for b<u>ir</u>d, <u>r</u>ee<u>v</u> for <u>l</u>i<u>v</u>e. Deaf students typically delete sounds that are not clearly visible such as k, t, s, ch, sh, and r.

Many Asian languages are composed of consonant-vowel (C-V) combinations, while English is typically made up of C-V-C words and syllables. Consequently, some foreign students tend to omit final consonants. Example: "<u>I wih go to suhkooh foh te moh yea</u>" (I will go to school for ten more years).

Additionally, students with neurological impairments such as cerebral palsy and cranio-facial malformations such as cleft palate may pronounce words differently. Stutterers repeat or prolong initial sounds.

- <u>Suggestions</u> Advise students to take a course such as "Voice and Articulation" before taking the public speaking course. Paraphrase the student's message for the others in the class.

Syntax The rules for the orderly placement of words in relationship to one another is called syntax, and each language has different rules for the ordering of ideas. For instance, "For native land our great with courage fight we," is a sensible word order in Latin syntax, while it is nearly incomprehensible in English. A foreign student might say, "I not go my country three year."

Syntax also includes the rules of grammar. For example, "I seen it" does not follow the formal rules for word order considered to be "correct" in Standard English. (However, "I seen" communicates the same idea, and many people use this phrase informally or in other dialects of English--it is nonstandard, not "bad" speech.)

Foreign students often fail to add an "s" to plurals, possessives, and third person singular verbs. Example: "My two daughter enjoy playing on the grasses."

- <u>Suggestions</u> On the written critique form, write the standard grammatical form. Advise students to take courses to improve their skills in Standard English grammar.

[5] A. Wierzbicka. (1991). *Cross cultural pragmatics: The semantics of human interaction.* Berlin: Mouton de Gruyter. p. 37.

Semantics Semantics is the study of the meanings of words. As Chapter 4 pointed out, some people know more words than others, and some students have smaller vocabularies than others. Furthermore, there are often other layers of meaning implied by a single term. Example in the text: the Japanese student said, "the car door was distorted," rather than "dented" or "caved in." Idioms often cause difficulties in understanding.

- <u>Suggestions</u> Be alert for nonverbal cues that students are confused. Define words that may cause problems; explain idioms and colloquialisms that might be misunderstood.

Pragmatics The study of how people actually use language in various contexts is called pragmatics. Language operates in a social and a psychological world at any given time, meaning that the identities of the participants, the time and place in which they meet, the beliefs, knowledge, and intentions they have all contribute to meaning.

For example, native speakers of a language can detect whether a speaker saying, "Pragmatics fascinates me," is being sarcastic when the speaker says the sentence using the cultural patterns meaning "sarcasm." Foreign students would be more likely to take the statement literally.

One way pragmatic issues enter a classroom is in the cultural patterns for question and answer sequences. Many co-cultural groups such as Native Americans and African Americans have different question and answer sequences than Euro-American patterns. Also, Asian patterns typically differ.

- <u>Suggestions</u> Direct requests for information may be less successful than open-ended questions ("What did you think about . . . ?") or invitations to participate ("Give me an example of . . . ").

B. B. Whaley, J. M. Yingling, & A. Langlois. (1991, October 31-November 3). Diverse student populations in the basic course: Speech and language production essentials for instructors. Paper presented at the Speech Communication Association. Atlanta, Georgia.

C. Morris. (1946). *Signs, language, and behavior.* New York: George Braziller.

Teaching Idea 12.3: Gender Differences in Speaking

Purpose: To highlight gender differences in language usage by presenting an example from another culture.

Procedure: Duplicate and distribute copies of "Traditional Japanese Women's Speech" found on the following page. Have students read it then discuss the differences the author mentions. [Note that globally, cultures are changing at a rapid pace, and many contemporary young Japanese women use *both* the masculine and feminine forms.]

Ask students if any of them come from speech communities where there are differences between masculine and feminine speech patterns. If so, what differences exist? Elicit cultural reasons that might explain such linguistic variation. (Examples: different traditional role expectations for men and women, public and private spheres of influence, etc.)

Then discuss gender variations in the U.S. You'll find some gender differences discussed in Research Note 13.1 (above) and in Appendix A in the text.

Traditional Japanese Women's Speech

Sex differences in speech are well documented in many of the world's languages. Scholars often cite Japanese in demonstrating these differences, as several aspects of traditional Japanese women's speech vary from forms used by Japanese men.

Throughout their educational years, Japanese boys and girls learned to speak in different ways. Although all were taught polite, more formal usages, Japanese females were taught to use more of these forms. In addition, women were supposed to use more indirect ways of saying things than men. For example, men could say "boku" for "I," while women were to use "watashi," a more polite, less direct form that either sex could use, but women should use.

Women also learned to soften statements with "kashira" (I wonder) or "wa" (don't you think?). For instance, a man could say, "Samuji yo," which means "It's cold, I say." Women, however, should say "Samui wa," which translates as "It's cold, don't you think?"

Men could use the suffix "-kun" when they address one another. This suffix has a backslapping, locker room type of connotation that is a familiar greeting to other men. It was not appropriate for women to use this term when addressing men. Instead, they used the suffix "-san."

Speaking norms are changing in Japan; now many women use a combination of masculine and feminine forms. However, the *New York Times* (1991) reported that there is still a great deal of pressure for women to use less assertive linguistic forms. This affects their ability to share equal status and to be on familiar terms with their male colleagues.

Rudolph, E. (1991, Sept. 1). Women's talk. *The New York Times Magazine.* p. 8.

Chapter 13

PRESENTATION AIDS

In a media-saturated culture this chapter is essential. People generally learn and remember better when the ideas they hear are presented with visual, and sometimes audio, as well as verbal support. Because this chapter focuses on skills, you'll find a lot of bulleted lists throughout. Have fun. This is one of my favorite chapters, because I, not surprisingly, get to use lots of interesting visual aids to present the information found here. (I continue to use Figure 13.3 because my nephew drew it; I grew up in New Mexico and we used to visit the kiva in Aztec, and it goes with the diversity theme of the text.)

Chapter Goals

<u>At the end of this chapter your students should be able to:</u>

- Explain the purpose of presentation aids
- Create a plan for visual, audio, and multimedia aids
- Choose specific presentation aids, including three-dimensional and two-dimensional visual and audio resources
- Determine the advantages and disadvantages using various presentation technologies
- Apply principles of visual design
- Understand guidelines for using visual aids

Chapter Outline

I. **Presentation aids** are found in the forms of visual, audio, and multimedia support, not just decorative additions to your slides or posters.
   A. Used well, they help and audience engage, understand, and remember information.
   B. Used poorly, audiences think you either lack skill or are not committed to the project.

II. The purpose of presentational aids relates to **dual coding theory**; we use **dual processing**, so hearing and seeing relevant images during a speech creates better retention.
   A. Presentational aids are important for clarifying ideas, providing emphasis, holding attention, and appealing to a variety of learning styles.
   B. Determine where you *need* additional support for a concept that is hard to describe in words alone.
   C. Ask where support would illustrate but is not essential.
   D. Find places where support could gain or maintain attention.
           <u>Stop and Check: Begin Your Audiovisual Aid Plan</u>
III. Plan the best type of visual aids, not necessarily the ones that are easiest to make.
   A. Three-dimensional objects are useful, especially in demonstration speeches.
       1. Things to touch, smell, and taste can be incorporated into talks.
       2. Objects can be inappropriate (live animals) or illegal (firearms).
       3. Tips for using objects include:
           a. Be sure everyone can see the object.
           b. Don't pass it around.
   B. Use a model when an object is an unrealistic choice.
       1. Scaled-down models depict large objects.
       2. Enlarged models can show objects too tiny for audiences to see.

160

© 2013 Cengage Learning. All Rights Reserved. May not be copied, scanned, or duplicated, in whole or in part, except for use as permitted in a license distributed with a certain product or service or otherwise on a password-protected website for classroom use.

C. Use people--friends, audience volunteers, or the speaker.
D. Two-dimensional visuals are many times more practical and appropriate than actual objects or models and can be text-based or image-based.
    1. Lists are text-based visuals that rely on written words to communicate; tips include.
        a. Don't put too much information on it.
        b. Follow the six-by-six rule (only six lines, six words per line).
        c. Don't write out sentences and read them to the audience.
    2. Image-based visuals rely on some sort of figures or pictures.
        a. **Charts** include *flowcharts* and *organizational* charts.
        b. **Graphs** include *line graphs*, *bar graphs*, *pie graphs*, and *pictographs*.
    3. **Photographs** are effective if everyone in the audience can see them.
        a. Don't pass photographs around.
        b. Don't show pictures from a book.
    4. *Diagrams*, *drawings* and *maps* can stand alone or serve to decorate or supplement other visuals.
        a. Drawings have many uses and can substitute for illegal, impractical, or unavailable objects.
        b. Cartoons can add humor to a talk.
        c. Diagrams are line drawings or graphic designs that explain instead of realistically depict an object or process.
    5. Maps visually represent spaces in a number of ways.
        a. Political maps show national and state borders; they can change rapidly during times of political upheaval.
        b. Geographic maps show natural features like mountains or rivers; they don't get quickly outdated.
        c. Blueprints and floor plans are maps of buildings.

IV. Audio and video recordings take extra planning and preparation.
A. Audio resources are especially good for topics relating to music, but creative thinking can lead to other types of sound clips.
B. Video resources can add to a speech as long as they supplement, rather than replace the speaker's words.

Diversity in Practice: Visual Aids and Culture
Stop and Check: Continue your Audiovisual Aid Plan

IV. It's important to plan the right type of presentation technology.
A. Presentation software and LCD projectors are very common.
    1. Used in a speech, PowerPoint requires a data projector.
    2. Not everyone uses PowerPoint effectively.
    3. Follow tips for using presentation software:
        a. Include visuals in your presentation plan.
        b. Simplify and remove unnecessary words or images.
        c. Use only high-resolutions that display clearly.
        d. Create slides first in black and white, adding color sparingly to emphasize   significant points.
        e. Rehearse without slides at least once to ensure they don't substitute for your message.

Ethics in Practice: Can a Visual be Unethical?

B. Document cameras and overhead projectors are readily available and easy to use.
    1. Before you begin speaking, turn on and adjust the focus, then turn it off till your are ready to use your visual.
    2. Draw listener's attention by pointing on the visual, not on the screen.
    3. If you use a visual to highlight material repeatedly, use a bland transparency over the material and mark on that using wet erase markers to keep your originals clean.

C. Chalkboards or whiteboards are standard equipment in many settings.
   1. They are good for explaining unfolding processes.
   2. They aid in informal, speaker-audience interactions.
   3. They have three major drawbacks.
      a. Visuals can't be prepared carefully beforehand.
      b. Most people don't write well on boards, so visuals look unprofessional.
      c. You must turn your back to the audience.
   4. Boards are evolving; for example, **Interactive whiteboards** can connect to a document camera or computer.

Diversity in Practice: Traveling and Talking

D. Poster board and flip charts are convenient and economical for speeches given repeatedly.
   1. Posters are good for small audiences who can see their details clearly.
   2. Following some tips will result in more professional-looking posters.
      a. Use rulers or yardsticks to make lines straight.
      b. Use more than one color to attract and hold attention.
      c. Use adhesive letters or computerized text for a professional look.
      d. Cover your posters when being transported.
   3. Flip charts are unlined or lined tablets that can function similarly to a chalkboard.
      a. They're good for brainstorming sessions.
      b. They help speakers build diagrams (which can be sketched lightly in pencil beforehand) in front of the audience.
      c. If you use the same presentation for different audiences, use heavier-weight tablets, expose each new visual as it is being discussed.
      d. Their stiff covers can function as easels, displaying the visuals when other equipment is unavailable.

E. Handouts are common in businesses and organizations.
   1. Brochures, handouts, photocopies, and reports free audiences from note-taking.
   2. Be sure handouts supplement, not replace, your message.
   3. Following several tips makes for more effective use of handouts.
      a. Distribute them face down before the speech and ask the audience to use them when discussing the material on them.
      b. In training sessions, provide space for notes, or blanks for listeners to fill in during the speech.
      c. Project identical material on a transparency and highlight the points of emphasis.
      d. Distribute handouts with only supplementary information after the speech.

Stop and Check: Continue Your Audiovisual Aid Plan

V. Apply proven design principles to create visuals.
   A. Use general design principles
      1. *Proximity* means to group related items together.
      2. *Alignment* connects every item on a page to something else on a page.
      3. *Repetition* is using the same fonts, colors, and so on throughout all visuals.
      4. *Contrast* adds visual interest with colors or formatting.
      5. *Space* uses the "Rule of Thirds," dividing page by thirds and placing important elements along those lines.

Practically Speaking: Consult a Consultant

   B. Choose a readable **font** (a complete set of letters and numbers of a particular design).
      1. Choose title or sentence case and avoid using all capital letters.
      2. A **serif font** is easier to read; **sans serif fonts** are good for titles.
      3. Choose fonts that are consistent from visual to visual.
      4. Letters should be large enough to be seen and indicate information importance.
   B. Use formatting features wisely.

1. Attributes (boldfacing, underlining, italicizing) can help audiences see relationships.
2. Use these features sparingly for the greatest impact.
C. Color adds interest and emphasis to visuals.
   1. Colors have cultural associations.
   2. Use colors for text and images that contrast with the background color.
   3. Use no more than three colors per slide and one color per word.
   4. Emphasize ideas through color.

<u>Stop and Check: Complete Your Presentation Plan</u>

VI. Successful presenters suggest many guidelines.
   A. Make sure the audience can hear or see the audio or visual aid.
   B. Don't create a visual for its own sake.
   C. Display visuals only when you discuss them.
   D. Talk to the audience not the visual.
   E. Rehearse using the visuals.
   F. Don't show visuals that will offend or shock the audience.
   G. Have a Plan B in case of equipment failure.

<u>Speech Video: Artificial Gills, Casey Millerick</u>

Suggested Videos

Book CourseMate. Casey Millerick's speech, "Artificial Gills," is featured throughout the chapter and at the end. Casey created a series of visual aids and used transition and build features. Review the design principles found in the text, then have students evaluate the slides using the following questions:

- How does the variety of presentation aids enhance his message?
- Are his slides designed well?
- Is color used effectively?
- What transitions and build features does he use?
- What specifically does he do well as he uses his slides?
- How would evaluate his use of an online animated diagram?
- What advice might you give him to improve him use of visual support? (synthesis, evaluation)

Interactive video activities also include "The *Dun Dun* Drum" by Josh Valentine (Chapter 16 resources), which has audio as well as visual support. "Pumpkins" by Anna Riedl (Chapter 13 resources), "Advergaming" by Kelsey Bennett (Chapter 6 resources), and "Shakespeare" by Hillary Carter-Liggett (Chapter 10 resources) also feature presentation aids. Hillary's speech is an example of excellent content with poor visuals. Because the context was a competitive speech tournament she used posters. Show the speech and ask some or all of the following questions:

- What kind of visual or audio support is used?
- What display technology is used?
- How well does the speaker transition between visuals? (knowledge, comprehension)
- Is color used effectively?
- Are the visuals designed well?
- What specifically does the speaker do well?
- What advice would you give for improvement, either in the VA or in its use? (synthesis, evaluation)

Professional Speeches. TED (www.ted.com) is especially useful for visual aid speeches on highly complex topics. Browse the collection and select one that would interest your audience. Ask some of the questions listed above. Edith Widder's speech, described at the beginning of the chapter, is maintained on **weblink 13.1**.

Discussion Topics

Purposes for Presentations (pp. 219-220) This chapter gives you many opportunities for "show and tell."Use **Suggested Videos**, Teaching Idea 12.1 in **Supplemental Resources**, or show other visual aids you have collected over time. This chapter distinguishes between text based visuals--those that depend on words for their meaning--and image based visuals that require a figure or other image. (application, analysis, evaluation)

Ethics in Practice: Can Visuals Be Unethical? (p. 228). Ask students to read the feature, and, working in groups, to answer the discussion questions that follow.

Presentation Technology (pp. 227-231) Here are more "show and tell" opportunities. Go over various technologies for presenting visuals, showing and discussing their advantages and disadvantages. Put a diagram on a transparency, write on the board, bring a flip chart (desk size or larger), distribute handouts, use computer-projected visuals, and so on. (knowledge, comprehension, application)

PowerPoint (p. 227) Is PowerPoint overused? There's an interesting article on InfoTrac titled, "Is PowerPoint the Devil?" Julia Keller wrote it for the Knight Ridder/Tribune News Service, December 30, 2002. Keller says that on a daily basis 30 million PowerPoint presentations take place globally. PowerPoint has moved from the boardroom to the classroom – not always with the best results. Many of her ideas would be suitable for classroom discussion. For a more positive appraisal, look for the March 2004 article, "PowerPoint: Devil in a Red Dress," by Stephen Abrams. He has some good tips for creating PowerPoint slides.

Diversity in Practice: Traveling and Talking (p. 230) Discuss some of the challenges that speakers face when they speak in other countries. (comprehension)

Stop and Check: My Presentation Plan (p. 232) The purpose of this chapter is to have students actually create and present visual aids that supplement a speech. Throughout the chapter, you'll find Stop and Check features that direct them to complete parts of their plan. (application)

Use Proven Design Principles to Create Visuals (pp. 232-235) The principles here can be used for posters, handouts, slides, and so on. Bring a computer and projector into the class and demonstrate major features of a presentation program like PowerPoint. Ask students who've worked with the program to demonstrate some things it can do. Change colors, fonts, bullets, spacing, and so on to create a balanced, esthetically pleasing visual. (application, synthesis)

Practically Speaking: Consult a Consultant (pp. 232-233) Ask students to read the feature, and, working in groups, to answer the discussion questions that follow.

Application and Critical Thinking Exercises

1. If you use journals or blogging in your class, for one week have students keep a "visual-aids-in-real-life" list, identifying the type of visual and the occupation of the user--either recording their findings in their journal or in email postings. At the end of the week, tally up the types of visuals used. As a group, discuss the questions in this exercise. (They'll probably see a lot of overhead projectors and few, if any, flip charts.) (application, synthesis, analysis, evaluation)

2. Have students identify classes in which they would have learned more had the instructor used visuals. Ask them what kind of visual or audio support would be most helpful, given their particular learning style. (application, analysis)

3. Transfer a cartoon to a transparency to show to the class. Then ask them to decide on several possible ways to display it in various contexts. Which would be most effective? Least effective? Why? (application, evaluation)

4. Have students do an "equipment assessment" of their specific speaking situation. Then use the questions here for an in-class written response on the day you present the material about displaying visuals. (analysis, application)

5. For years I demonstrated the principles of making visual aids by using posters. No more. I now ask students to create visuals using a presentation program such as PowerPoint. I usually bring a laptop computer and an LCD projector to class and demonstrate the program—pointing out its features and inviting competent students to demonstrate the skills they've developed on the program. I encourage them to experiment all they want but to create visuals for class that will enhance, not detract from their speeches. (application)

6. The bulleted list could form the basis for an in-class review of the *possible* and the *best* type of visual(s) to use with a specific topic. (evaluation)

7. Here are a few articles you can refer students to: 1) in *ABA Banking Journal,* June 2000, "Visual aids: How much is too much?" by H. Dennis Beauer; 2) in *St. Louis Business Journal,* April 10, 2000, "Visual aids should enhance, not take over presentations," by Sue Greenberg; 3) in *Presentations,* April 2002, "Props help bring content into the visual realm," by Andrea Neirenberg. (This article is fun to read.)

8. Give students time in class to design a visual package for a speech found in this text. Instruct them to begin by plainning slides on paper using principles in this chapter, then have them make the slides on the computer. You could use this as a contest and have students vote on the best package. Provide a small prize or bonus points for the winning package. (application, evaluation)

9. Many hits are from .com companies that have a vested interest in marketing products. Students should be aware of their commercial bias. You might want to direct students to the University of Kansas's excellent site; it has many links as well as a tutorial.

10. Give students the assignment of presenting a visual aid speech with NO PowerPoint permitted. After introducing the assignment (which may be unpopular as many speakers LOVE PowerPoint) lead students in a discussion about alternatives to computerized presentational aids. When would they be most useful? Least useful? (application, analysis)

11. Do this activity in class. Why would Lincoln's speech lose impact in Powerpoint?

Internet Activities

The CourseMate for Public Speaking, accessible through http://login.cengage.com, offers a broad range of resources that will help students better understand the material in the chapter, complete assignments, and succeed on tests. The CourseMate also features speech videos with critical viewing questions, speech outlines, and transcripts. It also offers interactive practice activities, self-quizzes, and a sample final exam.

Supplemental Resources

- Teaching Idea 13.1: Evaluating Visual Aids
- Research Note 13.1: Learning from Positive and Negative Instances

Teaching Idea 13.1: Evaluating Visual Aids

Purpose: To evaluate the effectiveness of visuals by comparing and contrasting a number of student-made posters or transparencies.

Procedure
1. Make a collection of the "best" and "worst" posters or transparencies you can find. (Often students will give you their visuals after their speeches. They never intend to use them again, and they are often flattered that you will use their work as a model.) In addition, check around the department for posters that students have made and discarded in previous terms. Be certain to remove all identifying marks from the visual aids to avoid potentially embarrassing students.

2. Divide the class into groups of three and give each group 3 or 4 visuals, well done and poorly done. Have them identify the best and the worst and discuss the reason for their judgment. After they have made their decisions, have members of the group explains which ones the group decided were best and worst, and why.

3. Alternatively, make a copy of good and bad PowerPoint slide shows. Present them to the class for evaluation.

Research Note 13.1: Learning from Positive and Negative Instances

Cognitive research shows that we learn concepts from seeing both positive and negative instances. Here is a summary of some findings that can guide you can as you present examples of both good and bad visual support:

*   Students learn concepts most easily when the positive and negative instances are clearly distinct.

*   Learning is best when you present positive instances first, then mix positive and negative instances.

*   Sometimes learners must pay closer attention to negative instances in order to identify the attributes and rules of the concept being presented.

*   Learning is enhanced when you present positive and negative instances side by side.

Robert M. W. Travers (1982). *Essentials of learning: The new cognitive learning for students of education, 5th ed.* New York: Macmillan.

Chapter 14

DELIVERING YOUR SPEECH

This chapter focuses on what many identify as their greatest public speaking worry--actually performing the speech. Good delivery requires the management of nonverbal behaviors, the display of skills such as eye contact, vocal variation, appropriate appearance, and gestures. Hopefully, by analyzing the elements of good delivery, students will feel a sense of control--a sense that they can do something to create and manage the impressions their audience has of them.

Chapter Goals

At the end of this chapter your students will be able to:

- List four methods of delivery and explain when and how to use each
- Describe how you can enhance your use of personal appearance, clothing, and accessories
- Plan ways to use gesture effectively
- Build eye contact skills
- Vary your voice effectively in presentations

At the end of this chapter you should be able to:

- Evaluate a videotape of yourself teaching this class. Have a student videotape you in the classroom, then set some goals for self-improvement. (Personally, I hate to do this, but I know it helps me teach more effectively.)

Chapter Outline

I. Competent speakers put together the elements of **delivery** to communicate in a way that's personally effective and socially appropriate.
   A. Begin by selecting the appropriate type of delivery.
      1. **Manuscript delivery**, reading the speech word for word, can lessen speaker-audience interactions; however, some occasions (highly formal speeches, mediated speeches) call for this type of delivery.
         a. Manuscript deliver is appropriate when precise working is important.
         b. It is also useful when exact timing is essential.
         c. Practice till it is conversational.
         d. Many professionals use a **TelePrompter**; this requires practice.
      2. **Memorized delivery** is common in oral cultures but uncommon in the United States; forgetting adds stress and delivery is often not natural sounding.
      3. **Impromptu delivery** involves little preparation beforehand; speakers draw from their experiences and knowledge for speech materials.
      4. **Extemporaneous delivery**, the most common type, features careful planning in advance, with specific wording selected during the speech itself.
         <u>Practically Speaking: Kendra Phillips, Student Serve Day Coordinator</u>

II. Speakers should maximize personal appearance to create and manage the impression listeners have of them. Good grooming, pleasing gestures, and smiles are important in **impression management.**
   A. Physical appearance discloses information.
      1. You can see someone's approximate age, racial background, height, sex, weight, and body type.
      2. In a culture that highlights physical perfection, many people worry about their appearance; choosing an interesting topic and creating a compelling introduction is a good strategy for drawing attention to the speech, not the speaker.
   B. The **Impression management** concept says we create and maintain impressions as if we were on stage.
      1. Audiences form an overall impression on facial expressions, posture, gestures and grooming.
      2. Clothing can create a positive impression and show you take the assignment seriously.
      3. To avoid embarrassment, check out clothing expectations before the speech.
      4. **Accessories** matter; keep them simple, appropriate, and of the best quality affordable.

<u>Ethics in Practice: Managing Impressions</u>

   C. Impression management has ethical implications.
      1. **Sincere** speakers believe the nonverbal and verbal messages they are sending.
      2. **Cynical** speakers choose strategies to create false or misleading impressions that they themselves don't believe.

III. Effective mannerisms enhance delivery. To develop effective mannerisms:
   A. Control your gestures.
      1. Plan gestures to be purposeful.
      2. Practice gestures till they seem natural.
      3. Watch a recording of yourself and analyzes where you can improve.
      4. Eliminate nervous mannerisms.
      5. Maintain pleasant facial expressions.
      6. Use movements to emphasize your speech structure.
      7. Control nervous gestures.
   B. Make eye contact.
      1. In the U.S. eye contact communicates honesty and trustworthiness.
      2. Making ey econtact can be difficult, but can be developed:
         a. Look in at least three general directions.
         b. Divide the group into a grid—make eye contact with a friendly fact in each.
         c. Hold your gaze for three to five seconds.
         d. Don't just zero in on those you think are powerful, like your instructor or boss.
         e. Don't look at one gender more than another.
         f. If your gaze makes someone uncomfortable, don't focus on that person's eyes.
      3. Expectations common in the U.S. are not universal.
         a. In Japan, downcast or closed eyes demonstrates attentiveness and agreement.
         b. Nigerians and Puerto Ricans consider prolonged eye contact with superiors to be disrespectful.
   C. Vary your vocal behaviors.
      1. **Vocalics**, or **paralinguistics**, deals with all aspects of spoken language but the words.
         a. Work on clear pronunciation.
         b. **Articulation** is the pronunciation of individual sounds.
         c. **Stress** is the accent on syllables or words.
      2. Regions differ in pronunciation and articulation.
         a. How long the sounds are held differs; southern speakers often hold out their sounds (drawl).
         b. Some add sounds (the Bostonian "r" at the end of words).
      3. Tips for improving pronunciation and articulation include:
         a. Consult a dictionary if you are unsure of a word's pronunciation.

    b. Work on sounds or words that cause you difficulty.
    c. Slow down during rehearsals to articulate clearly.
    d. During the speech itself, speak slowly to avoid slurring or dropping words.
    e. Consider a professional speech therapist for serious articulation problems.

<u>Diversity in Practice: Culture and Delivery</u>

D. Vocal variation is important for volume, pitch, and rate.
  1. **Vocal variations** make listening easier.
  2. Listeners associate vocal characteristics with personality traits such as dynamic (loud/fast) or composed (soft/fast).
  3. Speakers can use vocal characteristics to work for them.
    a. Show emotional attitude with your voice.
    b. Babble during one rehearsal, but use vocalics to express emotions.
    c. Rehearse parts that could use more energy.
  4. Vocal variations affect meaning.
    a. Speak loudly enough to be heard throughout the room.
    b. Relax your throat before you speak.
    c. Use the lower ranges of your voice.
    d. Speak naturally and conversationally.
    e. Use a slower rate for key points, slow up for background information.
    f. If audience appears to be losing interest, change vocal inflections.
E. Pause for effect.
  1. Effective pauses are intentional; they give listeners time to think.
  2. Ineffective pauses or hesitations disrupt fluency.
    a. **Unfilled pauses** are silent.
    b. **Filled or vocalized pauses** ("um") are common but potentially distracting.

<u>Stop and Check: Think Critically about Delivery</u>

Suggested Videos

Book CourseMate. You'll find examples of most of the types of delivery described in the text. If you want longer examples, use the following videos:
- <u>Memorized.</u> Hillary Carter-Leggett's (Ch. 10) and Hans Arian's (Ch. 11) speeches were memorized for participation in competitive speech tournaments.
- <u>Extemporaneous.</u> Anna Reidl (Ch. 13) and Josh Valentine (Ch. 16) illustrate this delivery mode.
- <u>Manuscript.</u> Linnea Strandy' speech (Ch. 18) uses manuscript delivery. Lishan Zeng (Ch. 16) reads from a teleprompter.
- <u>Impromptu.</u> Tape a segment off of the question-and-answer part of a press conference to show impromptu delivery.
- Have students evaluate the effectiveness of each type of delivery, given the topic and the speaking situation. (comprehension, application, evaluation)

Nonverbal Delivery. Show sample speeches of your choice without the sound to summarize the various aspects of delivery. Discuss their observations. (comprehension, application, analysis)

Personalized Student Speeches. If you are having students record their own speeches, here is a good place to have them watch and comment on their own delivery. Have them D-R-E (<u>describe</u> what they see and hear, <u>respond</u> emotionally, and <u>evaluate</u> what is and what is not effective) and then plan strategies to improve their own delivery.

Discussion Topics

Personal Appearance (pp. 245-246) Use the **Suggested Videos** for the section on maximizing personal appearance. (comprehension, application, analysis, evaluation)

Ethics in Practice: Managing Impressions (p. 245) Use these questions or question #1 (**Application and Critical Thinking Exercises**) to discuss ethical implications of impression management. You could also use the clip from the feature film *Elizabeth* that's described in **Suggested Videos, Chapter 2**. Instead of focusing on extemporaneous delivery, focus on her strategies for impression management. Is she putting on a front? Is this cynical? (comprehension, analysis, synthesis, evaluation)

Gestures (pp. 246-247) Play a speech from the suggested videos with the sound turned off, with at least a section on fast forward. (The extra speed really accentuates annoying or unnecessary gestures.) Concentrate on the speaker's eye contact and movements. Look for emblems, illustrators, and adaptors. Discuss the overall effectiveness of the delivery. (application, analysis, evaluation)

Varied Vocal Behaviors (pp. 241-244) There are many interesting ways to reinforce the concepts here:
- Teaching Idea 14.1: "Vocal Variation and Meaning" (**Supplemental Resources**) provides an in-class exercise.
- Question #2 (**Application and Critical Thinking Exercises**) is similar.
- Have students bring a children's picture book to class and read it to a small group of fellow students-- of course, they must use the vocal traits appropriate to each character. (The book should take no longer than four minutes to read.) If there's time, invite each group to select a person to read her or his book to the whole class. (application, synthesis)

Stop and Check: Think Critically about Delivery (p. 252) Do we vote based on a politician's image? Do we discount the words of unattractive people? Explore the relationship of image and effectiveness by using up-to-date examples of political candidates. Extend the application to include other speakers – members of the clergy, professors, and so on. (analysis, synthesis, evaluation)

Types of Delivery (pp. 241-244) Use guidelines in the **Suggested Videos** to present examples of the four modes. (comprehension, application, evaluation)

Application and Critical Thinking Exercises

1. Use this as a class activity. Are there cultural rules for delivery that may not be included in the text?

2. This exercise asks students to consider people who put on a front and appear to be something that they're not. How does this happen? What are the ethical implications of fronts? Use this question with the Ethics in Practice: Managing Impressions (p. 245). (analysis, synthesis, evaluation)

3. The point of this exercise is to have students vary their vocal behaviors to create different impressions. They can do this exercise as is, or they can practice reading an advertisement of their choice--either audio taped or performed live for a small group of their classmates; their vocal variation should match the words and mood of the ad. (application)

3. This is one of the most valuable learning experiences students can have. I normally ask students to buy a videotape which will be used to record every one of their speeches. At the end of the term they write a self-evaluation, noting what they did well, what they improved, and what they still need to work on. (analysis, evaluation)

4. This extends the previous exercise. (synthesis)

5. This is an example of peer coaching. (analysis, synthesis, evaluation)

6. This develops the concept, presented in Chapter 2, of classrooms as mini-cultures. (application, synthesis)

7. On-line courses are a fact of life; on-line public speaking courses are currently offered by some institutions. Because public speaking, almost by definition, is a performance class in which the students give speeches to one another, how can an on-line course work? Looking at actual sources on the Internet prepares them for this exercise. (analysis, synthesis)

Internet Activities

The CourseMate for Public Speaking, accessible through http://login.cengage.com, offers a broad range of resources that will help students better understand the material in the chapter, complete assignments, and succeed on tests. The CourseMate also features speech videos with critical viewing questions, speech outlines, and transcripts. It also offers interactive practice activities, self-quizzes, and a sample final exam.

Supplemental Resources

- Teaching Idea 14.1: Vocal Variation Associated with Specific Characters
- Teaching Idea 14.2: Vocal Variation and Meaning
- Research Note 14.1: Ums--Those Pesky Filled Pauses

Teaching Idea 14.1: Vocal Variation Associated with Specific Characters

Purpose: To have students create various vocal personae.

Procedure: Clip enough advice column letters and answers for each student to have one. (The late Ann Landers' columns can be found on the Internet.) Form groups of four or five. Give each group member a letter/answer and have them read through it silently. Then ask one person at a time to read his or her letter, using a character "voice" that you assign, changing characters on command. It goes like this:
- Have Person #1 in every group start with a "four-year-old girl" voice. After about 20-seconds, say "football announcer," and they switch to that accent.
- After about a half minute, say "Person #2," and all the #2 persons start reading their letter as a football announcer might... after a few seconds, I provide another character voice . . .
- Continue around the circle this way.
- Possible voices include: teenaged airhead, used car salesman, politician, Barney (the TV character), the Nanny (Fran Drescher), a French or Russian accent, southern accent, mother comforting a sick child, coach in the locker room, voice for a perfume ad.

Teaching Idea 14.2: Vocal Variation and Meaning

Purpose: To vary a speaker's vocal cues to match the contents of a message.

Procedure: Make one or more photocopies of the material on the following page (or make your own scripts) and cut along the dotted lines. Distribute the scripts to student volunteers. Give them a few minutes to mark the text for emphasis then have them read the script to the class, using the vocal variation appropriate to the character that's given. Discuss the vocal adjustments they made in rate, volume, inflection, pauses, and so on.

Next, have volunteers read the same ad in a voice that doesn't "match." For example, use a Valley Girl voice for the perfume ad, a perfume voice over for the sports announcement, a confident style for the cruise ship promotion.

(sports announcer) **WELCOME TO FRIDAY NIGHT FOOTBALL. TONIGHT THE UNBEATEN PIT BULLS TAKE ON THE EMERALD CITY AXMEN. EMERALD CITY IS CURRENTLY 4 AND 1, AND THE TEAM ENTERS THE STADIUM TONIGHT, LOOKING TO AVENGE THEIR DEFEAT AT THE HANDS OF THE PIT BULLS LAST SEASON.**

(used car sales person) **COME OUT TO AUTO ROW TODAY AND BUY A NEW CAR FROM ONE OF OUR WELL-TRAINED SALES REPRESENTATIVES.**

--NO MONEY DOWN. NO MONEY UNTIL JANUARY.

--JUST THINK. YOU CAN BE DRIVING A NEW TAURUS--THAT'S A NEW TAURUS--FOR NO MONEY DOWN, NO PAYMENTS UNTIL JANUARY!!

(voice over for a perfume commercial) **ROMANCE . . . THE NEW PERFUME FROM PARIS. WEAR IT TO CELEBRATE ALL THE ROMANCES IN YOUR LIFE.**

(conversational style) **GET AWAY FROM IT ALL!**

HAVEN'T YOU WANTED TO LEAVE YOUR TROUBLES BEHIND AND RELAX FOR A WEEK ON THE LUXURIOUS WHITE, WARM SAND OF A TROPICAL ISLAND?

WELL, OUR SPECIAL VACATION PACKAGE OFFERS YOU THIS AND MORE--

--AIRFARE FOR TWO--TO AND FROM THE ISLAND.

--A WEEK IN A LUXURY HOTEL OVERLOOKING THE BEACH.

--GOURMET MEALS.

--USE OF A HEALTH SPA.

CALL YOUR TRAVEL AGENT TODAY AND ASK FOR DETAILS.

Research Note: 14.1: Ums--Those Pesky Filled Pauses

Do you find yourself saying "um" as you teach? I'm always self-conscious when I present the material on delivery . . . especially the "filled pause" section, because, I confess, I'm an ummer. Several years ago, I read that one reason people say "um" relates to the amount of options they have. For instance, a math teacher won't say, "Two (um) plus two (um) equals (um) four." No, there's one answer, one choice for this teacher. However, we in the humanities have so many possible directions to take a discussion--or so many possible examples to illustrate a difficult concept--that we often pause to think . . . but we pause aloud.

Christenfeld (1994) examined the relationship between choices and ums by having students describe a number of mazes ranging from simple (one route) to complex (many alternative routes). He found that students describing a difficult maze produced a lot of ums . . . but students describing the simplest maze were regular ummers, too. Options did seem to contribute to filled pauses, but Christenfeld suggests that breaking up the rhythm of the speech may also result in ums.

In a sense, I'm thankful for student ums when they indicate extemporaneous rather than memorized or manuscript delivery!

Source. Christenfeld, N. (1994). Options and ums. *Journal of Language and Social Psychology, 13*, 192-199.

Chapter 15

TELLING NARRATIVES

Storytelling is universal. Besides that, storytelling is fun. Because narratives function in every culture, and because narrative speaking is enjoyable, I include a stand-alone chapter on the topic. Narratives are powerful; they explain and motivate and entertain. We reason through our stories, but we should test their merit. This chapter presents a number of guidelines for telling good stories, and it provides a pattern--the exemplum pattern--that speakers can adapt for use in a variety of settings.

Chapter Goals

At the end of this chapter your students will be able to:

* Explain how narratives function to explain, to persuade, and to entertain
* List elements of narratives
* Give guidelines for using language effectively in narratives
* Identify the parts of an exemplum
* Apply three tests for narrative reasoning

Chapter Outline

I. We have been called *homo narrans*, the storytelling animal because **storytelling** is an enjoyable oral art that has many cultural functions, primarily to inform, persuade, or entertain.
   A. Some narratives are informative.
      1. They explain natural phenomena.
      2. They explain society and its institutions.
         Ethics in Practice: Who Should Tell Native Stories?
      3. Narratives attempt to explain ultimate realities and answer philosophical questions.
   B. Narratives can be persuasive; Aristotle classified narrative reasoning as a type of **deliberative speaking** that gives people information and motivates them to make wise decisions about the future.
      1. Motivational narratives provide a rationale for a belief, attitude, or action.
         Practically Speaking: Applied Storytellers
      2. Stories also provide cautions against certain behaviors; horror stories can be powerful.
      3. Visionary narratives (the **rhetoric of possibility**) show what might be, not what is.
   C. Entertaining narratives (jokes, scary stories, quirky stories) are told for enjoyment.
         Stop and Check: Your Narrative Purposes

II. It is important to organize narrative stories for greatest impact.
   A. There are major guidelines for weaving narrative elements together.
      1. Identify the purpose or function for the narrative.
      2. Set up the story.
      3. Develop the characters.
         a. Characters can be fictionalized humans and animals.
         b. Their distinctive characteristics and backgrounds influence their choices.
      4. Develop the **plot** or action in which characters face challenges, respond, and inevitably change.
      5. Format your speech as a story.

175

D. Select vivid language.
1. Detailed descriptions at the beginning, at crucial elements of the plot, and at the climax invite listeners in to the story.
2. **Constructed dialogue** adds realism to stories and can be amplified by skilled delivery.
3. **Create lists**, as audiences can create mental images for each listed item.
   Diversity in Practice: Analyzing a Folktale

III. Use a narrative pattern
A. The **exemplum** pattern is a useful narrative pattern with a long history.
1. First, state a quotation or proverb.
2. Identify the author and/or source of the quotation or proverb.
3. Rephrase the point or general theme of the quotation.
4. Illustrate the central theme of the quotation with a narrative.
5. Apply the point to the audience.

IV. It's important to evaluate narrative reasoning in three major ways.
A. The story should have **narrative coherence**, meaning that it is understandable.
B. The story should make sense within the cultural framework; it should have **narrative fidelity**.
C. The story should **merit** being told.
1. Ethical issues arise when a story can create problems for the people involved but can have a cautionary or helpful message to the hearers.
2. Stories don't have to be true to be good--fiction is useful--but false, harmful stories are wrong to tell.
   Stop and Check: Judging Stories
   Student Speech with Commentary: My September 11, Benjamin Hargrove

Suggested Videos

Book CourseMate. Have students watch Gail Grobey's speech, "Spanking: There's Gotta Be a Better Way" which is printed in Appendix C.
- Show this speech as a model of how to incorporate details and dialogue in essential places.
- Have some students focus on details at the setting; others on details at the key action point; still others on details in the climax or the story.
- Discuss the effectiveness of details in each of the three places.
- Evaluate the effectiveness of the dialogue. Should she have included more? If so, where? (comprehension, analysis, evaluation)

Visionary Narratives. To highlight the concept of visionary narratives, show a clip or trailer from a movie that provides a negative vision of what might be. Examples: *Contagion* (2011) or *The Manchurian Candidate* (1962) or other conspiracy theory movie.
- Review the section "Visionary Narratives."
- Show the clip; have students take notes on what they see.
- Ask them to explain how such a movie might make people want to do something now that would prevent such a castrophe later. (comprehension, synthesis)
To highlight the power of narratives, show the clip from *The Great Debaters* (2007) mentioned in the text, page 258.

Native American Stories and Legends. Many myths, stories, and legends are available on YouTube. Use the questions in the Diversity in Practice box on page 264 to guide your discussion.

Discussion Topics

Laura Simms, Applied Storyteller (p. 259) Use Application and Critical Thinking Exercise #1 to discuss ways that stories bring about healing and help to people who are in difficult situations.

Diversity in Practice: Who Should Tell Native Stories (p. 257) Ask students when it is and when it is not appropriate to tell someone else's personal or group story.

Deliberative Speaking (p. 258) When we face a decision like "What should we do about social security reform?" we typically deliberate or ponder various courses of action before we formulate laws or policies. Select a campus or local issue and ask students to come up with narratives that would help a committee make a policy decision regarding the matter. Let's say the issue of roadside memorials is being discussed as a traffic safety hazard: one student tells how putting flowers at a friend's roadside memorial helped her gain closure regarding the friend's death; another tells how the memorial re-minded him to slow down on a rainy night when he was speeding; a third describes how a driver who was distracted by the memorial nearly collided with her oncoming car. (comprehension, application)

Visionary Narratives (p. 260) Use short clips from several science fiction or thriller feature films to illustrate how stories show possiblities. (See **Suggested Videos**.) (comprehension)

Entertaining Narratives (p. 260) Invite students to tell a joke in class. Be sure to give them guidelines so they don't present anything inappropriate. (synthesis)

Stop and Check: Your Narrative Purposes (p. 261) This exercise asks students to analyze the reasons they tell narratives. Ask them to divulge their percentages to the class and make a rough estimate of the percentage of stories an average person devotes to each purpose. (analysis)

Stop and Check: Analyzing a Folktale (p. 264) By comparing and contrasting a folktale from another culture, students can better understand the functions and elements of good narratives. (analysis, evaluation)

The Exemplum Pattern (p. 265) This is a very useful pattern, especially for inspirational speeches. I usually assign a student exemplum early in the semester--sometimes nongraded. Most students can use the pattern successfully and gain the self-confidence they need to do more difficult speeches. Part I in this manual provides guidelines and an evaluation sheet. (synthesis)

Application and Critical Thinking Exercises

1. Have students use this as the basis for a "cultural artifact" speech. Instruct them to find an item from their lives that represents a culture they belong to, using a narrative. To get students used to the idea, I present students with a toy Ford Mustang. Since I am from Detroit, I tell the story of everyone I knew buying new cars every two years. This cultural story clashed with my husband's family, who only buy cars when the old ones are no longer drivable. Have the audience take notes, asking them later to summarize a classmate's speech. (application, analysis, synthesis.)

2. – 3.   These questions, in combination, invite students to apply chapter concepts by analyzing the narratives that frame their view of life, of history, and of ultimate realities. Clashes occur between creationists and evolutionists; between Muslims and Jews; between sons of slaves and daughters of slave owners; etc. These two questions are appropriate as journal entries or as in-class, small group, or email discussion topics. (application, analysis, evaluation)

5. Use this as a class project—assign students to give a narrative speech on their favorite travel story. Have students develop outlines with classmates to encourage peer learning. (application)

6. Have students take a look at snopes.com, a web page devoted to proving wrong urban myths. Ask your students if they have ever fallen prey to one of the far too common pleas for money from a friend who had to go to London suddenly and was robbed and has no money or passport, or the lottery notification they had one a prize. What makes stories such as these believable?

6. Inspirational stories are quite widespread. In some religious groups, for example, it is common to hear "testimonies" or personal accounts of an adherent's spiritual journeys. Sports is another arena where storytellers recount the feats of heroes and of last-second wins against all odds. Sales managers tell stories of "diamond" salesmen or of persevering women who sold enough cosmetics that they could afford that pink Cadillac they'd always wanted. (application, analysis)

7. Here's a chance for students to apply what they know about the exemplum pattern to identify appropriate topics and sketch out speeches for the various contexts. (application)

8. Ask students to contrast Lewis and Clark's or the Whitmans' account of Anglo-Nez Perce relationships with those given by Chief Joseph. How does each group use storytelling to rationalize their behaviors and explain their social realities? Can differences in these stories be reconciled? If so, how? Can all these stories make sense at the same time? If so, how? (analysis, synthesis, evaluation)

9. Some stories have never been written down; they provide an oral history of a family, a team, a living group, and so on. Have students respond in journal entries or in an on-line discussion. Some of these stories may be distorted in the telling. For example, I recently used the Internet to try to track down the truth about some family legends. For example, my Swedish-immigrant grandmother once worked for "Mrs. Chase." I always thought it was the "Chase" of Chase Manhattan Bank. However, Internet research proved this wrong. I'm still trying to identify the right Chase family. Also, a great-great-great-great-grandmother was a Crockett. I'm still trying to piece together the story of how her family got to America. (analysis)

10. Have students discuss their favorite stories. What about the story did they enjoy as children? Does the story have different significant for them as adults?

11. Try this with a speech already completed. Is it easier to outline as a narrative? How about to deliver? Why are narratives sometimes easier to organize than speeches?

12. One of my favorite activities is to have students bring in and present their favorite children's'book. Either use this as a growth activity, or use it for something graded. Have students indicate why the book is significant to them to give the assignment more substance and educational weight. (analysis)

13. Try this in class as well. Try giving each group one of these topics as a 'skit' to try to frame the narrative.

Internet Activities

The CourseMate for Public Speaking, accessible through http://login.cengage.com, offers a broad range of resources that will help students better understand the material in the chapter, complete assignments, and succeed on tests. The CourseMate also features speech videos with critical viewing questions, speech outlines, and transcripts. It also offers interactive practice activities, self-quizzes, and a sample final exam.

Supplemental Resources

Teaching Idea 15.1: Narrative Purposes in Children's Books

Teaching Idea 15.1: Narrative Purposes in Children's Books

Purpose: To help students identify narrative purposes found in children's literature.

Procedure: Ask students to bring an illustrated children's book to class. The book should be short enough to read through in 3-5 minutes.

- Have them identify the book's purpose. Does it explain a natural, social, or ultimate reality? Did the author hope to persuade children to choose positive behaviors and reject negative ones? Does it present possibilities? Or is the book simply entertaining? (Even entertaining books often have an explanatory or persuasive purpose.)
- During the class session, have them read their books aloud to a small group of 3-5 students, displaying the pictures as they do so.
- Use this teaching idea in conjunction with Chapter 14's **Discussion Topics**, "Varied Vocal Behaviors." That is, have them use different voices for different characters, and have them vary their volume and rate or use accents, when appropriate.
- In a whole-class discussion, identify ways that all cultures use narratives, beginning in the members' earliest childhood, to shape their ideas of the world.

Chapter 16

INFORMATIVE SPEAKING

Most professors assign at least one informative speech, so the chapter begins with guidelines for analyzing and adapting to the level of understanding the audience brings to the speech. It describes how to give speeches in several broad categories including demonstrations and instructions, descriptions, reports, and explanations. The chapter closes with seven guidelines for making information interesting, relevant, memorable, and understandable.

Chapter Goals

At the end of this chapter, your students should be able to:

- Describe the global importance of information
- Analyze an audience's knowledge of the subject
- Create several types of informative speeches including demonstrations and instructions, descriptions, reports, and explanations
- Use guidelines to make your informative speeches more effective

Chapter Outline

I. Information is important globally in this, the **Information Age**.
    A. A product of modern technology, the **electronic superhighway** has created an information explosion in which huge amounts of disconnected, irrelevant facts bombard people.
    B. It's easy to feel like there's an overload of information, with overwhelming amounts of data.
        1. Speakers should help audience members understand how information relates to their lives.
        2. Good information can empower audience members and help them make wise decision.
    C. Article 19 of the Universal Declaration of Human Rights says that the right to information should be protected by international law.
        1. Article 19 recognizes that **information imbalance** exists and that some have access to information and others are left out.
        2. Information is a valuable resource.
                Ethics in Practice: The Right to Information

II. Speakers should analyze their audience's knowledge about the topic.
    A. Sometimes the information is new.
        1. Speakers should provide basic introductory facts.
        2. They should define terminology and jargon and explain and describe things clearly.
        3. Give detailed, vivid explanations and descriptions.
        4. They should make links to the audience's knowledge and compare the topic to something familiar.
        5. Help audience understand why they should know about your subject.
    B. Some speakers provide supplemental information to an audience already familiar with the topic.
        1. Speakers should dig deeper and discover less well-known information.
        2. Go beyond the obvious—add details and explanations.

3. Narrowing the topic to a novel subtopic can increase audience knowledge overall.
C. Some audiences need a review or an update about a familiar topic.
   1. Speakers should approach these subjects from different angles and perspectives.
   2. Be creative and use supporting material that captures and holds attention.
   3. Humor can make these topics more interesting and engaging.
   4. Present the most updated information; data can be quickly outdated.
D. Speakers commonly counter misconceptions and misunderstandings.
   1. Prepare for emotional responses, sometimes negative.
   2. Scientific information, especially quantification, may be more convincing.
   3. It is important to define terms carefully.
   4. Highlighting positive aspects of a topic may help counter negative reactions.

III. There are several types of informative speeches; methods for organizing them includes **division** and **classification**.
   <u>Stop and Check: Analyze Your Audience's Knowledge</u>
A. Demonstrations and instructions answer the question, "How do you do that?"
   1. **Demonstration speeches** show and tell how to do a process or how to use an item.
      a. First, think through all the stages or steps and arrange them in order.
      b. Second, work on the content of the speech.
      c. Planning visual support is also important.
      d. Timing is essential; the process must be presented in the allotted time frame.
         1) For lengthy processes, supplement a demonstration with a how-to handout.
         2) Or prepare several versions of the item, each at a different stage of completion.
   2. Instructions give tips or guidelines for subjects like conflict resolution or the listening process.
B. Descriptions answer the question, "What is it like?"
   1. Some provide vivid details that help listeners form precise images of a particular place.
   2. Some describe objects by explaining their origin, how they're made, their characteristics, how they work, how they are used, and so on.
   <u>Practically Speaking: Informative Speaking on the Job</u>
   3. Descriptions of events or occurrences often use chronological or topical patterns.
C. In a report, speakers tell what they have learned about a person or subject.
   1. Reports about people are generally organized in a chronological, topical, or narrative pattern; linking the person to the audience's interests is important.
   2. Reports about issues often present information about current subjects that impact the lives of individuals or the society as a whole.
      a. This speech is like an investigative report.
      b. Many patterns work well, including pro-con, cause-effect, and problem-solution.
   <u>Diversity in Practice: Informative Speaking in Africa</u>
D. Think of explanatory or **expository speeches** as the "speech to teach."
   1. Speeches of definition answer the questions, "What is it?" or "What does it mean?"
      a. They are common in educational and workplace settings.
      b. These speeches often have two parts:
         1) The denotative meaning explains the dictionary meaning.
         2) The connotative meaning uses realistic life experiences to clarify and elucidate the idea.
   2. Explanations or translation speeches put complex or information-dense concepts into more easily understood words and images.
      a. Break complex concepts into component parts.
      b. Define terminology and avoid technical jargon.
      c. Use analogies to compare the concept to something listeners already understand.
      d. Use detailed examples of concrete situations when possible.

181

IV. Several guidelines make informative speeches more interesting and understandable.
   A. Do an obstacle analysis of the audience; identify what they might find difficult to understand.
   B. Organize materials carefully; build in transitions and other structures that help listeners link ideas; use **discourse consistency,** a repetitive style, to help listeners identify and connect ideas.
   C. Personalize material by helping listeners see the connection between the topic and their lives.
   D. Compare what the audience already knows and then move to the unknown.
   E. Choose vocabulary that clarifies, rather than obscures, the ideas.
   F. Build in repetition and redundancy.
      1. **Repetition** is saying the same thing more than once.
      2. **Redundancy** is repeating the same idea in different ways.
   G. Strive to be interesting.

Stop and Check: Do an Obstacle Analysis and Strategic Plan
Student Speech Video: The Chinese Valentine's Day, Lishan Zeng

Suggested Videos

Book CourseMate. "*The Chinese Valentine's Day"* was created by an international student from China. The text is at the end of the chapter, and the video is in the resources for Chapter 16.

- Ask questions like these: What do you think the audience already knew about the topic? Did the speaker do a good job of analyzing the audience's level of knowledge? Are all the elements of the introduction and conclusion included? Are they effective? What could improve? What organizational pattern is used? What other patterns might work, given the topic? Are the main points clear? Does the speaker use adequate supporting material? What might he add? Subtract? Is the speech interesting?
- The speaker presents information about a holiday in his country. Have students discuss how well the speaker analyzed and adapted to the U.S. audience's need to know.
- Discuss how well the speaker followed the guidelines for informative speaking presented in the text? (comprehension, analysis, evaluation)

In addition, "Shakespeare" by Hillary Carter-Liggett (found with Chapter 10's interactive video resources) informs the audience of the controversy surrounding the authorship of the works attributed to Shakespeare. She compares and contrasts the two leading theories. Other informative speeches include "Neuroimaging" by Jennifer Salame (Chapter 7), Emily Smith's "Biliary Atresia" (Chapter 11), and "Pumpkins" by Anna Reidl (Chapter 13).

Professional Speeches. The hundreds of informative speeches on www.ted.com, include explanations of complex concepts and descriptions of scientific processes. For example, in a 4:19 minute speech, "Art Made of Storms," artist Nathalie Miebach gives a "how to" speech on the process of taking weather data and turning it into sculptures and music. Todd Kuiken's 18:51 minute speech, "A Prosthetic Arm That 'Feels,'" is just one example of a longer explanatory speech that might interest your students. If you don't have time to show the entire speech in class, you could assign students to watch it as homework and then come to class prepared to discuss the speaker's ability to communicate a technical topic.

Discussion Topics

The Importance of Information Globally (p. 272) Radio Free Europe/Radio Liberty online (www.rferl.org) monitors countries that restrict access to the Internet--usually by forcing citizens to subscribe to a state-run Internet Service Provider (ISP). Several countries are "real enemies of this new means of communication." Some totally prevent citizens from Internet access. Others control one or several ISPs, installing filters blocking access to unsuitable web sites or forcing users to officially register with the authorities. For more information on Radio Free Europe, link to "Historical Account of RFE/RL." Question #2 in **Application and Critical Thinking Exercises** is relevant here. (comprehension)

Ethics in Practice: The Right to Information (p. 273) Ask students to read the feature, and, working in groups, to answer the discussion questions that follow.

Stop and Check: Analyze Your Audience's Knowledge (p. 276) This exercise helps students analyze their topic in relationship to their classmates' knowledge. You can also use questions #1, #3 and #4 in **Application and Critical Thinking Exercises** here. (application, analysis, synthesis)

Types of Informative Speeches (pp. 275-285) Use clips from television shows as described in **Suggested Videos**. (application, analysis, evaluation)

Practically Speaking: Informative Speaking on the Job (pp. 279) Ask students to read the feature, and, working on groups, to answer the discussion questions that follow.

Diversity in Practice: Informative Speaking in Africa (p. 282) Direct students to Internet sites such as www.abantu.org (click on Programmes), or have them do a google search for "Rebecca Lolosoli," a Kenyan woman who leads an all-female village of ostracized women, girls running from forced marriages, and so on. Lolosoli speaks truth to power. (application)

Guidelines for Informative Speaking (pp. 285-286) Show sample speeches and have students evaluate how well the student followed the guidelines presented here. (analysis, application)

Stop and Check: Do an Obstacle Analysis and Strategic Plan (p. 286) Students can do this exercise online and email you a copy. (analysis, synthesis)

Application and Critical Thinking Exercises

1. As a group, have students brainstorm topics they find interesting for informative speaking. In addition, I ask students to make a list of topics they never want to hear again. This activity helps to limit the number of 'boring' speeches presented each semester. I like to tell students if they think their topic is boring to please not present it to the class—we don't want to be bored either! (application)

2. I often suggest that students consider an informative topic from the field of communication. This introduces them to other courses in our department and reinforces the importance of effective communication skills in every area of life. See a list of possible topics at the end of this chapter.

3. Students should be able to come up with several topics within each category. The misconceptions category might be the most interesting.

4. Here's another audience analysis opportunity. Select a few topics and have students identify the type of information that the persons sitting next to them need. For example, Topic: "how to write a resume." What type of information does Sally need? Information about the format? Information about how to frame the items for the person who'll actually read it? Or "social security." Does Roberto need

information about how the system works? About problems in the system that will probably affect his future? About alternative plans? About partially privatized accounts? (application, analysis)

5. You can use a clip from a television show (see **Suggested Videos**) with this question. Or provide an image such as the One-Pillar Pagoda on p. 295; they then use about five minutes of in-class writing time to create a descriptive word picture of the place. (application)

6. Much online material about informative speaking overlaps with textual materials. Reading someone else's examples and tips will reinforce students' learning.

Internet Activities

The CourseMate for Public Speaking, accessible through http://login.cengage.com, offers a broad range of resources that will help students better understand the material in the chapter, complete assignments, and succeed on tests. The CourseMate also features speech videos with critical viewing questions, speech outlines, and transcripts. It also offers interactive practice activities, self-quizzes, and a sample final exam.

Supplemental Resources

•   Teaching Idea 16.1: Informative Speeches on Communication Topics

Teaching Idea 16.1: Informative Speeches on Communication Topics

Purpose: To increase students' knowledge of the field of communication by having them do research and present an informative speech about a communication topic.

Procedure: Introduce students to the various areas of communication. Bring to class your college or university's catalog or a list of department offerings; also, bring some sample textbooks from various sub-disciplines like gender communication or nonverbal communication.

1. Use the course catalog or a list of department offerings to introduce various sub-disciplines within the communication field. Read aloud some course titles and write them on the board. For example, department offerings often include: "Interpersonal Communication," "Public Relations," "Gender Communication," "Nonverbal Communication," "Intercultural Communication," "Organizational Communication," and "Mass Media and Popular Culture."

2. Then list some possible topics from each sub-discipline. (Or duplicate and distribute the topic handout that follows.)

2. Show students how they can use communication textbooks both to find and to develop a topic. Use a textbook, say from interpersonal communication. (Most professors or departments receive many unsolicited texts from publishing representatives every year.) Direct students to the table of contents, and read aloud some of the possible subjects—Johari's Window, confirmation or disconfirmation, or friendships, for example. Then turn to the section within the text that discusses the subject.
    •   A topic like Johari's Wiindow is suitable for a classroom speech, because it provides a diagram, and the topic is narrowed enough for a student to present in a relatively short period of time. Topics

such as stages of relationships or types of family are already broken into subtopics which can become the main points of a speech. Students sometimes work on a subject together; one does stages of relationship build up; another does stages leading to termination.

4. Make the sample textbooks available to students to use in their research. I often keep a bookshelf outside my office and put the texts there, along with a sign out sheet. Another possibility is to put the books on reserve in the library.

Potential Communication Topics

Below you'll find some sub-disciplines within the broader area of communication studies. Each is followed by a number of possible topics. Select one of these topics, or find another communication topic of your choosing.

Interpersonal Communication

Stages of relationship development
Listening styles
Response styles

Effective listening
Friendships
Johari's Window

Intercultural Communication

Barriers to intercultural communication
Learning a second language
Cultural patterns
High- and low-context cultural patterns

Ethnocentrism
Intercultural friendships
Intercultural competence
Hofstede's cultural patterns

Nonverbal Communication

Classifications of touch (types and functions)
How we use space and/or territory
Dress for success
Facial expressions

Olfactory communication (smells)
Eye contact
Time as a communication system
Body language (gestures)

Gender Communication

Differences between men's and women's speech
Nonverbal differences between men and women
Men's friendships and women's friendships

Gender in other cultures
Sexual harassment
Stereotypes of men (or of women)

Family Communication

Disciplining children
The family life cycle
Characteristics of effective family communication

Sibling communication
Blended families
Family types

Mass Media

Research about television violence
Models of mass media communication
Oprah Winfrey (or another famous personality)
Censorship

Media in other countries
Six media revolutions
Talk radio
The Oscars

Small Group/Organizational Communication

Communication climates
Handling conflict
Group roles (task, maintenance, or blocker roles)
Phases of group development

How to write a resume
Interviews: Types of questions
Types of interviews
Types of public relations work

Chapter 17

FOUNDATIONS OF PERSUASION

Most professors assign at least one persuasive speech, and topic selection can again be a challenge. Consequently, this chapter discusses topic and purpose in a fairly detailed way. It emphasizes additional analysis of the audience's interwoven beliefs, values, attitudes and motivations--core resources introduced in Chapter 1 and described in some detail in Chapter 5. The chapter concludes with a number of organizational patterns that are especially useful in persuasive speeches.

Chapter Goals

At the end of this chapter, your students should be able to:

- Diagram and explain Toulmin's model of reasoning
- Explain how reasoning strategies vary across cultural groups
- Identify ways *ethos*, speaker credibility, functions as an element of reasoning
- Explain the role of *pathos*, or emotional proofs, in reasoning
- Explain four basic types of *logos*, or rational proofs, and know how to test each one
- Recognize several kinds of fallacious reasoning
- Identify elements of invitational rhetoric

Chapter Outline

I. Use Toulmin's reasoning model to create an **argument**.
   A. Make a **claim**, a disputable assertion about a fact, value, or policy.
   B. Support it with **grounds, data**, or **evidence** (facts, examples, quotations, statistics, and comparisons as described in Chapter 8); otherwise, your **assertion** is unsupported.
   C. Connect the evidence to the claim through a **warrant** or reasoning that justifies your conclusion.
   D. Provide **backing** or reasons to support or defend the warrant.
   E. Use **qualifiers** to limit the scope of the claim.
   F. Prepare to deal with **rebuttals** or objections and counterarguments.
      Diversity in Practice: The Influence of Culture on Reasoning

II. Ethos, or speaker credibility, comes from your personal qualities, and is made up of four components:
   A. Exhibit **good character** by choosing topics that matter to your and stick by your convictions, even when unpopular.
   B. Express **goodwill** by developing *identification* through areas of *common ground*.
      Ethics in Practice: Developing Good Character
   C. Demonstrate **good sense**, made up of:
      1. *Intelligence*, by showing you have a broad understanding of your topic.
      2. *Sound reasoning*, by supporting your claim with trustworthy evidence and logical connections.
      3. *Composure*, by maintaining poise in a stressful situation.
      Diversity in Practice: Composure in Other Cultures
   D. Showing **dynamism** influences credibility and is linked to extroversion, energy, and enthusiasm.
      Stop and Check: Evaluating Ethos

III. Including **pathos**, or emotional proofs, shows the speaker understands the audience's motivation and needs.
    A. Appeal to positive emotions such love, peace, pride, approval, and hope, etc.
    B. Appealing to **negative emotions** can be risky, but *fear, anger*, and *guilt* can motivate us to avoid real dangers.
    C. Appealing to **needs** primarily follows the work of Maslow, and includes:
       1. Basic needs.
       2. Security and safety needs.
       3. Love and belonging needs.
       4. Esteem needs.
       5. Self-actualization needs.
    E. Understanding needs, wants, emotions, and values overlap, but four factors are important in emotional appeals:
       1. Sometimes you have to choose between two desirable goals or feelings.
       2. Motives vary according to our circumstances.
       3. Our responses often come out of mixed motives.
       4. Motivations are often group centered.
    F. Emotional appeals should be tested to be sure you are not playing on irrational fears.
       1. Ask yourself if guilt is reasonable or if anger is rational.
       2. Make sure emotion is used ethically.

Ethics in Practice: Demagoguery

IV. Use *logos* or rational proofs, the verbal arguments that relate to the subject.
    A. Both figurative and literal **analogies** compare a less familiar item with one that's better known.
       1. Figurative analogies (**reasoning by metaphor**) compare two generally different things that share a recognizable similarity.
          a. Metaphors are fundamentally dialogical because listeners must actively make connections.
          b. Metaphors guide actions and arouse emotions.
          c. Use of metaphors is fundamental and universal and related to our oral heritage.
          d. Metaphor use is typical of African and African-American speakers.
       2. **Literal analogies** or **parallel case reasoning** compares likeness between two similar things and argues that what happened in one case is likely to happen in another one that's similar.
       3. Use three tests for analogies.
          a. Ask if the metaphor clarifies and illuminates the concept.
          b. Ask if the parallel case is really alike.
          c. Ask if the case is alike in essential details.
    B. **Inductive reasoning** begins with specific instances or examples, then formulates a reasonable generalization or conclusion.

Diversity in Practice: Reasoning and the Sexes

       1. It is typical of ethic speakers and women who form conclusions out of experience.
          a. Absolute accuracy requires observation of 100 percent of a population, which is usually impossible.
          b. Survey research takes a sample from a population and forms generalizations from that sample.
       2. Test inductive reasoning in three ways.
          a. Ask if enough cases are represented.
          b. Ask if the cases are typical or representative of the population.
          c. Ask if the examples are up-to-date.
    C. **Deductive reasoning** applies a generalization (premise) to a specific instance.
       1. A syllogism has a major premise, a minor premise, and a conclusion.
          a. A sure premise allows conclusions to be stated confidently.

      b.   Most premises have a measure of uncertainty and speakers should qualify both their premises and their conclusions.

    2.   An **enthymeme** leaves some parts of the syllogism unstated, so listeners dialogically fill in what's unsaid.

    3.   Test deductive reasoning in two ways.

        a.   Ask if the premise is true or highly probable.

        b.   Ask if the conclusion logically follows the premise.

  D. **Causal reasoning** shows that an effect follows a particular condition as a matter of rule; the second would not exist without the first.

    1.   The belief in causation is typical of Euro-American thinking.

    2.   Some links are well established; others are not as well proved.

    3.   Test causal reasoning in three ways.

        a.   Ask if there is a real connection between the conditions or if they just exist at the same time.

        b.   Ask if other, more important causes or factors contribute to the effect.

        c.   Ask if the cause is strong enough for the effect.

  E. Recognize logical **fallacies** or failures in logical reasoning that lead to unsound, misleading arguments.

    1.   In an **unsupported assertion**, a claim is offered without evidence or grounds.

    2.   The *ad populum* or bandwagon appeals to popular opinion; the majority can be wrong.

    3.   *Ad hominem* or personal attack discounts or demeans the messenger, ignoring the arguments.

    4.   **Overgeneralization** is an inductive fallacy which draws conclusions from too few instances.

    5.   The **red herring** argument happens when the speaker dodges the real argument and introduces a side issue in an attempt to divert attention; one clue is the thought "That's irrelevant."

    6.   A **false analogy** compares two things that aren't similar enough to warrant the conclusion drawn.

    7.   *Post hoc (ergo propter hoc)* means "after this, therefore because of this"; it is a fallacy of causation.

    8.   **False dichotomy** sets up an either-or choice without presenting other reasonable possibilities.

Stop and Check: Identifying Fallacies

V. Incorporate principles and forms of **invitational rhetoric**.

  A. Invitational rhetoric combines three principles.

    1.   **Equality** recognizes the importance of the audience.

    2.   **Nonhierarchical value of all** means speakers respect listeners as equals.

    3.   **Self-determination** emphasizes the principle of choice; the audience may not change.

Practically Speaking: Jeanne M. Edwards, Accuntant

  B. Invitational rhetoric includes two forms.

    1.   **Offering perspectives** means speakers share their understandings and invite others to do likewise; using **re-sourcement,** they creatively reframe an issue to be less divisive.

    2.   **Creating conditions** uses absolute listening and reversibility of perspectives to make audiences feel safe, valued, and free to offer perspectives.

Student Speech with Questions: The Benefits of Hunting

Suggested Videos

Book CourseMate On Chapter 17's resources you'll find several persuasive speeches including "Peace Corps," "Cyber-Bullying," and "Needed: A Grief Support System on Campus."

- Review the chapter—elements of reasoning: ethos, pathos, and logos.
- Watch a speech of your choice.
- Afterwards, ask why they think the speaker chose the topic. How is his or her credibility established and maintained? What type of emotional appeals are used? Are they valid? How effective is the speech overall? (comprehension, application, synthesis, evaluation)

Gail Grobey's speech, "Spanking? There's Gotta Be a Better Way" (in Appendix C resources) is an example of invitational rhetoric. Ask students to focus on the way Gail's narrative invites, but does not demand, her listeners to share her perspectives.

Feature Films. Many classic or current movies show situations you could use to teach this chapter.
- Show a courtroom scene from a movie such as *Twelve Angry Men* (1957, 1997), *A Few Good Men* (1992), or *To Kill a Mockingbird* (1962). Have students diagram the prosecution and defense arguments using Toulmin's model (Figure 17.1).
- Alternatively, have students watch courtroom scenes for logical arguments, emotional appeals, and speaker credibility. Show short clips of your choice and discuss the interwoven nature of the various proofs.

Discussion Topics

Stop and Check: Evaluating Ethos (p. 297) As a class, watch and compare two TED speeches (Weblink 17.1). Have students determine which speaker they believe is more credible. Discuss the role of demonstrating good character, goodwill, good sense, and dynamism. (analysis, application)

Ethics in Practice: Demagoguery (p. 301) Have students make a list of speakers they currently view as demagogues. What do the speakers have in common? How do they use emotional appeals to prove their arguments? (analysis, application).

Stop and Check: Identifying Fallacies (p. 307) Try this discussion topic as a class activity. Provide students with examples of fallacies from a variety of sources, including personal, print, TV, radio, and internet samples. Have students identify fallacies they themselves have fallen prey to.

Practically Speaking: Jeanne M. Edwards, Accoutant (p. 308) Ask students to read the feature, and, working in groups, to answer the discussion questions that follow.

Student Outlines with Commentary and Student Speech with Commentary (pp. 312-313) Review the anonymous speech on "The Benefits of Hunting." How does the speaker use emotional appeals to prove his/her point? Is their logic rational? What types of fallacies in logic does the speaker introduce? Also, in Appendix C, you'll find an outline and videotaped speech on overconsumption of sugar.

Application and Critical Thinking Exercises

1. Revisit the Casey Anthony trial from 2011 (in which Casey Anthony was tried and declared not guilty for the alleged murder of her daughter). Diagram the case against Anthony. Is the 'not guilty' verdict she received logical according to the Toulmin model? Why or why not?

2. Use the work of Stephen Toulmin to introduce the world of argumentation. Why is his work studied so carefully? What does his work contribute to the world of persuasion? (analysis, evaluation)

3. My students enjoy finding their own favorite commercials to share with the class. Have them discuss the emotional appeals in their ad, as well as how it adapts to audience needs. (analysis, application)

4. Have students try this activity in small groups during class. Use the lists of speech topics as idea starters for students own classroom speeches.

5. If you have an online school newspaper, use an article from it to analyze types of reasoning, then evaluate the arguments. Do they pass the reasoning tests? (analysis, evaluation)

6. Have students watch *12 Angry Men*. Have them diagram the case against the boy using Toulmin's model. Was the jury decisions in this case logical? (application, analysis)

7. Have students conduct a real debate in class. To make the assignment more interesting, ask students to debate opposite their true positions. Is it possible, logically speaking, to debate against your true convictions? Why or why not? Once students have debated against their believes, allow them to choose their true positions for an additional debate. Which position is most compelling? (application, evaluation).

8. Try this activity in class. At this point in the semester, students should have a clear understanding of what works in this speech and what doesn't.

Internet Activities

The CourseMate for Public Speaking, accessible through http://login.cengage.com, offers a broad range of resources that will help students better understand the material in the chapter, complete assignments, and succeed on tests. The CourseMate also features speech videos with critical viewing questions, speech outlines, and transcripts. It also offers interactive practice activities, self-quizzes, and a sample final exam.

Supplemental Resources

- Research Note 17.1: Theories of Persuasion

Research Note 17.1: Theories of Persuasion
What makes audiences listen to speakers and become convinced of the truth of their arguments? What moves them to act? Several theories attempt to explain the reasons why listeners are persuaded to modify their beliefs, values, attitude systems, and actions.

Speaker Credibility. Some researchers focus on characteristics of the communicator that make the speaker more persuasive. For example, chapter 5 discusses prior, demonstrated, and terminal credibility, and in this chapter we focus on ethos.

Audience Characteristics. Other researchers focus on characteristics of audiences that result in persuasibility differences among individuals. Several factors seem to be significant:*

- Age. Children are easy to influence until about the age of nine. Then their persuasibility declines until adolescence when it levels off.
- Gender. Women are more willing to change than men are. The essence of this theory is that women tend to be better listeners; in most teaching situations they learn more than men. Men don't listen well enough to be changed by the arguments.

- Intelligence. The situation determines the relationship of intelligence to persuasibility. Less intelligent listeners may not understand a complex argument; consequently, they'll be less moved by it; their more intelligent counterparts may be influenced by novel arguments. Moreover, less intelligent people may be persuaded by naive arguments that more intelligent people can see through.

- <u>Personality characteristics.</u> Dogmatic people are rigid, closed-minded, inflexible, and authoritarian. Persons scoring high on dogmatism scales avoid being exposed to inconsistent views. However, they have a low tolerance for dissonance, and when they are forced to encounter inconsistency, they may be highly susceptible to change. On the other hand, egalitarian (low-dogmatism) people are enterprising, calm, mature, forceful, and efficient. They can more easily tolerate inconsistency and as a result may be less susceptible to change.

Social Judgment-Involvement Theory by Carolyn Sherif, Muzafer Sherif, and Roger Nebergall.**
The <u>social judgment</u> aspect of the theory proposes that listeners have internal reference points called "anchor points." When making judgments, listeners first refer to the beliefs, attitudes, and values that comprise their *anchor points*. Each person has a *latitude of acceptance* and a *latitude of rejection* for new ideas.
- Individuals tend to accept ideas that are close to their anchor points.
- They consider ideas that are far from their anchor points too radical to accept, and they are immune to such arguments.
- There is also a latitude or range of non-commitment where the listener doesn't feel strongly either way. These individuals are open to persuasion in such areas.

The <u>involvement</u> aspect of the theory argues that the listener's *ego involvement* with the issue affects his or her persuasibility. Those with very strong feelings have incorporated the issue into their self-identity. Some make a social or public commitment to an issue. For example, a person might say, "I'm a card carrying liberal" or "I'm a born again Christian."
- Highly-involved people tend to affiliate socially with like-minded people.
- Those who are highly involved take pro- or con- positions with little or no middle ground.
- Individuals who are less involved are less polarized and can see both sides of an issue.

* This research is summarized in R. M. W. Travers. (1982). *Essentials of learning: The new cognitive learning for students of education (5th ed.).* New York: Macmillan.

** C. W. Sherif, M. Sherif, and R. W. Nebergall. (1965). *Attitude and attitude change: The social judgment-involvement approach.* Philadelphia: W. B. Saunders.

Let's say a speaker tries to convince a listener that abortion (induced or spontaneous) of a first pregnancy is statistically linked to development of breast cancer in later life and that the medical establishment is suppressing studies that show this link.
The listener will refer to her anchor points: her knowledge of scientific tests, her understanding of politics, her experiences with a friend who had an abortion, her beliefs and attitudes toward abortion and so on. If she has committed herself to a strong position on abortion and is socially affiliated with either a pro- or con- organization, this will affect her persuasiblity.
<u>Two other factors</u> influence the way people respond to new information:

- <u>Assimilation</u> (acceptance). A person will minimize the differences between her anchors and the new information.
- <u>Contrast effect</u> (rejection). People compare and distort positions that diverge from their own. They see a greater discrepancy than is really there.

Chapter 18

PERSUASIVE SPEAKING

In the 1950s the British writer, Dorothy Sayers, lamented that we were sending unprepared young people into a world in which they'd be bombarded with massive amounts of information. Imagine her concerns if she were writing today! The information explosion makes it even more imperative that students think critically about the claims and counterclaims, the emotional appeals, and the "character issues" that surround arguments today. This chapter explains reasoning strategies as they've been described across millennia. It uses terminology from Aristotle's classic text on *Rhetoric*, discusses fallacies using Latin terminology, and describes invitational rhetoric as proposed by feminist scholars in the 1990s.

Chapter Goals

At the end of this chapter, your students should be able to:

- Find a subject for a persuasive speech
- Decide on a claim of fact, value, or policy
- Analyze an audience's attitude toward a topic
- Develop a speech to convince
- Create a speech to actuate

Chapter Outline

I. Select your persuasive topics by asking four questions.
    Diversity in Practice: Persuasion in China
    A. What do I believe strongly?
    B. What arouses strong emotions in me?
    C. What social ideals do I support?
    D. What practices enrich my life?
    Stop and Check: Select Your Topic

II. Make a claim of fact, value, or policy, which generally build upon one another.
    A. Factual claims answer what, when, where, why or how something happened or will happen.
        1. **Debatable points** are disputable statements about things that did or did not happen or exist.
        2. **Causal relationships** argue something is the result of something that came before it and lead to it.
        3. **Predictions** contend that something will or will not happen in the future.
    B. Evaluating something as right or wrong, good or better, beautiful or ugly are value claims.
        1. Resolving value conflicts demands agreement on criteria.
        2. Convince an audience to accept your standards and they will more easily accept your judgment.
    C. Policy claims are statements about desirable actions using terms like *should* or *would*.
        1. When arguing against the status quo (existing state of affairs), the burden of proof is the speaker's responsibility to show policies should change.
        2. Some policy claims aim at personal behaviors.
        3. Claims in favor of the current situation and against change have presumption.
    Stop and Check: Make Fact, Value, and Policy Claims

III. Assess your audience's attitude to better identify how listeners will respond to your goal.
  A. Ask why when listeners are neutral toward your claim.
  B. When differences are mild, approach your audience directly.
  C. Rethink your options when listeners are negative toward your proposal.
  D. Approach common ground when audiences reject your proposal.
  E. If audiences are hostile toward you personally it is vital to emphasize common ground.
        <u>Stop and Check: Adapt to the Audience's Attitude</u>

IV. Choose a specific purpose or response you want from your listeners.
  A. A speech to convince is appropriate when audience members don't believe your claim or accept your value judgment.
    1. Convincing about facts requires some general strategies:
      a. Rely more on logical appeals.
      b. Define terminology and provide history of the issue.
      c. Use only high quality evidence with credibility.
      d. Cite sources to prove your competence.
      e. Show respect for your listener's intelligence and beliefs.
    2. Apply this model to be sure you consider your audience's response.
  B. Convincing about values involves getting others to share a judgment we hold.
    1. Using emotional appeals by linking values everyone can agree on.
    2. Appeal to authority if your sources are accepted by your audience.
    3. The criteria-satisfaction pattern is a strategy which answers audience questions.
      a. How do we make and apply judgements
      b. What criteria do we use?
      c. Where do these criteria come from?
      d. Why should we accept these sources?
  C. Convincing about policies involves answering stock issues.
    1. *Harm* or *ill* is showing the problem is significant enough to call for a solution.
    2. *Blame* is the cause part of the problem, linked to the effects established in the harm section.
    3. *Cure* is the solution section of the speech where you provide a plan and describe how it will create solvency.
    4. *Cost* is the feasibility part of the plan where you do a cost-benefit analysis and weigh advantages and disadvantages.
        <u>Stop and Check: Convincing Arguments</u>
        <u>Practically Speaking: A Mental Health Ambassador</u>
V. Sometimes you want to actuate an audience, or get them to change their actions.
  A. Cognitive dissonance theory explains why people behave in ways inconsistent with their beliefs or values.
  B. The Theory of Reasoned Action (TRA) adds a social component to motivating an audience and assumes humans weigh cost and benefits of acting.
    1. Our actions line up with our attitudes.
    2. Our subjective norms influence our perceptions of what people who are important think we should do.
    3. Perceived behavioral control is our opinion about our ability to accomplish the desired behavior.
  C. Monroe's Motivated Sequence is a commonly used persuasive pattern especially effective when purpose is to actuate an audience.
    1. Attention step involves gaining the audience's attention and drawing it to your topic.
    2. Need step is similar to the problem part of a problem-solution speech.
    3. Satisfaction step is a solution that will satisfy the need and includes as many as five parts.
      a. Statement
      b. Explanation

    c.   Theoretical demonstration
    d.   Practicality
    e.   Meeting objections
4.   The Visualization step is unique and asks the listeners to imagine the future in a positive or negative manner.
5.   The final call for action includes:
    a.   Naming the specific action, attitude, or belief you are advocating.
    b.   Stating your personal intention to act.
c.   Ending with impact.

<u>Stop and Check: Use Monroe's Motivated Sequence</u>
<u>Student Speech with Commentary: Fair Trade Coffee, Linnea Strandy</u>

Suggested Videos

Book CourseMate. On Chapter 18's resources you'll find "Fat Discrimination" and "Fair Trade Coffee." You can also use resources from Chapter 17.

- Review the chapter--finding a subject, making a claim, choosing a purpose, and organizing the information.
- Watch one of the speeches.
- Afterwards, ask why they think the speaker chose the topic. What is the major claim? What type of claim is it? What type of emotional appeals are used? Are they valid? How effective is the speech overall? How well does the speaker respond to listeners' beliefs, actions, values, and attitudes? (comprehension, application, synthesis, evaluation)
- Linnea Strandy's "Fair Trade Coffee" speech uses Monroe's Motivated Sequence to actuate her audience. Ask students to outline her speech using the information in this chapter.

Discussion Topics

<u>**Figure 17.1: Toulmin's Model**</u> (p. 292) Students should become familiar with the elements of this very common linear model of reasoning. I often use high profile trials or hearings to teach this diagram, because they illustrate Toulmin's model and they show how pathos (motive) and ethos (the character of the defendant, the lawyers, the witnesses) contribute to the argument. Or use questions #1, #7, and #8 (**Application and Critical Thinking Exercises**) and the corresponding **Suggested Videos** here. (knowledge, comprehension, analysis)

<u>**Stop and Check: Select Your Topic**</u> (p. 316) Have students do this exercise and share their topic with you. Speakers who choose their topic early--and stick with it--obviously have more time to analyze their audience, do appropriate research, and prepare their speech with care. It's also better if they care about their topic--but not too much. One student spoke on the high cost of auto insurance, a subject that made him so furious he could hardly talk about it! He, fortunately, harnessed his emotion for the speech, and it worked; he cared enough to make an impassioned appeal for change without losing control. (analysis, application)

<u>**Stop and Check: Make Fact, Value, and Policy Claims**</u> (p. 320) Many students don't realize how many claims can be made about a single topic; consequently, they create speeches that have no clear focus. Do this activity in class and have each group share its claims. Possible topics include (the often overused)

euthanasia, abortion, or capital punishment; discipline of children; television violence; hazards of smoking; campus issues; civil rights; etc. (comprehension, application, synthesis)

Stop and Check: Adapt to the Audience's Attitude (p. 322) This feature offers students the opportunity to apply the information to several scenarios.

Stop and Check: Convincing Arguments (p. 325) Have students use this information for their classroom speechces.

Theories of Persuasion (pp. 326-327) Most instructors save a discussion of persuasive theories for this chapter which briefly introduces the cognitive dissonance theory and the Theory of Reasoned Action. (knowledge, comprehension)

Practically Speaking: A Mental Health Ambassador (p. 326) Have students use the information and apply it to their own speaking situations.

Stop and Check: Use Monroe's Motivated Sequence (p. 329) This feature gives students practice working with this organizational pattern.

Application and Critical Thinking Exercises

1. Bring in popular magazines (*People, Us*, etc.) and conduct this activity using the latest issues of the day in the three categories. Divide the class into groups and have them each take a story to analyze. Use the lists to spur classroom discussion about the importance of valid sources. (analysis)

2. Instead of using a crime show, ask students to identify types of evidence they have used to prove facts in their personal lives (for example, showing an instructor a jury summons to show excused absences). How does this evidence differ from the type used in speeches? How is it similar?.

3. Show at least one professional speech in class. You can access this link through your CourseMate for *Public Speaking*, Chapter 18 resources. (analysis)

4. Go over Weblink 18.3 in class. Discuss the responses to hostile audiences and alternative strategies. Is the author credible?

5. Have students choose the controversial issue in class. Have them identify players in the debate on both sides of the argument. Who is more convincing? Why? (application)

Internet Activities

The CourseMate for Public Speaking, accessible through http://login.cengage.com, offers a broad range of resources that will help students better understand the material in the chapter, complete assignments, and succeed on tests. The CourseMate also features speech videos with critical viewing questions, speech outlines, and transcripts. It also offers interactive practice activities, self-quizzes, and a sample final exam.

Appendix A

SPEAKING IN SMALL GROUPS

Some instructors definitely want material on small group presentations. Others simply have no time for this topic. This appendix includes information on the advantages and disadvantages of groups and then guides students through the process of working with an investigative team and with a problem solving team. It provides information about how to conduct meetings and how to present the group's findings.

Appendix A Goals

At the end of this appendix, your students should be able to:

- List advantages and disadvantages of group work
- Describe how an investigative team works
- Explain what should happen in each team meeting
- Compare and contrast men's and women's speaking tendencies in small group interactions
- Describe five steps in a problem solving method
- Tell three common formats for presenting group findings

Appendix A Outline

I. Group work has both advantages and disadvantages.
   A. There are at least five advantages.
      1. Groups have access to more information and more knowledge than a single individual does.
      2. A variety of viewpoints lead to opportunities for more creative ideas to emerge.
      3. Group work provides a deeper level of involvement and learning.
      4. Many people enjoy working in groups.
      5. Group members co-create meaning in dialogical interactions.
   B. Groups also have several disadvantages.
      1. Working in groups takes more time.
      2. Some group members work harder than others do.
      3. Some members may dominate and monopolize the discussion.
      4. Members tend toward **groupthink**, when members conform to avoid conflict.
         Diversity in Practice: Male and Female Tendencies in Group Interactions

II. Investigative teams should have several meetings.
   A. In the first meeting, team members get acquainted.
      1. They share their interest in and knowledge of the subject.
      2. They sometimes choose a leader.
   B. Gatekeepers make sure that everyone participates and that no one dominates.
   C. Recorders take notes or minutes on what transpires during the meeting.
      1. They should divide up the topic and make assignments.
      2. Before breaking up, they set a date, place, and time for the next meeting.
   D. In additional meetings, members discuss their results of their investigations.
      1. Begin by reading minutes from the previous meeting.
      2. Use an **agenda** that lists in order the items for discussion.

      3.   Hold team members accountable for summarizing their assigned research.

      4.   Analyze the information, identify gaps, find themes, organize the material.

      5.   Have each member specify what she or he will do before the next meeting.

      6.   Continue meetings until information gathering and organization are finished.

   E. In the final meeting, team members polish the presentation, finalize details, and rehearse.

III. Problem solving teams commonly follow a process or method.

   A. Step one is to define the problem.

      1.   State the issue as a policy issue, using the word "should."

      2.   Use an open rather than closed question.

      3.   State the question objectively, eliminating overly emotional wording.

   B. Step two is to analyze the problem.

      1.   Look for facts and history.

      2.   Ask causes--both primary and secondary—and look for effects.

      3.   Identify cultural values that apply.

      4.   Find precedents or relevant policies.

   C. Step three: set criteria for deciding on the solution by asking what's required and what's desired.

   D. In step four, list possible solutions.

      1.   Brainstorm by inviting ideas without judgment from everyone in the group.

      2.   Revise criteria, as determined in step three, if necessary.

   E. Step five involves selecting the best solution.

      1.   Select the solution by comparing the solution against the criteria.

      2.   Eliminate some options immediately.

      3.   Weigh the merits of the remaining choices and find one that group members will accept.

IV. Present the group's findings both in written and oral form.

   A. Create a final report in which only one member speaks for the group.

   B. Present group findings in a panel format.

      1.   All group members participate in dialogical interactions.

      2.   A moderator or leader guides the discussion topics and participants.

   C. Use a symposium format.

      1.   All group members participate, one at a time.

      2.   Each prepares a presentation on only a part of the whole topic.

      3.   Often a question-and-answer period follows.

Appendix B

SPEAKING ON SPECIAL OCCASIONS

A common form of public speaking includes a variety of short speeches that provide an integrative function in organizational settings. One way to give students practice in special occasion speaking is to require or allow (non-graded or for extra credit) these speeches on a regular basis throughout the term. Discuss how such speeches serve to integrate the class to the classroom culture or to the culture of the larger institution.

Appendix B Goals

At the end of this appendix, your students should be able to:

- Explain what is meant by organizational culture
- Explain the integrative function of special occasion speaking
- Know the elements of seven kinds of special occasion speaking
- Give a special occasion speech

Appendix B Outline

(Appendix B opens with a brief introduction but has no Stop and Check features or summary.)

I.   Introductions provide information about people.
    A.   Introduce a newcomer to an established group.
        1.   Provide her or his name and job title.
        2.   Provide relevant details about background and personal characteristics.
        3.   Welcome the newcomer to the group.
    B.   Introduce a guest speaker.
        1.   Greet and/or welcome the group.
        2.   Make a statement about the occasion.
        3.   Announce the speaker's name and topic.
        4.   Provide relevant information about the speaker's background and personal characteristics.
        5.   Be prepared to follow the speech with a few remarks that provide closure.

II. Say farewell as one who leaves or as one who stays behind.
    A.   Say good-bye when leaving a group.
        1.   Remind people what they've meant to you personally.
        2.   Share lessons you've learned from them.
        3.   Tell humorous stories that will be happy memories.
        4.   Express sadness but hope for the future and invite them to keep in touch.
        5.   Invite people to write or visit you in new location.
    B.   Say good-bye to a person for a group.
        1.   Recognize ways the person benefited the group.
        2.   Note memorable positive personal traits.
        3.   Tell funny stories.
        4.   Express personal sadness and the group's sense of loss.

5. Wish the person well.
6. When appropriate, present a going-away gift.

III. Give an announcement to keep informed and motivated to attend.
    A. Draw attention to the event.
    B. Provide details like who, what, when, where.
    C. Give cost and benefits of attending.
    D. End with a summary of important information.
<u>Diversity in Practice: Organizational Culture</u>

IV. Present an award at rituals that express a group's common values.
    A. Name the award and describe its significance.
    B. Summarize the reasons this individual was chosen as recipient.
    C. Say how appropriate the award is for the recipient.
    D. Express good wishes to the person.
    E. Remember that some cultures hesitate to single out individuals and praise a group instead.

V. Give an acceptance speech.
    A. Thank those who gave the honor.
    B. Acknowledge others who supported you along the way.
    C. Personalize how special it is.
    D. Express appreciation for the honor.

VI. Nominations introduce the candidate and explain his or her suitability for the position.
    A. A direct method or statement of reasons pattern works well.
    B. Criteria satisfaction patterns are especially suited.

VII. Give a commemorative speech to emphasize a group's common ideals, history, and memories.
    A. Build the speech around a theme.
    B. Be inspirational.
    C. Pay special attention to language.
    D. Use humor appropriately.
    E. Be brief.

VIII. Tributes highlight and reinforce important cultural beliefs, values, and behaviors.
    A. Indicate why the subject is significant or worthy of the honor.
    B. Identify a few ideals the subject represents.
    C. Consider using a statement of reasons pattern.
    D. Develop each point with illustrations from the person's life.
    E. Although not an informative speech, you probably need to include information about the subject.

IX. A eulogy is possibly the most difficult type of speech to give.
    A. Ask the family if there is something you should (or should not) say.
    B. Draw from your memories to identify positive things about the deceased.
    C. Humor or poetry can be appropriate.
    D. The wave pattern works well.
    E. Lines from poetry or lyrics often work well.
    F. Don't worry about showing emotion during delivery.
    G. Be brief; ten minutes or less is usually best.

Suggested Videos

High School Graduation Speech by Alexandria Reed This speech is at the end of Chapter 1 and on the text website videos. An archive of professional giving commencement addresses is online at www.humanity.org/voices/commencements/.

Eulogy by Cher (available on www.americanrhetoric.com) Actress and singer Cher eulogizes her former husband, Sonny Bono.

Inaugural Address by John F. Kennedy. You can find the script of this speech in Appendix C. An audio and video version is available on www.americanrehtoric.com

Part III

TEST QUESTIONS

and

ANSWERS TO TEST QUESTIONS

Chapter 1

INTRODUCTION TO PUBLIC SPEAKING AND CULTURE

TRUE-FALSE: Most of these questions test <u>knowledge</u> and <u>comprehension.</u>

1. By definition, public speaking occurs when one person prepares and delivers a presentation to a group that generally fake listens without interrupting the flow of ideas. <u>False</u>. (2)

2. Taking a public speaking course will prepare you to listen more effectively, and you will probably listen to more speeches than you give during your lifetime. <u>True</u>. (2)

3. You must feel confident to be a competent communicator. <u>False</u>. (3)

4. According to the text, effective communication skills are vital in most higher-paying jobs and positions. <u>True</u>. (3)

5. Darrell is planning to be an engineer; he is right to think that his oral communication skills won't much matter in his career. <u>False. Most employers value oral communication skills, and public speaking skills are helpful in a wide variety of careers.</u> (3)

6. "Rhetoric," by definition, is less important than action. <u>False. Rhetoric is defined as the art of persuasive public speaking.</u> (2)

7. The oldest book in existence is from China; it gives advice on speaking and listening. <u>False. Although the book does talk about speaking, it's from Egypt not China. (5)</u>

8. A diversity perspective is important in a community that's not very diverse. <u>True.</u> (4)

9. You can pretty much tell the most important things about a culture by observing its visible characteristics such as patterns of dress, art, food, and language. <u>False. You can't see the culture's fundamental worldview.</u> (4)

10. Rhetorically sensitive people are those who can adapt their communication behaviors and perform reasonably well in a variety of social settings. <u>True</u>. (9)

11. Our core cultural resources consist of an I/Thou behavior system. <u>False</u>. (6)

12. Attitudes are our mental acceptance of something as being true or false. <u>False. Those are beliefs; attitudes are tendencies to evaluate something as positive or negative.</u> (6)

13. In oral cultures, people must store all their knowledge in their memories. <u>True</u>. (7)

14. Many African cultures highly value verbally skilled people. <u>True</u>. (7)

15. The dominant United States communication style includes a problem orientation. <u>True</u> (7)

16. Cultural factors can influence how comfortable you feel speaking in public. <u>True</u> (9)

17. Traditional Chinese and Japanese cultures had a tradition of debate where people publicly disagreed with one another. <u>False. It was improper to disagree publicly</u>. (9)

18. The Ibo woman mentioned in the text has problems moving from her home culture where she's expected to be docile and content as a wife and mother to conferences where she presents academic papers. <u>False. She never confuses her two selves.</u> (9)

19. Non-verbal skills add little meaning to a message. <u>False. Non-verbal skills add meaning to the message</u> (10)

20. Conversations and public speaking have little in common. <u>False. The dialogic theory of communication states that these two are linked.</u> (10)

21. Teachers do much of their speaking in order to transmit important cultural elements to the next generation. <u>True.</u> (10)

22. The police chief speaks to her community after a devastating hurricane. She is speaking to transform her community. <u>False. She is speaking to restore or repair the community</u>. (5).

23. According to the dialogical theory, all communication is based on conversations. <u>True.</u> (10)

24. The Russian scholar associated in the text with dialogue is Mikhail Barishnikov. <u>False.</u> (10)

25. As a general rule, public speeches should be conversational but more formal than everyday conversations. <u>True.</u> (10)

26. We use models to depict or explain communication phenomena. <u>True.</u> (12)

27. When you listen to your classmates give their speeches, you and your fellow listeners are passive. <u>False. Although audience members do not generally interrupt, they are actively co-creating meaning.</u> (10)

28. Both you and your listeners decode messages when you give a public speech. <u>True.</u> (11)

29. Roman educators largely ignored the ethical implications of public speaking. <u>False; *vir bonum dicendi peritus* is a phrase emphasizing ethical speaking.</u> (8)

30. Learning public speaking can improve your civic engagement. <u>True.</u> (3)

MULTIPLE CHOICE QUESTIONS: These questions test <u>knowledge</u>, <u>comprehension</u>, and <u>application.</u>

1. Rhetoric is _____
   a. the ability to talk in a way that obscures the real issue.
   b. a formerly important element of a liberal arts education that is unimportant today.
   c. <u>the study of persuasion in its various forms. (2)</u>
   d. the opposite of action.
   e. the ability to discern the speaker's intentions and biases.

2. All of the below are good reasons to study public speaking, except:
   a. It will almost guarantee that you will get a good job. (2) [There's no guarantee.]
   b. You can develop your critical thinking skills.
   c. You join a long list of people historically who have studied the skills of rhetoric.
   d. The course can help you feel more confident.
   e. The course can help you be more competent.

3. The world's oldest manuscript, which talks about public speaking, came from _____
   a. Mesopotamia.
   b. Egypt. (5)
   c. Sumeria.
   d. Greece.
   e. Rome.

4. Culture is best defined as _____
   a. an integrated system of learned beliefs, values, attitudes, and behaviors that a group accepts and passes along. (4)
   b. the invisible, underlying world view of a group.
   c. the predictable, observable behaviors of a society.
   d. patterns of dress, art, food, language, and rituals that affect the group's actions.
   e. patterns derived from the oral tradition that shape the dominant institutions of this society.

5. The Amish are a group whose worldview or belief system sets them apart from the dominant culture. They are a(n) _____
   a. co-cultural group. (4)
   b. ethnic minority.
   c. culture.
   d. multivocal group.
   e. example of rhetorical sensitivity.

6. Which of these is NOT a cultural resource as defined in the text?
   a. actions or behaviors
   b. attitudes
   c. beliefs
   d. diversity (6)
   e. values

7. A mental acceptance that something is true or false, correct or incorrect, valid or invalid is ____
   a. a belief. (6)
   b. a value.
   c. an attitude.
   d. an action.

8. Joe emphasizes *hard work* as he argues for his ideas. He's appealing to a core U.S. ____
   a. belief.
   b. value. (6)
   c. attitude.
   d. action.

206

9. Our preferences or tendencies to have positive or negative opinions about people, places, objects, and situations are our _____
    a. beliefs.
    b. values.
    c. attitudes. (6)
    d. actions.
    e. core assumptions.

10. Public performers in cultures without print are like a "walking library"; these public performers store the group's knowledge in their minds; theirs is a(n) _____ culture.
    a. oral (7)
    b. nonexpressive
    c. expressive
    d. narrative
    e. dramatic

11. Expressive cultures ____
    a. encourage their members to give their opinions and let their feelings show in all situations.
    b. do not permit much variation for shy persons.
    c. are typical of Japanese and Native American cultures.
    d. teach negative attitudes toward verbalization, emphasizing nonverbal skills more.
    e. encourage their members to present their words and emotions in dramatic fashion. (7)

12. Public speaking varies across cultures in all these ways EXCEPT_____
    a. the amount of expressiveness that's encouraged.
    b. how the speaker presents her or his ideas.
    c. what topics are considered appropriate.
    d. whether or not the culture has public speakers (6-9)
    e. who speaks.

13. Which is NOT a component of the U.S. style of communication identified in the text?
    a. problem oriented
    b. impersonal (9)
    c. direct
    d. informal
    e. explicit

14. The Nigerian woman who speaks competently in the dominant culture while participating competently within her own speech community is _____
    a. bicultural. (9)
    b. nonexpressive.
    c. expressive.
    d. co-cultural.

15. When President W. Bush went to New Orleans after Hurricane Katrina, his narrowed purpose was to _____ the city's culture.
    a. produce
    b. transmit
    c. reinforce
    d. restore (5)
    e. transform

16. Inspirational speakers who urge donors to continue supporting charities speak with the narrowed intention to _____ their actions.
    a. initiate
    b. transmit
    c. reinforce (5)
    d. restore
    e. change

17. Which of these is NOT true about both conversation and public speaking?
    a. Both conversation and public speaking rely on nonverbal cues as well as words.
    b. Each type of speaking has predictable structures, functions, and lengths.
    c. In both, meaning depends on the context.
    d. Co-creation of meaning occurs in both conversation and public speaking.
    e. Public speaking and conversation are similarly informal. (8)

18. The term _____ refers to the give-and-take interactions we engage in as we co-create meanings.
    a. dialogue
    b. respons-ibility (10)
    c. communication
    d. speech genre
    e. transaction

19. After a fight with your significant other, you focus on what you didn't say and tune out a classroom speech. In the transactional model of communication shown in the text, this is _____
    a. nonverbal communication.
    b. negative feedback.
    c. noise or static. (11-12)
    d. the situational context.
    e. the cultural context.

20. You're giving your speech; two people frown when you say "abortion." In the communication model shown in the text, their frowns are _____
    a. the channel.
    b. feedback. (11)
    c. noise or static.
    d. decoding.
    e. the cultural framework.

21. The Latin phrase *vir bonum, dicendi peritus* means _____
    a. speaking well, listening effectively.
    b. a sound mind, a sound body.
    c. reading and writing, listening and speaking well.
    d. the good person, skilled in speaking. (8)
    e. to be good, speak well.

22. Which of these examples is typical of a collectivist culture?
    a. Mitch gets an A on his exam and runs home to tell his mother and father about it.
    b. Darlene works hard to hit the softball further than anyone else on her team so she will be honored by her coach.
    c. Darren doesn't tell his friend about a job Darren really wants because he's afraid the friend will apply for and get the job.

d. Even though Kyle knows that Mark was the one who took the teacher's pen, he says quiet while the entire class is punished for it rather than singling Mark out. (7)

e. Laura is does not understand what the teacher said, and she raises her hand and asks for further explanation.

FILL IN THE BLANK: These questions test <u>knowledge</u>, <u>comprehension</u>, and <u>application.</u>

1. The "art of persuasive public speaking" is Aristotle's definition of _____ <u>rhetoric.</u> (3)

2. Within the US, Jewish-Americans are considered a _____ <u>co-culture.</u> (4)

3. Callista can effectively adapt her communication behaviors and be reasonably effective with her friends, in on-the- job speaking, and in her public presentations; she has _____. <u>rhetorical sensitivity.</u> (9)

4. Wycliffe Bible Translators go all over the world to small tribes in which there is no writing at all; the type of culture they are seeking is _____ <u>an oral culture.</u> (7)

5. Cultures that place high value on silence and privacy, and value keeping emotions and ideas to oneself are _____ cultures. <u>nonexpressive</u> (7)

6. A culture's preferred way of communicating, given its core beliefs, values, attitudes, and behavioral norms is called its _____. <u>communication style.</u> (8)

7. The _____ theory contends that all human communication, including public speaking, is based on our earliest conversations. <u>dialogical</u> (10)

8. The communication model that shows communication as a process in which speakers and audiences work together to create mutual meanings is called the _____ model. <u>transactional</u> (10-12)

9. You send a schedule request to your boss via email. The internet is the _____ part of the communication model depicted in the text. <u>channel</u> (11)

10. *Vir bonum, dicendi peritus* means _____. <u>The good person [lit. man], skilled in speaking.</u> (8)

11. _____ refers to knowing and applying different rules and expectations for two different cultures. <u>bicultural</u> (9)

12. Beliefs, attitudes, values, and behaviors that combine to suggest what is right, wrong, allowed, and forbidden are called _____. <u>core cultural resources</u> (6)

SHORT ANSWER: These recall questions test <u>knowledge</u> and <u>comprehension.</u>

1. Give two reasons for requiring public speaking courses. <u>Student answers should include these ideas: public speaking skills courses emphasize critical thinking and provide instruction and practice in specific communication skills you can use in your personal and professional life.</u> (2-4)

2. List and give examples of at least four ways that public speaking affects culture. <u>Answers should include four of the following: speakers transmit, reinforce or maintain, restore or repair, transform, or improve cultures. Examples will vary</u>. (5)

3. Using your first classroom speech as an example, draw and label the elements of the transactional model of communication. <u>Refer to the diagram and labels on pages. (10-11)</u>

ESSAY QUESTIONS: These include <u>application</u> and <u>synthesis</u> levels of thinking, based on the students' <u>knowledge</u> and <u>comprehension</u> of chapter concepts.

1. Design a brochure that the communication department might distribute to explain the advantages of taking a public speaking course.

2. Your best friend asks you what "culture" has to do with public speaking. Isn't "diversity" just another form of political correctness? What do you say?

3. Describe the ways culture influences public speaking.

4. Use the example of an influential person or persons (such as Martin Luther King, Jr., Abraham Lincoln, or Hillary Clinton) to illustrate specifically how public speaking transmits, reinforces, restores, or transforms cultural elements.

5. Using an example from your life, explain a recent conversation using the transactional model of communication.

Chapter 2

GIVING YOUR FIRST SPEECH: DEVELOPING CONFIDENCE

TRUE-FALSE QUESTIONS: These questions assess <u>knowledge</u>, <u>comprehension</u>, and <u>application</u>.

1. The five canons of rhetoric include invention, disposition, audience, memory, and delivery. <u>False. Audience is not a canon; style is.</u> (17)

2. Principles in the canon of invention help you gather the materials you need, analyze the audience and situation, and select a purpose for your speech. <u>True.</u> (17-18)

3. Once you've analyzed your audience, you are in a better position to choose a speech topic. <u>True.</u> (18)

4. Revealing something unusual about yourself shouldn't be done in a classroom speech. <u>False.</u> (18)

5. Your speech purpose is determined by the response you want from your audience. <u>True.</u> (19)

6. The Internet contains excellent as well as poor and even fraudulent data. <u>True.</u> (20)

7. When you organize facts and examples into main points with supporting materials, you're following principles in the canon of disposition. <u>True.</u> (20-21)

8. The major function of a speech introduction is to give your audience as much background information about your topic as they need. <u>False. This is not listed as one of the four major functions.</u> (20)

9. It is important in the conclusion to provide closure and give the audience something to take away from the speech. <u>True.</u> (21)

10. Speech connectives are the emotional high points of the speech, designed to increase the audience's emotional responses by relating to their lives. <u>False. Connectives tie the parts of the speech together.</u> (21)

11. The principles in the canon of style apply to writing as well as speaking. <u>True.</u> (21)

12. In rhetoric, your "style" is the way you walk, talk, dress, and present yourself. <u>False. In rhetoric, style means language.</u> (21)

13. In literate cultures, the canon of delivery is often called the "lost" canon. <u>False. The canon of memory is "lost."</u> (22)

14. Memorizing your speech takes the risk out of speechmaking. <u>False. Memorizing can be risky because of the danger of forgetting under stress.</u> (22)

15. Men and women typically experience PSA similarly. <u>False. Women typically have stronger physical and psychological reactions than men.</u> (23)

16. The fight-or-flight mechanism is a basic component of psychological anxiety. <u>False. It is an element of physiological anxiety.</u> (24)

17. Seth will probably experience his greatest anxiety during the adaptation milestone in the middle of his speeches when he suddenly realizes everyone is looking at him. <u>False. Anxiety is usually greatest during the introduction</u>. (24)

18. Carefully planning your introduction may, surprisingly, help you deal with anxiety. <u>True.</u> (25)

19. Use of visual aids during your introduction will distract you and cause increased anxiety. <u>False.</u> (25)

20. Internal Monologue (I-M) is defined as self-talk, and negative I-M can make you more anxious about public speaking. <u>True.</u> (26)

21. According to the text, athletes use a strategy called "cognitive modification" that you can adapt to help yourself overcome PSA. <u>False. The text associates athletes with visualization.</u> (27)

22. Because of the process of habituation, your anxiety lessens when you speak repeatedly and the negative outcomes you expect aren't all that bad. <u>True.</u> (27)

23. Communication apprehension (CA) is identical to public speaking anxiety (PSA). <u>False; PSA is a specific type of CA, and people can be apprehensive in arenas other than public speaking.</u> (16)

24. Segev is avoiding his public speaking class because he knows the more he speaks in public, the worse his CA will become. Is Segev's assertion true or false? <u>False. Many students say their anxiety decreases.</u> (25)

25. Behnke and Sawyer found that anxiety peaks in the anticipatory period just after the speech is announced. <u>True.</u> (24)

26. Stage fright refers to the feelings of dread many people have at the thought of giving a speech. <u>True.</u> (16)

27. Impromptu delivery is more useful for formal ceremonial talks. <u>False. Manuscript delivery is more useful.</u> (22)

MULTIPLE CHOICE QUESTIONS: These questions assess <u>knowledge</u>, <u>comprehension</u>, <u>application</u>, and <u>analysis</u>.

1. When you first learn a new skill, such as public speaking, you probably do all these EXCEPT___
   a. fear the unknown.
   b. learn through observation, study, and practice.
   c. follow the guidelines more closely at first.
   <u>d.</u> give a speech from a previous class. (17)
   e. wonder how to do it.

2. A canon is a _____
   a. creative unit in a speech.
   b. small unit in a speech.
   <u>c. body of principles.</u> (17)
   d. Roman method of memory training.
   e. moment of great intensity in your speech.

3. The canons of rhetoric are _____
   <u>a. delivery, style, invention, disposition, and memory.</u> (17)
   b. reading, writing, listening, speaking.
   c. oral, literate, and electronic.
   d. to inform, to persuade, to entertain.
   e. audience analysis, topic selection, research, and organization.

4. Mary Ann will use the principles in the canon of invention when she _____
   a. memorizes her speech.
   b. actually gives her speech.
   c. analyzes her audience and researches her topic. (17-18)
   d. selects language for her ideas.
   e. organizes her main points.

5. Which is NOT necessarily considered when preparing a speech?
   a. Demographic information about an audience.
   b. Psychological information including attitude about a topic.
   c. The situation in which you will speak, including time of day and equipment available.
   d. All of the above. (18)

6. In her self-introductory speech, Carly showed a videotape of herself in the delivery room giving birth to her son. She ran the danger of violating which of the following speech guidelines?
   a. Be sure you understand the assignment.
   b. Choose to reveal something unusual.
   c. Consider your listeners' sensibilities. (19)
   d. Select a significant incident.

7. The general purposes identified in the text are _____
   a. to inform, to persuade, to entertain, to commemorate. (19)
   b. to introduce, to persuade, to inform, to highlight cultural ideals.
   c. to convince, to convert, to educate, to introduce.
   d. to explain, to demonstrate, to convince, to entertain.

8. Kim has great ideas, but she doesn't know how to order them so that they flow well. She needs to learn the principles in the canon of _____ .
   a. invention.
   b. disposition. (20)
   c. style.
   d. memory.
   e. delivery.

9. Jim has a great topic for his speech, has organized it flawlessly, but forgets to make eye contact with his audience and sways from side to side. Jim needs to improve in ____
   a. the canon of style.
   b. the canon of invention.
   c. the canon of delivery. (22)
   d. the canon of disposition.

10. The mode of delivery most commonly used in the classroom is _____ .
    a. memorized.
    b. manuscript.
    c. impromptu.
    d. extemporaneous. (22)

11. Before he speaks, Rajin's heart races, he begins to perspire, and his stomach has "butterflies." He is experiencing _____
    a. memory loss.
    b. <u>the "fight or flight" mechanism.</u> (24)
    c. the butterfly phenomenon.
    d. withdrawal.
    e. disruption.

12. Engaging in physical exercise, such as brisk walking, running, or lifting weights helps to
    a. promote positive thoughts about the audience.
    b. <u>counteract physical tension.</u> (24)
    c. understand the anxiety process.
    d. assess your public speaking anxiety.
    e. rehearse through visualization.

13. According to research, anxiety is highest _____
    a. <u>before the speech.</u> (24-27, Figure 2.2)
    b. about the time you make the transition from the introduction to the body of the speech.
    c. during the body of the speech.
    d. during the conclusion.
    e. during the question and answer period following the speech.

14. If you tell yourself your topic is boring and no one wants to hear you speak, you are not _____
    a. <u>controlling your internal monologue.</u> (26)
    b. understanding the anxiety process.
    c. refining your personal style.
    d. "psyching" yourself up.
    e. rehearsing through visualization.

15. About an hour before his class, Jon finds a quiet place and thinks through all the aspects of his speech. He "sees" himself beforehand; then he "observes" himself going to the podium, setting up his visual aids, and giving his speech. Finally, he mentally thinks through the question and answer period and "watches" himself returning to his seat. He's rehearsing by _____
    a. controlling his internal monologue.
    b. knowing the speechmaking process.
    c. physical relaxation.
    d. <u>visualization.</u> (27)
    e. understanding the anxiety process.

16. After she finished the course, Judy was much more confident. She gave several speeches and the negative outcomes she expected weren't so bad after all. This is the process of _____
    a. cognitive modification.
    b. visualization.
    c. <u>habituation.</u> (27)
    d. internal-monologue.

17. If you are afraid of speaking out because you think something negative will result, people will think you're stupid or you might get a bad grade; for example, you are suffering from _____
    a. <u>communication apprehension. (6)</u>
    b. process anxiety.
    c. performance anxiety.
    d. all of these.

FILL IN THE BLANK: Most of these questions assess <u>knowledge</u> and <u>comprehension</u>.

1. Knowing the _____ process and learning strategies to deal with _____ are two ways to overcome anxiety. <u>speechmaking</u> . . . <u>nervousness</u> or <u>anxiety</u> (16)

2. The canon of _____ is often called the lost canon. <u>memory</u> (22)

3. Principles for outlining your speech are in the canon of _____ <u>disposition</u>. (20-21)

4. Words and phrases you use to tie your ideas together are _____ <u>connectives</u>. (21)

5. Principles of language usage are found in the canon of _____ <u>style.</u> (21)

6. When you give a spur-of-the-moment speech, you are using _____ delivery; when you prepare your speech carefully in advance and rehearse but use note cards and choose the exact wording as you go, you are using _____ delivery. <u>impromptu</u> (22) . . . <u>extemporaneous</u> (22)

7. The sudden burst of energy you get when you're nervous--the pounding heart, the butterflies in your stomach--are part of the _____ mechanism. <u>fight-or-flight</u> (24)

8. Negative self-talk that may contribute to feelings of anxiety is ___. <u>Internal Monologue (I-M).</u> (26)

9. _____ is a strategy for controlling anxiety in which you mentally observe yourself successfully giving your speech from beginning to end. <u>Visualization</u> (27)

10. You use _____ delivery when you write out your entire speech and then read it to your audience. <u>manuscript</u> (22)

11. Stage fright is another name for _____. <u>Public speaking apprehension or PSA</u> (16)

ESSAY QUESTIONS: These questions deal with <u>application</u>, <u>analysis</u>, and <u>synthesis</u>.

1. You are the personnel director of a company who is in charge of training new employees to make speeches on an occasional basis. You have been asked to prepare a 1- 2 page guide for these inexperienced speakers. Using the five canons of rhetoric, briefly outline the speechmaking process.

2. Give an example of how to use visualization before a speech. Include the steps outlined in this chapter.

3. Give guidelines for choosing a subject for your classroom speech of self-introduction.

4. Analyze your personal speech anxiety. What internal and external effects are you liable to experience? Describe a realistic plan for dealing with your nervousness. [If you do not experience anxiety about public speaking, analyze why this is so.]

5. Your friend confesses to you that she is terrified about taking a public speaking class--but she has to do so to graduate. What would you tell her to do to overcome her anxiety?

Chapter 3

ETHICS IN A DIVERSE SOCIETY

TRUE-FALSE: These questions test <u>knowledge</u>, <u>comprehension</u>, and <u>application</u>.

1. Disagreement and different points of view are the foundations of democracy. <u>True</u>. (36)

2. In our diverse society you are regularly called on to make ethical choices. <u>True</u>. (34)

3. The Constitution of the United States allows for freedom of speech. Period. <u>False. Things like slander are illegal as is yelling FIRE! in a crowded theater</u>. (32-33)

4. "Rightsabilities" means we can do whatever is within our rights. <u>False</u>. It means we should try to balance what we *can* do and what we *should* do. (34)

5. Heckling is common in political gatherings, but university audiences are too sophisticated and open-minded to shout down a speaker. <u>False. Heckling often occurs on campuses nationwide</u>. (43-44)

6. Diversity is rarely divisive at the minimum end of the maximum-minimum scale of differences. <u>False. Even small differences can divide people</u>. (34)

7. Brianna marches in a protest against the World Trade Organization; she's encountering diversity with resistance. <u>True</u>. (35)

8. According to Deborah Tannen, the U.S. is an "argument culture" partly because we often use metaphors about storms and dangerous weather in our public discourse. <u>False. Tannen is more concerned about the widespread use of war metaphors</u>. (35)

9. People who respond to diversity by assimilation may create alternative institutions. <u>False. This characterizes resistance not assimilation</u>. (35)

10. Caitlin goes away to college where her political beliefs are challenged. She decides to reject or surrender them. Her response is assimilation. <u>True</u>. (34)

11. A multivocal society is one that permits certain voices to be heard. <u>False. A multivocal society</u>. (35)

12. Accomodating groups allow themselves to rethink ideas and hear diverse ideas from a variety of perspectives. <u>True</u>. (35)

13. Occasionally, intense heckling forces a speaker to stop mid-speech. <u>True.</u> (44)

14. Dialogue involves a set of rules including equality, empathy, and examination. <u>False. Dialogue is more of a mindset or attitude than it is a set of rules</u>. (40)

15. A dialogical speaker generally does not have personal biases or strong beliefs that he or she wants the audience to share. <u>False. The key is to present the ideas honestly in a noncoercive manner</u>. (40)

16. A dialogical perspective and invitational rhetoric both invite others into dialogue and create contexts that facilitate dialogue. <u>True</u>. (40-41)

17. According to Amitai Etzioni, it's important to deal with every issue when you engage in dialogue with others who have major disagreements with you. This prevents you from sweeping less important matters under the rug. <u>False. You don't have to deal with every issue</u>. (40-41)

18. The United Nations was created in the belief that dialogue can triumph over discord. <u>True</u>. (41)

19. Traditionally, Arabs gathered in tents to express their opinions and discuss important issues respectfully. <u>True</u>. (41-42)

20. According to the *Credo for Ethical Communication*, unethical communication threatens the well-being of nations as well as individuals. <u>True</u>. (37-38)

21. If you find a study saying that chocolate helps the heart, but discover that a chocolate manufacturer funded the research, it's unethical to use this information. <u>False. The data is not necessarily inaccurate; just be cautious and check other sources</u>. (47)

22. The emphasis on civility developed as a reaction to the type of communication features on *The Jerry Springer Show*. <u>False. Ancient Greeks and Asian cultures also emphasize civility</u>. (38-39)

23. When you disagree with a speaker, it's all right to heckle her loudly so that other people can't hear her false information. <u>False. Heckling is a way to silence speakers, and in this culture everyone has the right to speak</u>. (42)

24. One way to silence a speaker is by whispering to a friend during the speech. <u>True</u>. (42-43)

25. Ethical listeners expose themselves to a variety of arguments and listen with an open mind. <u>True</u>. (42-44)

26. Responsible listeners listen only to the side of an issue that they agree with so that they can give the speaker a fair hearing. <u>False. Responsible listeners expose themselves to both sides of arguments</u>. (43-44)

27. Plagiarism is making up information. <u>False; that's fabrication</u>. (44-47)

28. The Internet has made plagiarism more common. <u>True</u>. (46)

29. A good way to avoid plagiarism is to cite your sources within your speech. <u>True</u>. (44-45)

30. All you have to do to avoid plagiarism when you cut and paste material from the Internet is to change a few words here and there and cite the Internet source in your references at the end of your outline. <u>False. This is improper paraphrase. You need to cite the source in the text as well as at the end of the outline</u>. (45).

31. If I accidently forget to cite someone, it isn't plagiarism. <u>False. Plagiarism is still plagiarism if done out of ignorance</u>. (45)

32. When you download a picture from the Internet onto a PowerPoint slide, if you don't include on the slide the URL of the website where you got the picture, you are plagiarizing. <u>True</u>. (46)

33. Rules of plagiarism require you to document results of experiments you personally conduct. <u>False. It is not necessary to document your own experiments</u>. (46)

34. The U.S. rules against plagiarism are applicable in every culture globally. <u>False. Some cultures don't have the same rules about intellectual property</u>. (47)

35. Shaura needs seven sources in her speech; she only has five, so she makes up citations from *Time*, the *New York Times*, and the *Boston Globe*. This unethical behavior is called fabrication. <u>True</u>. (47-48)

MULTIPLE CHOICE: These questions test <u>knowledge</u>, <u>comprehension</u>, and <u>application</u>.

1. Lakshmi came from India, became a Christian, married a man from Montana, and never again spoke her native language. Her response to diversity is called _____
   a. resistance.
   b. activism.
   <u>c. assimilation</u>. (34)
   d. accommodation.
   e. multivocal.

2. Manuel responds to diversity by acknowledging real differences between himself and members of other cultural groups, but he shows a willingness to listen to their ideas and evaluate them fairly. His response is called _____
   a. resistant.
   b. defiant.
   c. assimilation.
   <u>d. accommodation</u>. (35)
   e. multivocal.

3. Deborah Tannen, which language makes our culture an "argument culture"?
   a. 'Culture wars'
   b. 'Fighting for your rights'
   c. 'Battleground states'
   d. 'shoot down ideas'
   <u>e. All of the above</u> (35)

4. In the *Magic of Dialogue,* Daniel Yankelovich defines empathy as
   a. putting aside a know- it-all attitude.
   b. scrutinizing your own assumptions with an open mind.
   c. regarding each other's opinions as important.
   <u>d. understanding other perspectives and identifying emotionally.</u> (40)
   e. avoiding demonizing the other side.

5. Your concern with ethics should begin ____
   a. at the point when you begin gathering information.
   b. at the time you decide upon a persuasive purpose.
   <u>c. as soon as you get the speech assignment.</u> (36)
   d. when you have questionable information and must decide whether or not to present it.
   e. when you begin your audience analysis.

6. According to Daniel Yanelovich, dialogue requires which of these sets of conditions:
   a. *respons*-ibility and authenticity.
   b. mutuality, synergy, openmindedness.
   c. <u>equality, empathy, examination. (40)</u>
   d. accommodation, authenticity, active listening.
   e. inclusiveness and invitational rhetoric.

7. Which is NOT a characteristic of dialogical listening and speaking?
   a a belief that the whole is greater than the sum of the parts
   b. <u>an attempt to control one another's reactions</u> (40)
   c. a value on mutuality
   d. active involvement of both speakers and listeners
   e. both speaker and audience willing to change as a result of the speech

8. Using a dialogical perspective provides for all but which ability?
   a. <u>the ability to guarantee that dialogue will resolve contentious problems (40)</u>
   b. the ability to engage in dialogue in response to another's invitation to do so
   c. the ability to invite others into dialogue
   <u>d</u>. the ability to create contexts that facilitate dialogue

9. Which of the following is NOT one of Amitai Etzioni's rules of engagement for productive dialogue?
   a. Don't demonize the other side or depict it as completely negative.
   b. Don't feel you must deal with every issue.
   c. Don't abandon your personal convictions.
   d. <u>Talk more about non-negotiable rights than needs, wants, and interests. (40-41)</u>
   e. Don't offend the other party's deeply held moral commitments.

10. President Obama's speech after the shooting in Tuscon, Arizona, was an attempt to lead people to engage in a practice called: _____
    a. McCarthyism.
    b. Accommodation.
    c. <u>Civility. (37-38)</u>
    d. Demonization.
    e. Diversity.

11. According to the text, a major reason to develop a habit of research is _____
    a. the information you find will most likely be interesting.
    b. you are practicing civility when you do so.
    c. you are being more dialogical as a speaker.
    d. you will be less likely to plagiarize speech materials if you do extensive research.
    e. <u>you owe it to your audience to know what you're talking about. (36-37)</u>

12. Drive-by debating might be thought of as the opposite of _____
    a. <u>civility. (38)</u>
    b. fairness.
    c. truthfulness.
    d. monologue.

13. The social virtue, _____, involves self-control or moderation and results in persuasion, consultation, bargaining, compromise, and the like as means for resolving differences. Many cultures across space and time have valued it.
   a.   courtesy
   b.   civility (38)
   c.   tolerance
   d.   assimilation
   e.   accommodation

14. You're listening to a speaker who's giving false information, playing on emotions, and otherwise manipulating listeners. You think you should say something, but you don't want to embarrass the speaker or make a scene. This is a(n) _____
   a.   ethical dilemma. (42-43)
   b.   dilemma about heckling.
   c.   quest for truthfulness.
   d.   unwillingness to hear a diverse perspective.

15. Two students quoted word-for-word the same example about killer bees; neither credited the source, and they worked on their speeches separately. This is called _____ .
   a.   plagiarism. (44-45)
   b.   unsubstantiated material.
   c.   quoting material out of context.
   d.   fabrication.

16. Dan borrowed a speech his roommate gave the previous semester and presented it as his own. This type of plagiarism is called _____
   a.   improper paraphrase.
   b.   cut-and-paste plagiarism.
   c.   cultural plagiarism.
   d.   deliberate fraud. (45)
   e.   accidental plagiarism.

17. A history professor downloaded a map from the Internet onto a PowerPoint slide, not realizing that she needed to put the URL of the source on her slide. This is an example of _____
   a.   improper paraphrase.
   b.   cut-and-paste plagiarism.
   c.   cultural plagiarism.
   d.   deliberate fraud.
   e.   accidental plagiarism. (45)

18. You need to cite your source when you _____
   a.   give your personal insights about your topic.
   b.   quote a unique phrase spoken by a character in a television comedy. (46)
   c.   provide generally accepted facts.
   d.   tell the audience about experiments you personally conduct.
   e.   paraphrase a well-known folktale.

19. Kevin made up a survey he used on his speech about texting and driving. This is called _____ .
   a.   plagiarism.
   b.   exaggeration.
   c.   fabrication. (47)
   d.   rumormongering.

FILL IN THE BLANK: These questions test <u>knowledge</u> and <u>application</u>.

1. _____ is a term that Professor Vernon Jensen coined to describe the balance between what we can do and what we should do. <u>Rightsability</u> (34)

2. Jean deals with diversity by refusing to risk changing her ideas. She attacks the traditions of others and defends her own beliefs and values. Her response is _____ <u>resistance</u>. (35)

3. A _____ society actively seeks out a variety of opinions to be heard with respect. <u>multivocal</u> (35)

4. _____ is the conscious decision to speak and listen in ways that are honest, fair, right, and helpful to others as yourself. <u>Ethical communication</u> (34)

5. The three conditions necessary for dialogue are _____, _____, and _____. <u>equality, empathy, examination</u>. (40)

6. Dialogical principles focus more on _____; democratic guidelines focus more on the ethical issues involved in _____. <u>the relationship between the speaker and the audience; the creation of the speech itself</u> (40)

7. A person who taunts, insults, ridicules, or shouts down a speaker is called a _____. <u>heckler</u> (42)

8. Giving the words and ideas of others as your own without crediting the source is called _____. <u>plagiarism</u>. (44)

9. Sean found his roommate's take home exam from the Econ class he took last semester. Since he has the same professor this semester, Sean put his name on his roommate's exam and turned it in as his own. This is called _____. <u>deliberate fraud</u>. (45)

10. Downloading entire sections of material from the Internet and putting it into your document is called _____. <u>cut-and-paste plagiarism</u>. (45)

11. Malek made up a story about his infant sister who passed away as a result of a drunk driving accident. Later it was proven Malek never had a sister. This is called _____. <u>fabrication</u>. (47-48)

SHORT ANSWER: These questions test <u>comprehension</u>.

1. Give examples of responses to diversity. Explain how each response functions for a particular group. (<u>Answers should include resisting, assimilating, and accommodating. Examples will vary</u>.) (35-36)

2. Identify and explain three conditions that are required if true dialogue is to take place. (<u>Answers should include equality or mutual respect; empathy or mutual attempts to understand each other's perspectives; examination or the willingness to examine one's own as well as the other's assumptions with an open mind</u>.) (40)

3. List and explain three common guidelines for ethical speaking in a democratic society. (<u>Answers should include 1) Develop a habit of research or searching through several sources representing a variety of perspectives; 2) Be honest and fair or present material truthfully and in a balanced way; 3) Practice civility or exercise self-control, moderation, compromise</u>.) (36-39)

4. What responsibilities do ethical listeners have to themselves? To other listeners? To the speaker? (Ethical listeners should openmindedly expose themselves to more than one viewpoint; they should not distract others who want to listen; they should hear out a speaker and encourage him or her to meet ethical standards.) (42-43)

5. Explain two kinds of ethical breaches to avoid during research and preparation. Tell how to avoid them. (Plagiarism is copying the work of others and not giving credit to the source. There are several types of intentional and unintentional or accidental plagiarism. Fabrication is making up information or passing along unsubstantiated information or rumors.) (44-47)

ESSAY QUESTIONS: These questions test application, analysis, and synthesis.

1. Identify an area in our society that causes strong disagreements. (Examples: euthanasia, abortion, religion.) Create three hypothetical characters who respond to the issue in different ways. Describe and analyze their responses. Then outline some principles for ethical speaking and listening these people can use to live together peacefully within a pluralistic culture.

2. Using information from this chapter, explain what you can personally do to help create a multivocal society?

3. Describe dialogical speaking and listening, and identify ways you can become a more dialogical speaker.

4. You want to be an ethical speaker. Define and give examples of two mistakes you might make that would make you less than ethical. Then explain what you can do to avoid these mistakes.

5. In public discourse, many people are irresponsible listeners. What guidelines would you give a group of people who were concerned about this problem and wanted to listen more ethically?

6. A friend asks to use your informative speech from your public speaking class next semester. How do you respond? Give a complete discussion of your reasoning.

7. Identify ways that the Internet has added to the problem of plagiarism in academia.

8. Compare and contrast ideas about plagiarism in the United States and in other cultural groups.

Chapter 4

EFFECTIVE LISTENING

TRUE-FALSE: These questions test <u>knowledge</u> and <u>comprehension.</u>

1. The average person spends about one third of her time listening. <u>False; it's about 50%</u>. (54)

2. If one is able to hear, they are also able to listen. <u>False; hearing is a physical process, listening is an active mental process</u>. (55)

3. According to research, the average student spends about 40 percent of his or her communication time speaking. <u>False; the average is 20 percent</u>. (55)

4. Most people have had classes in listening. <u>False. Listening is either incorporated into other courses or ignored</u>. (55)

5. We typically recall only about twenty five percent of what we hear. <u>True</u>. (55)

6. Ashley has just started a job in public relations; chances are, on the job she will use her listening skills more than she uses any other communication skill. <u>True</u>. (56)

7. You may have trouble understanding heavily accented English; this is an example of vocabulary differences. <u>False; it's an example of language differences</u>. (56)

8. Cultural allusions are pretty much the same the world over. <u>False. They vary from culture to culture</u>. (57)

9. Worries about an upcoming interview or concerns about a sick family member are examples of physical factors that hinder listening. <u>False. These are psychological factors</u>. (57)

10. Prejudice involves your negative or your positive pre-formed judgments of someone. <u>True</u>. (57)

11. Your speech-thought differential means you think about 350 words per minute faster than the average speaker talks. <u>True</u>. (58)

12. When you listen and follow the speaker's ideas but you disagree and stop trying to understand the speaker, and argue with her instead, you are going off on a tangent. <u>False; you are engaging in private argument</u>. (58)

13. Your schema for a wedding toast enables you to predict the types of things a speaker will typically say when your friends marry. <u>True</u>. (58-60)

14. In several Asian cultures, listeners see themselves equally responsible with the speaker for making communication successful. <u>True</u>. (62)

15. "Call and response" is typical of Japanese-American speaker-audience interactions. <u>False. It is true of African-American speakers</u>. (62)

16. Shoshanna is taking notes in her physics class; her major listening purpose is critical listening. <u>False. Her major goal is to learn or comprehend</u>. (60-62)

17. Looking for the organizational pattern the speaker is using is one way to improve comprehensive listening. <u>True</u>. (61)

18. When you're listening to comprehend, you should be suspicious of a speaker who is enthusiastic about and involved with her topic; she should be more detached and objective. <u>False. Intense involvement may signal that the topic is important and the speaker is confident about her information</u>. (60)

19. Critical listeners are following this advice: "If you don't have anything nice to say, don't say anything at all." <u>False Critical listeners are following this advice:</u> Don't believe everything you hear. (62)

20. Mr. Garcia is listening to an investment planner talking about mutual funds; Garcia really believes in investing in such funds and the planner is enthusiastically promoting them. In such a case, Mr. Garcia can just accept the planner's ideas without much critical evaluation. <u>False; he should be reflecting and weighing the merits of the appeal</u>. (62-63)

21. Where you sit in the classroom doesn't much matter. You probably get as much out of a lecture from any position in the room. <u>False. People who sit closer to the front and center arguably get more out of the lecture</u>. (65)

22. Good listeners can help a speaker become a better communicator. <u>True</u>. (56)

23. A loaded question, by definition, invites the speaker to provide a great deal of detail in the answer. <u>False. A loaded question may not really expect a precise answer</u>. (66)

24. An example of a closed question is "What is your opinion of on-campus food?" <u>False. It is open because it allows for any number of responses</u>. (66)

25. A request for elaboration is "Can you give us more details about DNA evidence?" <u>True</u>. (66)

26. Chinese and Japanese audiences typically ask clarification questions to make sure that they understand the speaker. <u>False. Questions reflect negatively on both listeners and speakers</u>. (66)

27. The statement "Your speech would be more effective if you used a visual aid with your statistics" would be classified as a *response* in the D-R-E Method. <u>False. It's an evaluation</u>. (67)

28. "During your speech, you said 'OK' seven times" would be classified as a *description* in the D-R-E Method of giving feedback. <u>True</u>. (67)

29. "Your examples made me want to do something to help children with AIDs in Africa" is an *evaluation* in the D-R-E Method of feedback. <u>False. The critic is giving a personal response</u>. (67)

MULTIPLE CHOICE: These questions test <u>knowledge</u>, <u>comprehension</u>, and <u>application</u>.

1. Zeno of Citium said _____
   a. <u>We have been given two ears and but one mouth so that we may hear more and talk less. (54)</u>
   b. Listening to people keeps them entertained.

c. Learning is a result of listening, which in turn leads to even better listening and attentiveness to the other person.

d. To listen is an effort, and just to listen is no merit. A duck listens also.

2. According to the text, these things are true about listening, EXCEPT _____
   a. Listening is the skill most often used on the job.
   b. Most people are better listeners than they think they are. (55)
   c. Good listening skills are good job skills.
   d. Being listened to is a basic human need.

3. Which of these is NOT a part of the Chinese character for listening?
   a. eyes
   b. ears
   c. heart
   d. mind (56)

4. Which is NOT a linguistic factor that hinders listening?
   a. accents
   b. pronunciation
   c. stress on syllables
   d. allusions (56-57)
   e. vocabulary

5. A speaker refers to David Hume, assuming her audience knows that he was an influential philosopher. Several listeners have no idea who he was, so they misunderstand her _____
   a. vocabulary.
   b. cultural allusion. (57)
   c. listening schema.
   d. jargon.

6. "Female professors are so much better than male professors at explaining the listening process!" is an example of _____
   a. a physical factor that hinders listening.
   b. a barrier to comprehension.
   c. a negative listening schema.
   d. a stereotype that hinders listening. (57)

7. Speech-thought differential is a term that means _____
   a. the difference between how fast you think and how fast the speaker talks. (58)
   b. the amount of time you spend in a departure from the communication line.
   c. you bring to the speech some personal worries that distract your attention.
   d. mental activity during which you think of examples that bolster the speaker's ideas.

8. During a speech, the speaker mentions a dog and one listener starts thinking about her dog, then about her veterinarian, then about her doctor, then . . . . The listener is _____
   a. taking a small departure from the communication line.
   b. going off on a tangent. (58)
   c. engaging in a private argument.
   d. taking a large departure from the communication line.

9. Jesse is listening to a speaker whose views on capital punishment widely differ from his. Although the speaker is making understandable arguments, Jesse closes his mind and counters everything the speaker says by mentally reciting his position. He is _____
   a. taking a small departure from the communication line.
   b. going off on a tangent.
   c. engaging in a private argument. (58)
   d. taking a large departure from the communication line.

10. You hear someone say, "Once upon a time in a faraway place. . . ," and you pull up your mental framework or blueprint that tells you are listening to a fairy tale. You are using a _____
    a. listening schema. (58-59)
    b. cultural allusion.
    c. jargon phrase.
    d. stereotype.
    e. narrative.

11. Listening to a lecture on post-Civil War economic history is an example of _____ listening.
    a. active
    b. comprehensive (60)
    c. critical
    d. dialogical
    e. cultural

12. To get more out of a classroom lecture and discussion, Omar should do all these EXCEPT ____
    a. prepare by reading the chapter before coming to class.
    b. think of examples and images that link the material to his personal experiences.
    c. tape record the lecture. (60-62) (this is not necessary for everyone)
    d. direct his attention by taking notes.
    e. look for the organizational pattern of the lecture.

13. Critical listeners ____
    a. question a speaker's goal. (62-63)
    b. use totally different skills than they use for comprehensive listening.
    c. can be less critical when they listen to a speaker who affirms their ideas.
    d. avoid speakers they disagree with.
    e. don't worry about comprehensive listening.

14. Michelle makes these nonverbal interactions with the speaker. Which makes her a less competent listener?
    a. She leans toward the speaker.
    b. Even though she is taking notes, she makes eye contact.
    c. She taps her pen and shuffles her papers. (64-65)
    d. She smiles and nods.
    e. She sits directly in front of the speaker in the second row.

15. "What year did Eisenhower take office?" is a(n) _____ question.
    a. loaded
    b. open
    c. disclosing
    d. clarification
    e. closed (66)

16. "What do you think our candidate should do to increase her credibility with voters?" is a(n) _____ question.
    a. loaded
    b. <u>open</u> (66)
    c. closed
    d. disclosing
    e. clarification

17. In Chinese and Japanese speaking traditions, listeners avoided asking questions because _____
    a. a question would be an admission that you are not intelligent enough to understand.
    b. asking a question would cast doubt on the speaker's ability to communicate.
    c. questioning the speaker's information does not help the speaker maintain face.
    d. <u>all of these</u>. (66)
    e. none of these.

18. The three elements of the D-R-E Method of feedback are ___
    a. determine, react, evaluate.
    b. discriminate, react, express.
    c. <u>describe, respond, evaluate.</u> (67)
    d. distinguish, react, evaluate.

FILL IN THE BLANK

1. The Chinese character for listening combines characters for _____, _____, and _____ <u>eyes, ears, heart</u> (56)

2. The president of the university didn't understand the valedictorian's reference to Eminem's new track. This is because they don't share the same _____. <u>cultural allusions</u> (57)

3. Janice dismisses a speaker who's discussing the need for adequate daycare by thinking, "Just another feminist giving just another tired old feminist song and dance!" Janice is employing the psychological barrier to listening known as _____ <u>stereotyping</u>. (57)

4. As Jack sat in the audience waiting for the Intelligent Design speaker to begin, he thought, "I won't agree with a thing this guy says." He is using the psychological hindrance known as _____. <u>prejudice</u> or <u>bias</u> (57)

5. We think about 500 words a minute and speak about 150 words a minute. The 350 word gap between speaking and thinking is called _____. <u>the speech-thought differential</u> (58)

6. _____ are the mental plans, blueprints, or models that you use to organize, compre-hend, and interpret the information you hear presented in speeches. <u>Listening schemas</u> (58-60)

7. The traditional African speaker-listener interaction pattern that is characterized by speaker statements that are punctuated by listener reactions to them is termed _____. <u>call and response</u>. (62)

8. Listening for information or listening to understand is called _____ listening. <u>comprehensive</u> (60)

9. Listening to evaluate the merit of various claims is called _____ listening. <u>critical</u> (62-63)

10. A question that seeks a brief, specific answer is a _____ question. <u>closed</u> (66)

SHORT ANSWER: These questions test <u>knowledge</u> and <u>comprehension.</u>

1. Explain three ways good listening skills will help you. (<u>Answers include the idea that we listen most so listening well will make our lives more productive; listening helps personal relationships; listening skills are important job skills.</u>) (55-56)

2. List and explain the importance of each element in the Chinese character for listening. (<u>Ears, eyes, and heart. Explanation should include the idea that hearing and paying attention, watching for the speaker's nonverbal cues, and getting emotionally involved all enhance listening.</u>) (56)

3. Identify and explain four specific thought patterns that are typical of listening. (<u>1) Taking small departures from the communication line can hinder--or help if they're used to elaborate on ideas given in the speech; 2) going off on a tangent seizes on one idea and stops listening to follow that idea, and the next, and the next; 3) engaging in a private argument happens when the listener challenges the speaker's ideas and forms a counter argument for everything she or he hears; 4) taking large departures from the communication line listens for awhile and then wanders off, comes back, and wanders off again.</u>) (57-58, Figure 4.2)

4. Identify four strategies you can use to comprehend material better. (<u>Include four of these: prepare in advance; direct attention toward the speech; take notes; enhance or elaborate on the meaning; look for organizational patterns; use specific strategies that complement your learning style; watch the speaker's manner of presentation.</u>) (60-62)

5. Give an example for each of the following: loaded questions, closed questions, open questions, clarification questions, requests for elaboration, comments. (<u>Answers will vary.</u>) (66)

6. Explain the D-R-E Method of giving feedback on a speech. (Students should explain the three elements: description, response, and evaluation.) (66-67)

ESSAY QUESTIONS: These questions test <u>comprehension</u>, <u>application</u>, <u>synthesis</u>, and <u>evaluation.</u>

1. You are an active listener. Describe what you do as you listen to a speech.

2. Give an example of a time you experienced a cultural barrier. How was your listening impacted?

3. You have a friend who is having trouble getting information from lectures. Give her several tips she can use to improve her comprehension of course material.

4. You've been asked to create a videotape that will help students in classes like yours understand what it means for speakers and listeners to participate actively in co-creating meaning. First, identify the concepts you'd want your viewers to understand. Second, plan your video, including a script (brief) and description (briefly) of the scenes you'd include. For instance, who would you show? Where would they be? What kinds of verbal and nonverbal interactions would illustrate the concepts for the viewers?

5. Identify the three elements of the D-R-E Method of written feedback, give an example of each, and tell how and why the three interwoven elements create a more meaningful critique than any of the elements would by itself.

Chapter 5

SELECTING YOUR TOPIC AND PURPOSE

TRUE-FALSE: These questions test <u>knowledge</u>, <u>comprehension</u>, and <u>application.</u>

1. There are three sure fire ways to decide upon a speech topic. <u>False. There's probably no single way, and certainly not three.</u> (72)

2. A speech demonstrating a common procedure like how to make coffee wastes listener's time. <u>True.</u> (72)

3. Curiosity is a speaker characteristic generally related to good public speaking. <u>True.</u> (72)

4. Audiences like to listen to speakers who are enthusiastic about their topics. <u>True.</u> (74)

5. It's considered cheating to use research for one class as speech material for another. <u>False. Not if the material is adapted to each audience.</u> (74)

6. International topics are usually appropriate for classroom speeches, because most students are interested in world events if linked to the audience. <u>True.</u> (72)

7. Giving one speech on communication and culture greatly increases a student's empathy. <u>False. One speech gives no significant gain in empathy.</u> (76)

8. The principle of narrowing a topic to fit within a designated time frame applies across all speaking contexts such as projects, farewell speeches, and sales presentations. <u>True.</u> (79-80)

9. "To persuade my classmates to purchase only product that have the Fair Trade certification label" is a general purpose. <u>Fasle. This is a specific purpose.</u> (79-80)

10. A "speech to teach" has "to inform" as its general purpose. <u>True.</u> (79-80)

11. A tribute has "to entertain" as its general purpose. <u>False; it's a commemorative speech</u>. (78)

12. Each speech has only one general purpose; there's no overlap of goals at this level. <u>False. A speech that persuades can also be entertaining and informative.</u> (78-79)

13. Targeting your listeners' emotions means you hope for cognitive responses. <u>False. Targeting emotions means you hope for affective responses.</u> (80)

14. "To inform my audience about important facts about the life of Chief Joseph" is an example of a central idea. <u>False. It is a specific purpose</u>. (80-82)

15. Another term for thesis statement is general purpose. <u>False. Another term for thesis statement is central idea.</u> (81)

16. Depending on your purpose, your thesis statement may be written in the form of one or more questions or declarative sentences. <u>False. It should be a single declarative sentence.</u> (81)

17. State or paraphrase your thesis statement in your speech--usually in the introduction. <u>True</u>. (81)

18. A thesis statement is exactly the same as the preview—a short summary of your major points. <u>False</u>. (81-82)

MULTIPLE CHOICE: These questions test <u>knowledge</u>, <u>comprehension</u>, and <u>application.</u>

1. Antoine's speech, "How to Make a Peanut Butter Sandwich," presented familiar, predictable information. What principle for choosing a topic or purpose should he have considered?
   a. Choose cognitive goals when you want your audience to believe something.
   b. Narrow the topic to a manageable size.
   c. <u>Take a novel approach</u>. (72-73)
   d. Relate the topic to listener concerns.
   e. Incorporate humor as one way to maintain attention.

2. Which of the following students needs help in topic selection?
   a. Oren speaks about his summer internship at the state capitol.
   b. Coral decides that no one needs to hear a speech about baking chocolate chip cookies.
   c. Tito goes to a newsstand and skims magazines such as *Time.*
   d. Yocheved carefully considers how her international topic can relate to her fellow students.
   e. <u>Eliyahu decides to give the same speech on "Cooking Israeli Food" he gave his anthropology class.</u>
      (71-76) (He can use the topic but must adapt the material.)

3. Which is NOT a factor to consider regarding international topics?
   a. <u>Audiences generally relate to these topics readily.</u> (76)
   b. Look into topics from your own heritage and experiences.
   c. These topics are increasingly important in a shrinking world.
   d. The U.S. media regularly covers international subjects.
   e. The topics might be linked to fundamental values.

4. One study on cultural topics showed that
   a. requiring just one diversity issue speech significantly increased students' ability to take diverse perspectives.
   b. students who chose a topic related to their ethnicity greatly increased in empathy.
   c. students who did extensive research in diverse sources increased in empathy.
   d. <u>in order to increase in empathy, students need to discuss diversity issues more than once during the term</u>. (76)

5. The next step after topic selection is _____
   a. <u>narrowing the topic to a manageable size.</u> (77-78)
   b. deciding on a general purpose.
   c. analyzing the audience.
   d. deciding on the desired audience response.
   e. tentatively formulating a central idea.

6. A mind map is especially useful for _____
   a. topic selection.
   b. <u>narrowing a topic</u>. (77)
   c. identifying a purpose.
   d. eliminating taboo or sensitive topics.
   e. pointing toward a logical thesis statement.

7. A comedian who does stand-up monologues in a nightclub probably has this goal:
    a. Although he uses humor, his general purpose is "to persuade."
    b. <u>His major purpose is "to entertain."</u> (78-79)
    c. His purpose is "to inform"—but in an entertaining way.
    d. His main goal is "to convince."
    e. He is attempting "to commemorate."

8. Professor Barram is a popular and entertaining lecturer in the business department on my campus; his major purpose for his lectures is ____
    a. <u>to inform.</u> (78)
    b. to convince.
    c. to persuade.
    d. to commemorate.
    e. to entertain.

9. At the recent 10 year anniversary of 9/11, speaker after speaker gave addresses about those who had fallen that day, with the purpose of ____
    a. informing.
    b. convincing.
    c. persuading.
    d. <u>commemorating.</u> (78)
    e. entertaining.

10. Your specific purpose in a speech, as opposed to your general purpose, focuses on _____
    a. information in the speech.
    b. <u>the desired audience response.</u> (80-81)
    c. background material.
    d. the broad topic.
    e. the narrowed topic.

11. The defense lawyer tries to humanize her client, who is on trial for murder, so that the jury sees him as a normal human being, not a monster. Her specific purpose is mostly _____
    a. cognitive.
    <u>b.</u> behavioral.
    c. informative.
    <u>d. affective.</u> (80)
    e. defensive.

12. If, at the end of your speech calling for a protest march, your audience charges out the door and begins to make placards to carry, that response is best called _____
    a. commemorative.
    b. cognitive.
    c. affective.
    d. <u>behavioral.</u> (80)
    e. informative.

13. Brittany wants her audience to believe that eliminating beer commercials on TV would lessen underage drinking. The main response she wants from her audience is _____
    a. <u>cognitive.</u> (80)
    b. affective.
    c. behavioral.
    d. humorous.

14. The following is an example of a well-written specific purpose statement:
    a. Giving a speech.
    b. <u>To convince my audience that learning principles in the five canons of rhetoric will improve their speaking skills</u>. (81)
    c. Why should you study the five canons of rhetoric?
    d. Principles in the canons of rhetoric will help speakers gather information, organize it, select appropriate language, learn their major ideas, and deliver their speeches.

15. The following is an example of a well-written thesis statement:
    a. Taking a hot air balloon ride.
    b. To convince my audience to take a hot air balloon ride.
    c. As a result of my speech, my listeners will take a hot air balloon ride.
    d. Why should you take a hot air balloon ride?
    e. <u>A hot air balloon ride will increase your enjoyment of life.</u> (81)

16. The following is an example of a well-written preview statement:
    a. Taking a hot air balloon ride with friends is an exciting social event.
    b. To convince my audience that taking a hot air balloon ride will be an enjoyable experience.
    c. To persuade my listeners that hot air ballooning is a beneficial activity.
    d. <u>Hot air ballooning is beneficial in three ways: it's relaxing; you meet new friends; and you fulfill your need for adventure.</u> (81-82)
    e. A hot air balloon ride will increase your enjoyment of life.

17. A speech that ends by asking listeners to fill out cards to become organ donors seeks which response?
    a. commemorative
    b. cognitive
    c. affective
    d. <u>behavioral</u> (80)
    e. informative

FILL IN THE BLANK: These questions test <u>knowledge</u>, <u>comprehension</u>, and <u>application.</u>

1. A diagram that you can use to find narrower topics within a broad subject area is a _____. <u>mind map</u>. (77)

2. When you explain, teach, describe, or provide your audience with a greater understanding of your topic, your general purpose is _____. <u>to inform</u> (78)

3. When your goal is to influence your audience's understandings and other mental processes, you are aiming at _____ responses. <u>cognitive</u> (80)

4. Gabriela wants her audience to appreciate gangsta rap music. She is targeting _____ responses. <u>affective</u> (80)

5. "To inform my audience of the controversy surrounding the 'repressed memory syndrome'" is an example of a _____. <u>specific purpose</u>. (80-81)

6. Another term for "central idea" is _____. <u>core idea</u> or <u>thesis statement</u> (78)

7. Your speech _____ lets your audience know how you will develop your thesis or central idea. <u>preview</u> (81)

SHORT ANSWER: These questions test <u>knowledge</u>, <u>comprehension</u>, and <u>application.</u>

1. How can beginning speakers add novelty to a speech? What is considered novelty? (<u>Speakers should either deal with something unfamiliar, or they should seek a fresh approach for a familiar topic</u>.) (72-73)

2. Summarize Carrell's findings on the relationship between empathy and the inclusion of diversity issues in a communication course. (<u>Basically, giving one diversity speech doesn't increase empathy significantly, but taking an entire course in intercultural communication does. And discussing diversity issues more than once increases empathy or the ability to take diverse perspectives</u>.) (76)

3. List and explain three major general types of responses a speaker desires from his listeners. (<u>Cognitive responses are related to their thinking, understandings, or beliefs; affective responses are related to their emotions; behavioral responses are related to their actions</u>.) (80)

4. Give guidelines for writing a good thesis statement. (<u>In their own words, students should include these elements: the central idea is a single, declarative sentence; it makes a statement about the subject matter; it summarizes the speech, simply but precisely</u>.) (81-82)

ESSAY QUESTIONS

1. Your roommate decides to give a speech on "How to make coffee." What guidance can you offer him or her about choosing an appropriate classroom speech?

2. Karla Banks is a member of the clergy who must prepare a sermon every Sunday for an audience comprised of people in various stages of religious belief. Let's say she's speaking on the importance of forgiveness. Explain how she will probably overlap the four general speech purposes as she presents her subject to her audience.

3. Select a broad topic such as crime, education, or sports. Then give a budding speechmaker some guidelines for creating a mind map that can help narrow this broad topic. Finally, create a mind map to illustrate how it's done.

Chapter 6

AUDIENCE ANALYSIS

TRUE-FALSE: These questions test <u>knowledge</u>, <u>comprehension</u>, and <u>application.</u>

1. Professor Wright's effectiveness is linked to her sensitivity to each audience at every step of preparation. <u>True</u>. (87)

2. In a random audience, participants are initially involved in another activity, but decide to pause and listen if the subject matter attracts their attention. <u>True</u>. (89)

3. A homogeneous audience can be either positive or negative toward a topic. <u>True</u>. (89)

4. When you do a demographic analysis of the audience, you survey their beliefs, attitudes, and values regarding a topic. <u>False. That's a psychological profile</u>. (93-96)

5. Salience is defined as the audience's perception of the speaker. <u>False. Salience means significance or importance</u>. (91)

6. Ethnicity includes skin color and facial features. <u>False</u>. (91)

7. Race is more of a social category than it is a physical category. <u>True</u>. (91)

8. Thinking about the audience's religious commitments is important only when the topic is religious in nature. <u>False. It's important in every speech</u>. (91)

9. When you see someone of the male sex, you can obviously assume he is of the masculine gender. <u>False. Gender and sex aren't the same</u>. (91)

10. The millennium generation is also known as the I-generation (the Internet-generation). <u>True (91-92)</u>

11. Although listeners at a sports banquet may differ in age, sex, religious affiliation, and ethnicity, their mutual interest in the sport is probably more salient than their other characteristics. <u>True</u>. (91)

12. A politician who gives the same speech in Denver, Miami, Boston, and Seattle is wise, because the culture in the U.S. is so similar throughout. <u>False. There are distinct regions</u>. (92-93)

13. Creating a questionnaire to assess their beliefs and attitudes toward a topic is a good way to assess the audience's psychological approach to a topic. <u>True</u>. (94-96)

14. Most of our beliefs are based on study or investigation of a subject. <u>False. Some are; many have little basis in fact or knowledge</u>. (93-94)

15. Attitudes are our tendencies to like or dislike something. <u>True</u>. (95)

16. The best scale for dealing with value questions ranges from strongly agree, agree, neutral or no opinion, disagree, strongly disagree. <u>False; "very important" to "very insignificant" is a better range</u>. (95)

17. The time of day you give your speech really has no bearing on how you give your speech. <u>False. Time of day and cultural times should be considered in assessing the situation</u>. (97)

18. If you speak in a country such as Brazil, you'll be expected to stick to precise time limits--with a plus or minus "grace period" of two minutes at the most. <u>False. Other countries (Brazil) have less precise timing</u>. (97)

19. The room you speak in and the weather outside are two aspects of the environment you should consider in your speech preparation. <u>True</u>. (97-98)

20. If the *Saturday Night Live* comic Andy Samberg were to visit your campus, he'd have prior credibility to talk about substance abuse, because he is a highly visible public figure. <u>False. Samberg would not necessarily be an expert on the topic of drug or alcohol abuse</u>. (98-99)

21. In general, Chinese, Japanese, and Native American cultures rate older speakers as more credible than younger ones. <u>True</u>. (99)

22. Once your speech is over, you can sit down relieved in knowing that your credibility is firmly established. <u>False. Terminal credibility comes after the speech, and additional factors may make people lose confidence in a speaker</u>. (99-100)

23. Audience demographics include age, sexual orientation, and religion. <u>True.</u> (90-91)

24. A rhetorical triangle has three sides: audience, speaker, and message. <u>False; they are audience, speaker, and situation.</u> (88, Figure 6.1)

25. Getting information from your audience by talking to focus groups is the direct method. <u>True.</u> (93-94)

MULTIPLE CHOICE: These questions test <u>knowledge</u>, <u>comprehension</u>, and <u>application</u>.

1. Considering the audience at every stage of speechmaking and discovering ways that you can most effectively communicate with this particular group is called _____
   <u>a. audience analysis</u>. (88-90)
   b. audience motivations.
   c. evaluating salience.
   d. demographic analysis.

2. A young woman approaches people walking through the mall and attempts to sell a new nail project. This is a(n) _____ audience.
   <u>a. random</u> (88-89)
   b. passive
   c. selected
   d. concerted
   e. hostile

3. An environmental activist who is addressing a group of builders and developers is most likely facing a(n) _____ audience.
   a. passive
   b. concerted
   <u>c. hostile</u> (89-90)
   d. absent
   e. organized

4. Students who are interested in obtaining advanced degrees in Communication Studies attend a meeting with graduate school representatives. They are a(n) _____ audience.
   a. random audience
   b. passive audience
   c. <u>motivated</u> (89)
   d. hostile audience
   e. unmotivated audience

5. Thinking of your audience according to cultural populations they represent is _____
   a. sexist and racist.
   b. perceiving their motivations.
   c. <u>demographic analysis.</u> (90-93)
   d. ethnicity.
   e. psychological profiling.

6. Janelle is aware of her Native American heritage when she goes to hear a speech about Zuni jewelry makers; then, her ethnicity is more _____ than when she attends her calculus lecture.
   a. androgynous
   b. <u>salient</u> (91)
   c. complex
   d. ambiguous

7. Demographic characteristics include all **but** _____
   a. ethnicity
   b. gender
   c. religion
   d. age
   e. <u>all of the above are demographic characteristics.</u> (94)

8. A mental acceptance that something is true or false, correct or incorrect, valid or invalid is ___
   a. <u>a belief.</u> (94)
   b. a value.
   c. a motivation.
   d. an attitude.

9. Austin has a negative opinion about politicians and a positive view of Disneyland; these are just two of his _____
   a. beliefs.
   b. values.
   c. <u>attitudes.</u> (95)
   d. actions.

10. Which is NOT a way to adapt sensitively to time factors?
    a. Consider the time of day.
    b. Consider your audience's cultural expectations about time.
    c. Be more animated when your listeners are tired.
    d. <u>Start on time wherever you are.</u> (97)
    e. These are all ways to be sensitive.

236

11. Which is NOT an environmental factor relating to public speaking?
    a. The color of the walls in the room.
    b. A lack of windows.
    c. <u>The clothing you select on your speech day</u>. (97-98)
    d. Sunshine outside the classroom.
    e. Not enough chairs for everyone to have a seat.

12. Newscaster Brian Williams brings speaker credibility with him because of who he is and the job he has. This is _____
    a. <u>prior credibility</u>. (98-99)
    b. demonstrated credibility.
    c. intrinsic credibility.
    d. terminal credibility.

FILL IN THE BLANK: These questions test <u>knowledge</u> and <u>comprehension</u>.

1. An audience whose members are similar in their attitude toward a topic--whether that attitude is positive or negative--is _____. <u>homogeneous</u> (89-90)

2. The group of students listening to the university president speak about the upcoming tuition increase—the third in three years—can be considered _____. <u>hostile</u> (92)

3. Sometimes particular characteristics of a listener, such as ethnicity or gender, are significant, meaning that they matter or become _____ in that setting. <u>salient</u> (91)

4. A group's common heritage and cultural traditions that usually stem from national and religious origins is called _____. <u>ethnicity</u> (91)

5. A rhetorical triangle of three sides-- _____, _____, _____--(<u>audience, speaker, situation</u>) comes together around a _____. <u>message</u> (88, Figure 6.1)

6. Assumptions about how someone will act because he is a man or she is a woman reflect the influence of _____. <u>gender</u> (91)

7. Researching your audience by asking other people about the group or getting information from websites is a _____ method. <u>indirect</u> (94)

8. When you want to take a _____ of the audience, you can use a questionnaire with questions that assess their beliefs, attitudes, values, and behaviors. <u>psychological profile</u> (93-94)

9. The standards we use to judge what is good or bad, right or wrong, moral or immoral, beautiful or ugly are our _____. <u>values</u> (95)

10. Rudy Giuliani was a college commencement speaker. Because of his expertise as mayor of New York City during the 9-11 crisis, he brought _____ credibility with him to the speech. <u>prior</u> (98-99)

11. Even though the students in the audience had heard good things about the speaker, he mumbled, swayed from side to side, and referred to the wrong school mascot through his speech. The type of credibility revealed in his speech itself is called _____ <u>demonstrated</u> or <u>intrinsic credibility.</u> (99)

SHORT ANSWER: These questions assess <u>knowledge</u>, <u>comprehension</u>, and <u>analysis.</u>

1. Distinguish between ethnicity and race. (<u>Ethnicity is the group's common heritage and cultural traditions, usually having national and religious origins; members may or may not have the same racial background; there are Jews of African origin, for example. Race categories are generally based on physical factors and may or may not be shared among ethnic groups. For example, many Asians might be classified in the same group racially but be Muslims from Indonesia. Generally, ethnic categories are more useful than racial categories.</u>) (91)

2. How is gender different than sex? Give examples of both. (<u>Gender is different from biological sex. Gender traits are those traits a culture labels as feminine or masculine; androgynous traits have characteristics of both.</u>) (91)

3. Identify four generational cohorts in the United States and give characteristics of each. (<u>The cohorts are: 1) seniors; 2) baby boomers; 3) generation Xers, and 4) the millennium generation. Description of traits will vary. Answers should include the type of technology that each generation grew up with.</u>) (92)

4. Explain how time and the environment affect a speaking situation; give examples. (<u>Answers should describe how the time of day and the cultural time system influence audience members; examples will vary. Environmental considerations should explain effects from specific elements in the room or in the weather.</u>) (97-98)

ESSAY QUESTIONS

1. Describe four types of audiences you might address (the book listed six). When might you address each one? What are your major challenges with each type? What strategies do you use to best meet these challenges?

2. A health educator is going to address a group of senior citizens in an assisted living complex on the topic of safer sex. What would you advise her to consider about her audience as she narrows her topic and selects her evidence?

3. Evaluate your classroom audience according to the categories identified in the text under "audience demographics."

4. Make a questionnaire that will help you get a profile of your audience's psychological approach to the topic of "Internet shopping." First, explain the factors you must measure in order to profile your audience and then create a questionnaire that will help you assess each factor.

5. Choose a public figure and use that person as a case study to explain credibility. (Examples: George W. Bush or Hillary Clinton; Jay Leno or Oprah, Eminem or the governor of your state.) Create an imaginary scenario (perhaps you invite him or her to campus) in which that person might speak; then explain what your person must do to be credible before, during, and after the speech.

Chapter 7

RESEARCHING YOUR SPEECH IN THE DIGITAL AGE

TRUE-FALSE: These questions test <u>knowledge</u>, <u>comprehension</u>, and <u>application.</u>

1. Principles for the researching a speech topic are included in the canon of disposition. <u>False. They're in the canon of invention. (108)</u>

2. Reference librarians are paid to help you during any stage of your research project. <u>True</u>. (108-109)

3. Commonly, students fail to budget as much research time as they need to get enough high quality information to create a good speech. <u>True</u>. 108)

4. Primary sources are those you consult first. <u>False. They come from sources directly involved in the event</u>. (110-112)

5. A piece of jewelry created by a Navajo craftsman is a primary source. <u>True</u>. (110)

6. Textbooks, scholarly analysis, and critical reviews are examples of secondary sources. <u>True</u>. (113)

7. Adding international and ethnic presses to your speech will cause your audience to distrust you. <u>False. Adding international and ethnic presses can offer perspective and alternative voices to be heard</u>. (114)

8. Interviewing a communication student to find out what needs to be improved in the college's communication department is a way of using a lay or peer source. <u>True</u>. (111)

9. Since a telephone interview is rarely as effective as a face-to-face interview, don't use one unless you must. <u>False. With careful preparation, they can be similarly effective</u>. (111-112)

10. Any lecture used in a classroom speech should have been attended live, to get the full effect of the event. <u>False. Many types of lectures and performances are recorded and effective as sources</u>. (112)

11. Wikipedia should never be used as a source for a classroom speech. <u>False. Although some sources are questionable, it is a good place to start.</u> (115)

12. Information found on The Internet should be evaluated critically. <u>True</u>. (116)

13. Search engines are web pages hand picked by humans and classified by subject. <u>False. That's a subject directory</u>. (116)

14. The invisible web refers to documents in specialized databases that are not linked to other web pages. <u>True.</u> (116)

15. Many databases charge a fee or require you to register before you can access their information. <u>True</u>. (116)

16. The Invisible Web includes millions of specialized databases that are not listed on subject directories but are visible to search engine spiders. <u>False. Spiders can't see them</u>. (116)

17. One difference between subject directories and search engines is that information on search engines is hand-picked by humans whereas materials in subject directories are collected by robots called spiders. <u>False. It's the other way around</u>. (116)

18. If you must choose between two equal websites, choose the one that's better organized. <u>True</u>. (117)

19. A domain suffix such as .edu or .gov helps you assess the credibility of the source. <u>True</u>. (115)

20. Many Internet sites contain plagiarized materials. <u>True</u>. (117)

21. OPAC stands for Online Public Academic Code. <u>False. Online Public Access Catalog</u>. (109)

22. When you search an online catalog, you can pretty much use the search strategies you use on search engines like google. <u>False. OPACs are less flexible</u>. (109)

23. When you do a computer search for a book, you can search for the title, the author, or the topic. <u>True</u>. (109)

24. Wikipedia is a new style encyclopedia that features community-generated knowledge. You can add or correct entries you find there. <u>True</u>. (115)

25. The *Congressional Digest* is a government publication that contains summaries of actual speeches given on the floor of Congress. <u>False. It looks at a single controversial issue each month</u>. (113)

26. The "elite media" are expensive newspapers and magazines used predominately by wealthy, influential business and government leaders. <u>False. They carry in-depth stories often used by smaller papers</u>. (114)

27. Using note cards can help you avoid cut-and-paste plagiarism. <u>True</u>. (119-120)

28. You use source cards to record bibliographic information. <u>True</u>. (119)

29. Using a photocopier to record research findings is as effective as using note cards for some people. <u>True</u>. (122)

30. When you use a mind map to record your ideas, it is important to keep the entire map on a single page. <u>False. Sometimes it helps to use a separate page for each point</u>. (119)

31. A good place to begin academic Internet research is with an online tutorial. <u>True</u>. (123)

32. Where you look online for information should depend on what kind of research you are doing. <u>True</u>. (111)

33. *Vital Speeches of the Day* and *Sports Illustrated* are both periodicals.
<u>True</u>. (113)

MULTIPLE CHOICE: These questions test <u>knowledge, comprehension, application, and evaluation.</u>

1. When formulating a research plan, you should NOT ___
   a. Analyze your topic.
   b. Budget enough time to research.
   c. Make use of the reference librarian.
   d. <u>Use library books for every topic you research</u>. (108-109)
   e. Identify key terms for your topic.

2. Which of these suggestions is the best way to avoid drowning in data?
   a. Do no more than four hours of research on the topic.
   b. Use only library sources like books and newspapers.
   c. Make critical evaluation a part of your plan from the very beginning. (111)
   d. Keep a running list of all the sources you search.
   e. Use a variety of credible sources.

3. Which is NOT a primary source?
   a. A diary written by a woman traveling in a covered wagon.
   b. A book of poetry by e. e. cummings.
   c. A newsreel showing a prison in Siberia.
   d. The Empire State Building.
   e. A movie review by Roger Ebert. (110)

4. Secondary sources are _____
   a. one step removed from the persons or events under study. (110-112)
   b. the materials you find in print.
   c. not produced at the time the event took place.
   d. just about the same value as primary sources.
   e. always associated with interviewees.

5. Drawing from your personal experiences is _____
   a. not recommended in the text.
   b. less believable than something from a book would be.
   c. useful in demonstration or how-to speeches. (108)
   d. essential for every topic.
   e. a secondary source.

6. Dr. Vered Braun has written and spoken extensively about the history of Israel. She would be a(n) _____ source for an interview.
   a. lay and primary
   b. primary and expert
   c. expert and secondary (110)
   d. peer and secondary

7. Which is NOT a tip for conducting a successful interview?
   a. Give the interviewee an idea of your topic in advance.
   b. Be on time.
   c. Be spontaneous; let the interview "happen." (111-112)
   d. Read your notes back to the interviewee so she or he can correct them.
   e. Ask permission if you want to tape the interview.

8. Which of these is NOT characteristic of the Invisible Web.
   a. They include specialized databases.
   b. The material on them cannot be seen by search engine spiders.
   c. All the materials on them are free. (116)
   d. InfoTrac College Edition is included.
   e. They are not linked to other Web pages.

9. The _____ suffixes such as .com or .gov _____
    a. URL . . . tell you whether or not the site is a blog.
    b. Web . . . link you to a responsible agency.
    c. rating . . . give you an idea of the quality of the information on the site.
    d. domain . . . indicate the provider's primary purpose and tax status. (119)

10. Which of the following is most important for evaluating Internet sources?
    a. Make sure the information is free.
    b. Use global sources.
    c. Consider the source. (116-117)
    d. Use only .edu and .gov sources.
    e. Make sure the information is organized well.

11. To be sure the information you get on The Internet is valid, you should do all BUT _____
    a. Be sure the information is free. (117)
    b. Look for a site rating.
    c. Determine the purpose of a site.
    d. Try to assess the bias of the site.
    e. Check the material against material you've found in other sources.

12. Primary sources include:
    a. A Tiffany engagement ring.
    b. "The Diary of Anne Frank".
    c. An old *People* magazine.
    d. All of these.
    e. "a" and "b" only. (119)

13. Collections and summaries of information on thousands of topics are called _____
    a. books.
    b. encyclopedias. (114)
    c. dictionaries.
    d. statistical sources.
    e. digests.

14. ____ is the community-created online encyclopedia that allows anyone, even you, to add or correct information on it.
    a. Wicktionary
    b. Www.fedstats.gov
    c. Merriam-Webster Online
    d. Wikipedia (115)
    e. Grolier's Encyclopedia Online

15. A monthly periodical featuring pro and con arguments surrounding controversial issues is (the)
    _____
    a. *Statistical Abstract of the United States.*
    b. *Congressional Digest.* (113)
    c. *Reader's Guide to Periodical Literature.*
    d. *New York Times Index.*
    e. Microsoft *Encarta.*

16. Newspapers such as the *New York Times* and the *Washington Post* are called _____ because they are influential, have reputations for good reporting, and are widely cited.
    a. <u>the elite media</u> (114)
    b. primary documents
    c. indexed papers
    d. syndicated
    e. opinion shapers

17. _____ is a monthly publication that translates, edits, and excerpts materials from papers outside the United States.
    a. *The Socialist Worker*
    b. *The International Press*
    c. <u>*The World Press Review*</u> (114)
    d. *The Reader's Guide to Periodical Literature*
    e. The *New York Times Index*

18. Which is NOT named as an advantage of the note card method of recording information?
    a. It is the most structured way to do research.
    b. <u>It takes less time than other methods.</u> (119)
    c. It can help you avoid cut-and-paste plagiarism.
    d. Cards are small enough to handle easily.
    e. You can shuffle the cards into piles with one for each main point and supporting materials.

19. If you use photocopied materials in speeches, it is helpful to have a _____ to emphasize ideas.
    a. note card
    b. computer
    c. <u>highlighter</u> (122)
    d. bibliography
    e. mind map

FILL IN THE BLANK

1. Librarians who are paid to help you find information are called _____ librarians. <u>reference</u> (110)

2. _____ sources are first hand; they come from people directly involved in events at the time they take place. <u>Primary</u> (112)

3. People who know about a subject because of in-depth study (like scholars who study single parent families) or because of occupational experience (like park rangers) are _____. <u>experts</u> (113)

4. Google, Yahoo! and Ask are_____." <u>Search engines</u> (116)

5. Most of the Web's total documents lie in _____. <u>Specialized Databases</u> (116)

6. A suffix in the URL such as .gov or .mil is called a _____. <u>domain</u> (119)

7. OPAC stands for _____ . <u>Online Public Access Catalog</u> (109)

8. A new style, user-created online encyclopedia is called _____. <u>Wikipedia</u> (115)

9. Library materials that are issued once a week, month, quarter, or year are called _____. <u>periodicals</u> (113)

10. Three ways to record your information are _____, _____, and _____. <u>note cards, photocopies or printouts of downloaded materials, mind maps</u>. (122)

11. The note cards you use for your bibliographic information are called _____ cards. <u>source</u> (119

12. Note cards you use to record ideas, statistics, examples, quotations, and the like are called _____ cards . <u>information </u>(119).

SHORT ANSWER

1. List three ways that every library book is catalogued. (<u>subject, author, title</u>) (120)

2. Explain what's meant by the term "elite media." (<u>Newspapers like the *New York Times* or the *Washington Post* that have good reputations and generate articles that smaller newspapers use.</u>) (123)

3. List and explain five ways to evaluate Internet sources. (<u>Source content: intent or purpose; bias; timeliness; accuracy; originality; and organization.</u>) (117)

4. List and explain three ways to record information you find during your research. (<u>1) Note cards-- standard sized cards with separate cards for information and sources; 2) mind maps--with a combination of drawings and web-like recording of information; and 3) photocopies--with sources identified and highlighters used for marking important material.</u>) (124-127)

5. Identify three different types of primary sources and explain how they could be used in your speech.(110)

ESSAY QUESTIONS

1. Explain the difference between primary and secondary sources and give examples of interview, Internet, and library resources in both categories.
2. You decide that information from interviews would best support your topic. Explain how you would identify sources to interview, how you would set up your interview(s), and how you could use electronic technology to gain access to interviewees who might otherwise be unavailable to you.

3. You get a work study job in the campus library. A student, who is clueless about research, comes in panicky about her upcoming speech. Describe how you'd go about explaining ways she can use electronic sources effectively--including Internet and library resources--in conducting research for her speech materials.

4. Your roommate is writing a speech and needs your help. Explain to your roommate how to use the Internet to yield the best results. Include guidelines that someone who isn't quite skilled in Internet research could use.

Chapter 8

CHOOSING SUPPORTING MATERIALS

TRUE-FALSE: These questions test <u>knowledge</u>, <u>comprehension</u>, and <u>application.</u>

1. Our cultural values affect what evidence we accept or reject. <u>True</u>. (131)

2. Global warming supporters and detractors can come to widely different conclusions, based on the evidence they choose to accept. <u>True</u>. (130)

3. A major test of factual information is that it be verified by more than one observer. <u>True</u>. (131)

4. A definition that is generally accepted by most members of a society is considered a fact. <u>True</u>. (131)

5. "Recycling is the most important issue facing our community today" is an example of a fact. <u>False. It's an opinion</u>. (138)

6. The details give facts; the choice of words make these facts easy to visualize. <u>True</u>. (132)

7. In general, statistics involve your audience and are very intesting to most. <u>False. In general, statistics do not involve your audience, and too many can be boring</u>. (141)

8. It's wise to check your facts in a variety of sources. <u>True</u>. (131)

9. Skillful use of examples may enhance your personal credibility with the audience. <u>True</u>. (133)

10. Using examples from your own experience hurts your credibility, because your audience thinks you haven't taken the time to do outside research. <u>False. They can help your credibility</u>. (133)

11. Hypothetical examples are rarely useful because people want to know that something really happened. <u>False. Sometimes they are more appropriate than real examples</u>. (134)

12. Speakers most commonly string together four or five brief examples to illustrate a main point. <u>False. The text suggests two or three</u>. (133)

13. The many details in extended example help the audience form emotional connections with the topic. <u>True</u>. (135)

14. Quoting culturally accepted authorities is one way of getting around the quesiton, "Who says?" <u>False. It is one way of answering this quesion</u>. (137)

15. Experts are never biased. That's what makes them experts. <u>Fasle. Experts are often biased</u>. (138)

16. It is rarely appropriate to paraphrase the words of an authoritative source. <u>False. When the quotation is long, it's often better to summarize</u>. (145)

17. A piece of art can be used as supporting material for a persuasive argument. <u>True</u>. (138)

18. When using testimony from a qualified but relatively unknown source, you need to cite the source's credibility. <u>True</u>. (148)

19. When speaking to middle school students, citing a young, attractive movie star who strongly believes in sexual abstinence is probably more effective than citing a middle-aged teacher or pastor who tells young people to postpone sexual activity. <u>True</u>. (137)

20. During your speech on teen arson, you quote your childhood friend who once lit a pile of leaves on fire. <u>False. This is peer testimony</u>. (139)

21. It is wise for Camille to quote philosophers her audience would recognize as great in her speech on honesty. <u>True</u>. (139)

22. Skillful use of statistics may increase your credibility, because in the U.S., people tend to like numbers. <u>True</u>. (131)

23. Using an exact number such as "234,569 families in this state have cocker spaniels" is advisable for it helps listeners get exact information. <u>False. The number changes almost immediately</u>. (141)

24. Because numbers are "hard" evidence, it's difficult to manipulate them. <u>False. Numbers can easily be deceptive</u>. (141-142)

25. It's often advisable to use visual aids to present statistics. <u>True</u>. (143)

26. It generally does not matter if your statistics are several years old. <u>False. Statistics should generally be up-to-date</u>. (144)

27. Making a comparison is also called making an analogy. <u>True</u>. (144)

28. "All the world's a stage" is an example of a literal analogy. <u>False. It's an example of a figurative analogy</u>. (144)

MULTIPLE CHOICE: These questions test <u>knowledge</u>, <u>comprehension</u>, and <u>application.</u>

1. How can some scientists think global warming is a huge risk to the world and other scientists believe other issues, like pure drinking water, are more pressing?
   a. They come from two different countries: the United States and Denmark.
   b. One man is smarter than the other.
   c. <u>Each man uses different supporting materials to support his conclusions.</u> (130-131)
   d. One uses biased materials; the other chooses more objective data.
   e. They are both blinded by their assumptions.

2. Which is NOT true about facts?
   a. In this culture, we like facts.
   b. Explanations are a form of factual information.
   c. Dictionary definitions are considered facts.
   d. <u>Facts, by definition, are true even if only one person observes them.</u> (131)
   e. A vivid description of a Navajo rug can be considered factual.

3. Which of these statements contains opinion rather than fact?
   a. George Washington died in 1799.
   b. <u>Washington was the wisest choice for our first president</u>. (145)
   c. Washington's horse was shot out from under him.
   d. Washington married a widow with two children.
   e. During his presidency, the cotton gin was invented.

4. Which is NOT true about examples?
   a. They attract attention.
   b. They can enhance the speaker's credibility.
   c. Longer examples are called narratives.
   d. <u>Hypothetical examples are more persuasive.</u> (134)
   e. They help listeners identify emotionally with the topic.

5. A hypothetical example is _____
   a. more persuasive.
   b. unethical because it's false.
   c. <u>often useful when dealing with sensitive issues</u>. (134)
   d. brief, by definition.
   e. the same as a narrative.

6. Focus groups in Kenya named _____ as the most convincing type of support.
   a. hypothetical examples
   b. vivid descriptions
   c. cultural proverbs
   d. percentages
   e. <u>personal examples</u> (134)

7. Using unexpected testimony can be powerful in persuasive speeches because
   a. the testimony is misleading.
   b. <u>listeners will reason that someone willing to go against his peers has probably thought through his own opinions carefully</u> (138)
   c. listeners will be unfamiliar with these sources.
   d. culturally accepted sources are more important than personally accepted sources.
   e. they define identity and reflect people's needs.

8. In the course of your research for a speech about the space program you find a quotation by a rocket scientist who worked on the first moon launch. Using his words in your speech is _____
   a. factual.
   b. a composite example.
   c. lay testimony.
   d. paraphrasing.
   e. <u>expert testimony (137)</u>

9. If you quote a teen gang member who states his opinions about gangs, what type of support are you using?
   a. hypothetical example
   b. narrative
   c. literal analogy
   d. <u>peer testimony</u> (139)
   e. expert testimony

10. Quoting a well-known conservative who supports a well-known liberal position can be powerful evidence because _____
    a. it agrees with the "conventional wisdom."
    b. it gives a voice to an opinion other conservatives probably share but are afraid to say.
    c. listeners reason if she is willing to go against her party, she has probably thought through her opinion carefully. (239)
    d. people would probably not hear this opinion otherwise.

11. Eleanor quotes Erasmus's opinion in her speech on loyalty. This will be effective only if _____
    a. she uses a direct quotation, not a paraphrase.
    b. the audience sees Erasmus as an authoritative source. (137)
    c. Erasmus had written a well-known book on loyalty.
    d. he speaks for other philosophers of his day.

12. Which is true about statistics _____?
    a. They are scientifically derived and thus hard to manipulate.
    b. They are never intentionally misleading.
    c. They may increase a speaker's credibility since they are commonly use in the US. (141)
    d. They are by nature more credible than examples.

13. Enumeration is another name for _____
    a. a count. (141)
    b. statistics.
    c. quantification.
    d. percentages.

14. The mean grade point average in a certain department is 2.94; this tells you that _____
    a. half the grade points lie above and half lie below 2.94.
    b. 2.94 is the average grade point. (141-142)
    c. some very low grade points probably skewed the figure.
    d. 2.94 is the most common grade point of the students.

15. The relationship of the part to the whole, represented by the number 100, is _____
    a. quantification.
    b. the mean.
    c. the median.
    d. a percentage. (142)
    e. the rate of increase.

16. Speakers often use ratios when _____
    a. the percentage is very small. (142)
    b. the baseline figure for the rate of increase is unknown.
    c. the statistics are out of date.
    d. the source of the statistics are unknown.
    e. the rate of decrease is minimal.

17. Two good ways to make numerical data more understandable is to _____
    a. use a visual aid and compare the number to something your listeners already know. (141)
    b. use exact numbers and explain every factor that might skew the mean.
    c. use rates of increase more often than you use ratios, and use visual aids.
    d. compare the number to something already in their experience, and enumerate.

18. _____are useful when you want to connect what is familiar with what is lesser known.
    a. <u>Analogies</u> (144-145)
    b. Contrasts
    c. Statistics
    d. Hypothetical examples
    e. Quotations from experts

19. Showing how one college excels in an academic area over another college is using what type of support?
    a. figurative analogy
    b. <u>contrast</u> (145)
    c. literal comparison
    d. hypothetical example
    e. expert testimony

20. A speaker who says that the human mind is like a filing cabinet with different areas for different functions is using what type of support?
    a. <u>figurative analogy</u> (144-145)
    b. contrast
    c. literal comparison
    d. hypothetical example
    e. opinion

21. Which is true about using comparisons? _____
    a. the items must be alike in essential details.
    b. <u>the comparison must be clear and sensible.</u> (145)
    c. the listeners must be able to see differences as well as likenesses.
    d. the comparison must be made between two familiar things.

FILL IN THE BLANK: These questions test <u>knowledge</u>, <u>comprehension</u>, and <u>application.</u>

1. A speaker who uses a _____ example often creates a composite of several different people who are representative of the type of person she is discussing. <u>hypothetical</u> (134-135)

2. A _____ example has actually taken place. <u>real</u> (139)

3. President Obama said, "Change will not come if we wait for some other person or some other time." This is a _____. <u>direct quotation</u> (148)

4. Giving a count is called _____. <u>enumeration</u> (141)

5. The _____ is the middle number in a set of numbers that have been arranged into a ranked order with half the numbers above and half below. <u>median</u> (142)

6. _____ are specific illustrations that enrich your speech. <u>Examples</u> (132-134)

7. Factual information is judged as being _____ or _____, _____ or _____. <u>true, false, accurate, inaccurate</u> (131)

SHORT ANSWER: These questions test <u>knowledge</u>, <u>comprehension</u>, and <u>application.</u>

1. Identify three of the five tests for using sources. (What is the person's expertise? Is the person recognized as an expert by others? Is the layperson supporting a similar opinion? Are the words taken out of context? Is the quotation accurate<u>?)</u> (138)

2. List and explain three tests for examples. (<u>Representativeness--is it typical, representative, or probable? Sufficiency -- are enough cases represented? Truth -- did or could something like it have happened?)</u> (136)

3. Define enumeration and give two tips for using it effectively in speeches. (<u>Enumeration means counting. Round the numbers up or down and make them vivid by relating them to something already familiar to the audience.)</u> (141)

4. Distinguish between figurative analogies and literal analogies. (<u>Figurative analogies or metaphors highlight similarities between dissimilar things, and listeners must make the connections; literal analogies point out similarities between similar things.</u>) (144-145)

5. What is the difference between a hypothetical example and a fabricated story? <u>A hypothetical example is an imagined example that the speaker reveals is imagined. A fabricated story is an imagined story that is passed off as real.</u> (135)

ESSAY QUESTIONS: These questions test <u>application</u>, <u>analysis</u>, <u>synthesis</u>, and <u>application.</u>

1. Explain why listening to speeches with lots of examples is generally more interesting than hearing one full only of facts and statistics. Then make a list of guidelines for various ways to use examples effectively in speeches.

2. One way to tie into cultural beliefs and values is to use testimony or quotations. Explain how you might use testimony or quotations in a speech about tolerance.

3. Discuss the strengths and weaknesses of numerical data, and provide guidelines for using numbers effectively in your speeches.

4. Identify at least four makes or models of cars whose name is a metaphor (example: Jaguar, Dart). Beside each car name, write several characteristics you think the auto maker wants potential buyers to associate with that make of car. Then, put in rank order (from least effectiveness to most effective) the way the four metaphors appeal to you personally (for example, would you rather have a sleek, fast, graceful jaguar or ride in an efficient, fast, powerful dart); explain your answer.

5. Revisit the idea of hypothetical example versus fabricated story. Give an example of each and discuss why one was acceptable (if it was) and one was not. Is it ever ok to use a fabricated story in a speech? What are the ethical considerations in using hypothetical examples?

Chapter 9

ORGANIZING YOUR SPEECH

TRUE-FALSE: These questions test <u>knowledge</u>, <u>comprehension</u>, <u>application</u>, and <u>evaluation.</u>

1. Guidelines for organization or arrangement are found within the Roman canon of invention. <u>False. It's the canon of disposition or arrangement</u>. (151-155)

2. You should start from the introduction and work straight through to the conclusion when organizing your speech. <u>False. You should organize the body of your speech before you write out the introduction</u>. (151)

3. Our minds remember material better when it's blocked into 7-9 major units. <u>False. 3-7 units is better</u>. (151)

4. Begin to organize your main points by returning to your thesis statement. <u>True</u>. (151)

5. If you've done your research well, the logical flow of points will be evident in every speech you create. <u>False. The logical flow is only apparent for some topics</u>. (157)

6. The most common organizational pattern is the chronological pattern. <u>False. It is the topical pattern</u>. (155)

7. The chronological pattern is especially good for organizing biographical speeches. <u>True</u>. (151-152).

8. The topical pattern is best for explaining a cycle, such as the sleep cycle. <u>False. The chronological pattern is better</u>. (151-152)

9. When your main ideas show a right-to-left or top-to-bottom direction, you are using a wave pattern. <u>False. This is a spatial pattern</u>. (153)

10. A speaker from a culture that believes it is futile to fight fate will probably choose a problem-solution organizational pattern. <u>False. This pattern is based on the belief that we solve problems through our efforts</u>. (154)

11. The cause-effect pattern is sometimes contained within the problem-solution pattern. <u>True</u>. (154)

12. Because you are advocating a specific solution, the problem-solution pattern is only used to organize persuasive speeches. <u>False. It can also be used for informative speeches</u>. (154)

13. After you've gathered your materials, you must search for the one way to organize your speech. <u>False. You have several options for the same topic</u>. (155)

14. Cheryl Jorgensen-Earp identified a number of less direct, more "organic" ways that women commonly organize their speeches. <u>True</u>. (160)

15. According to the text, Martin Luther King, Jr.'s "I Have a Dream" speech is the most familiar wave pattern speech. <u>True</u>. (160)

16. The "crest" in the wave pattern must restate the theme; you cannot introduce another major point as the crest. False. Repeating a phrase is not a requirement. (160)

17. The spiral pattern is often useful for speeches based on points that build in dramatic intensity. True. (161)

18. The star pattern is useful for a speaker who uses the same topic with a number of different audiences. True. (162)

19. To avoid confusion, use only one pattern of organization in your speech.. False. You can combine patterns within your speech. (163)

20. A circular pattern or wheel is typical in Japan. False, it is typical in Kenya. (158)

21. A speech on the history of the Ford Mustang and a speech on making mac n' cheese use the same patterns of organization. True. (151-152)

MULTIPLE CHOICE: These questions test knowledge, comprehension, and application.

1. Principles for organizing your speech are found in the canon of _____
   a. invention.
   b. disposition. (151-156)
   c. style.
   d. memory.
   e. delivery.

2. What is one "secret" for making a good business presentation?
   a. Organized ideas are easier to understand. (151)
   b. Working hard on your presentation will guarantee success.
   c. Taking a mental exit occasionally during your preparation relieves stress.
   d. Audiences like "stream of consciousness" presentations.

3. The first part of your speech to plan is the _____
   a. introduction.
   b. body. (151)
   c. conclusion.
   d. connectives.
   e. content outline.

4. Which is NOT a tip for organizing the main points of a speech?
   a. Limit the number of points to seven. (151)
   b. Return to the tentative central idea and begin to flesh it out.
   c. Arrange supporting data under the main points.
   d. Put the points in order for maximum effectiveness.
   e. Choose the pattern that best meets the topic, the purpose, and the situation.

5. Andrea wants to describe the public areas of Buckingham Palace. She should probably consider a _____ organizational pattern first.
   a. topical
   b. chronological
   c. spatial (162)
   d. causal
   e. star

6. Which is NOT an element of a speech in the Merina tribe of Madagascar?
    a. a period of excuses and expression of inability to speak
    b. a formula thanking God, the leaders, and listeners
    c. a proposal supported by proverbs, illustrations, and poems
    d. main points supported by facts and enumeration (158)
    e. a blessing on the audience

7. What is the organizational pattern, given this central idea? "The graduating class will need courage, wisdom, and a sense of humor."
    a. topical (155)
    b. chronological
    c. spatial
    d. causal

8. How would a speech about the life of the president BEST be organized?
    a. chronologically, from his birth until now
    b. topically, according to his major accomplishments
    c. pro-con, contrasting the views of his supporters and his detractors
    d. spatially, illustrating the travels he's made during his presidency
    e. depends on your purpose and supporting materials (151-156)

9. Alternative patterns such as the wave historically have NOT been commonly used by _____
    a. speakers in Madagascar.
    b. women speakers.
    c. members of ethnic minority groups.
    d. CEOs of major corporations. (160-164)
    e. Kenyan speakers.

10. Martin Luther King's speech, "I Have a Dream," is an example of a _____ pattern.
    a. wave (160-161)
    b. topical
    c. spiral
    d. star
    e. spatial

11. Hy wants to share anecdotes of the immigration of the founders of his 100-year old synagogue. Each one is more intense than the previous. According to the text, the _____ pattern is very good for this type of narrative speech.
    a. topical
    b. wave
    c. spatial
    d. star
    e. spiral (161-162)

12. The central idea that binds together the major points in the star pattern is the _____
    a. thematic circle. (162)
    b. preview.
    c. organic whole.
    d. peak moment.
    e. general purpose.

13. Process speeches or speeches which feature steps that follow one another in a logical sequence use which pattern?
    a. spatial
    b. <u>chronological</u> (151-152)
    c. topical
    d. causal
    e. star

14. In which of these lists are all items written as parallel points?
    a. Who suffers from brain cancer?, The symptoms of brain cancer, Types, What can you do?
    b. What kind of dog is best?, How many breeds are there?, How can you adopt a dog?, Benefits
    c. Elephants are poached for their ivory, Groups in Africa help save these elephants, What can you do to help?
    d. <u>TOMS is an organization that seeks to help others., When you buy a pair of TOMS another is donated to people in need of shoes., TOMS can be purchased from many online and in-person retailers, TOMS continues to expand by now offering eyewear and eyecare.</u> (157)
    e. Epstein-barr virus affects millions of people., Most people are immune to long-term infection., Symptoms, Long-term effects

15. Using words such as "first," "next," and "finally" in your speech are examples of using what?
    a. a transition
    b. <u>a signpost</u> (159)
    c. an internal summary
    d. an internal preview
    e. a parallel point

16. Carrie says, "Experts say that there are three main reasons for loss of retail merchandise, called shrink: internal theft, external theft, and shipping mistakes. First we will talk about …" Carrie's first sentence is an example of what part of a speech?
    a. a transition
    b. a signpost
    c. an internal summary
    d. <u>an internal preview</u> (159-160)
    e. a parallel point

MATCHING: These questions test <u>application.</u>

<u>Directions</u>: Match the organizational patterns to the central idea. (Some may be used more than once.)

    a. topical (155)
    b. spatial (153)
    c. chronological (151)
    d. causal (153)
    e. problem-solution (154)

1. Today we will look at what causes breast cancer, then examine the effects it has on the patient. <u>d. causal</u>

2. When travelling internationally, keep the "three Ps" in mind: Patience, practice, and persistence. <u>a. topical</u>

3. The museum has four floors, each with a North and South wing. b. spatial

4. There are five stages in the development of relationships. c. chronological

5. Smaller companies are leaving New York for many reasons; this has serious implications for the city. d. causal

6. Today we will look at Robert E. Lee's early years, his war career, and his final years.
   c. chronological

7. Robert E. Lee was a brilliant general, a great educator, and a generous human being. a. topical

8. Parking on campus is not going to get any better without identifying deficits in the current system, followed by determining a workable way to provide spaces for students, faculty, and staff. e. problem-solution

FILL IN THE BLANK: These questions test application.

1. You want to look at both sides of the controversial issue of legalizing drugs; the _____ pattern is excellent for this. pro-con (154)

2. Your topic is urban legends. Your main points are: horror stories, campus legends, and tales of government bungling. Your organizational pattern is _____. topical; the points could be in any order (155)

3. Sojouner Truth's "Ain't I am Woman?" speech uses a repetitive theme and features examples leading to a crest of emotions. This is the _____ pattern. wave (160-161)

4. A speech that's organized in a _____ pattern builds in intensity with each point more important or more dramatic than the previous one. spiral (161)

SHORT ANSWER QUESTIONS: These questions test application.

1. Using your most recent speech for your example, list the main points as parallel points. (Students should list their main points in parallel ways, either listing all points as questions or all points as declarative sentences.) (157)

2. Using the following main points, write an internal preview and an internal summary:

   RETAIL MERCHANDISE LOSS
   I. Internal shrink occurs when there is intentional theft or accidental removal of merchandise by an employee.
   II. External shrink occurs when someone not affiliated with the company removes unpaid merchandise from the store.
   III. Allocation shrink occurs when there is a mistake in what units a store is given or recorded to have been given.

(Students will write a preview and summary similar to the following examples. INTERNAL PREVIEW: "Retail merchandise loss can occur in three ways: through internal shrink, external shrink, and allocation shrink. First we will talk about ..." INTERNAL SUMMARY: "As I have demonstrated, retail merchandise loss can happen due to unpaid removal of merchandise by an employee, unpaid removal of merchandise by a customer, or due to allocation issues.") (159-160)

ESSAY QUESTIONS: These questions test <u>application</u> and <u>synthesis.</u>

1. You've been asked to nominate one of your friends for an important office. You decide to use an alternative pattern to organize your speech. Sketch out two different speeches using two alternative patterns showing ways you could nominate your friend.

2. Choose a broad topic area (some examples: vacations, your university or college, parenting) and then discuss how you could organize various speeches on aspects of that topic using at least four different linear organizational patterns described in the text. (For example, I might choose a broad topic such as health and then I'd plan: 1) a biographical speech about a famous doctor, using a chronological pattern; 2) an investigation of the causes of leukemia and effects of the disease on the body, using a causal pattern; 3) a descriptive "tour" of the new hospital in town, using a spatial pattern; 4) an investigation of the use of the drug Ritalin, using a pro-con pattern.)

3. The connective devices used in a speech can help the listeners keep their place as you talk. Develop an outline that shows which connectives should be where in a typical classroom speech. Discuss how the placement of these connectives will assist your audience.

Chapter 10

Introductions and Conclusions

TRUE-FALSE: These questions test <u>knowledge</u>, <u>comprehension</u>, and <u>application</u> .

1. The first part of an introduction is establishing your credibility to speak on the topic. <u>False. First, draw attention to the topic.</u> (173-174)

2. "When was the last time you slept at least eight hours at a stretch? Jose? Marylin?" is an example of a rhetorical question. <u>False. It's a participatory question that invites specific people to answer</u>. (169-170)

3. Vivid descriptions engage listeners mentally. <u>True</u>. (170)

4. If you use a description to gain attention, make sure it describes a real, not an imaginary, event. <u>False. You can describe either</u>. (170)

5. A quotation from your grandmother might gain attention as well as a quotation from a better known person. <u>True</u>. (170-171)

6. You should save audio or visual aids for the body of your speech to support your major ideas. <u>False. VAs are often good openers</u>. (170)

7. Jokes work well almost any time, because people like to laugh. <u>False. They may or may not be successful</u>. (172)

8. Beginning with a current event is a good way to establish common ground with an audience filled with strangers. <u>True</u>. (172)

9. Examples are generally better than statistics as a way to gain attention and involve listeners emotionally. <u>True</u>. (171)

10. Statistics are rarely effective as attention getters, because they're inevitably dry and boring. <u>False. They can be startling</u>. (171)

11. Before giving a speech in an unfamiliar organization, a good speaker finds out about the group's distinctive culture and then adapts her introduction accordingly. <u>True</u>. (172-173)

12. It's important in the introduction to link the topic to your listeners' lives and interests. <u>True</u>. (173-174)

13. Connecting a topic to a larger social issue is a good way to preview the topic. <u>False. It's a good way to relate to the audience</u>. (173)

14. Establishing one's credibility to speak on a topic can be optional. <u>True</u>. (174)

15. Even if you don't have experience with your topic, you can still be a credible speaker because of research you've done. <u>True</u>. (174)

16. Credibility is not fixed; you can be highly credible in one situation and minimally credible in another. <u>True</u>. (174)

17. A Navajo (Diné) speaker typically begins by previewing the main ideas he or she will cover. <u>False. These speakers begin by establishing their personal and clan identity</u>. (170)

18. The preview is a statement of some form of your thesis statement. <u>True</u>. (174-175)

19. If you plan your introduction and speech body carefully, the conclusion is not so important, because you've already demonstrated your credibility. <u>False. A poor conclusion can lessen a positive image</u>. (183)

20. Sometimes your transition to the conclusion can be nonverbal instead of verbal. <u>True</u>. (175-176)

21. Referring to the introduction provides psychological closure for listeners. <u>True</u>. (176-177)

22. To end your speech memorably, you can use similar material that you used to gain attention in the introduction. <u>True</u>. (177-178)

23. Reviewing your main ideas satisfies the, "tell them what you've told them" axiom. <u>True</u>. (176)

24. Using words like *next* or *additionally* signals the speaker you are coming to the end of your speech. <u>False. Using words like *finally* or *to conclude* signals the ending of your speech</u>. (176)

25. Ending a speech with "that's it" provides psychological closure for your audience. <u>False. Psychological closure links to an element of the introduction</u>. (176-177)

26. Many of the strategies used in the introduction can be used in the conclusion. <u>True</u>. (177-178)

27. To evaluate a conclusion, ask yourself how well the speech signals the end of the speech, reviews main ideas, provides psychological closure, and ends memorably. <u>True</u>. (178-179)

MULTIPLE CHOICE: These questions test <u>knowledge</u>, <u>comprehension</u>, <u>application</u>, and <u>evaluation.</u>

1. A good introduction answers all these listener questions EXCEPT _____
   a. What's this all about?
   b. Why does this matter to me?
   <u>c. How long will this take?</u> (169)
   d. Why listen to this speaker?
   e. What are the main ideas of the speech?

2. Which is NOT part of the introduction?
   a. a statement of the central idea
   b. establishing why you are competent to speak on the topic
   c. drawing attention to the topic
   d. showing the audience why they should listen to this topic
   <u>e. statistics to explain your main points</u> (169)

3. Which is a participatory question?
   a. When was the last time you had a relaxing day in the country?
   b. Who is your favorite basketball player?
   c. Who can tell me the name of the last president to die in office? (169)
   d. Do you ever wonder where your activity funds go?
   e. What motivates you to get out and volunteer?

4. _____ is an especially good way to invite the audience to respond internally to your topic.
   a. Asking a rhetorical question (168-169)
   b. Establishing your credibility
   c. Telling a joke
   d. Previewing your ideas
   e. Beginning with a visual aid

5. According to the text, these openings are especially effective for engaging the audience:
   a. rhetorical questions, statistics, and examples
   b. an intriguing question, reference to a current event, an example (172)
   c. quoting your grandmother, using an example, telling a joke
   d. statistics, jokes, current events
   e. visual aids, descriptions, a statistic

6. Which opening statement is best for a classroom speech about cloning?
   a. The purpose of my speech today is to tell you about the pros and cons of cloning.
   b. Hi. My name is Sam, and my topic today is cloning.
   c. Early in 1997, journalists flocked to England to see Dolly, a sheep who had been cloned there. (172-173)
   d. I came upon the most interesting topic in one of my science classes. It's the topic of cloning, and I'd like to tell you about it today.
   e. Hi. How's everybody doing today?

7. To answer the listener question "Why should I listen to this speech?" you must _____
   a. gain attention.
   b. relate to your listeners. (173)
   c. introduce your topic.
   d. establish personal credibility.
   e. preview your main ideas.

8. In her introduction to her speech about the prescription drug Ritalin, Maryssa tells her audience that she has a brother on Ritalin. She is _____
   a. gaining attention.
   b. relating to her listeners.
   c. personalizing her topic.
   d. establishing personal credibility. (174)
   e. previewing her main ideas.

9. "Today, we will first look at the problems associated with over-prescription of the drug Ritalin and then we'll look at some possible solutions" answers which of these listener questions?
   a. What's this about?
   b. Why should I listen?
   c. Why should I listen to you?
   d. What will you cover? (169)

10. In your conclusion, refer back to the introduction in order to _____
    a. <u>provide your listeners with psychological closure</u>. (176)
    b. end memorably.
    c. leave the audience in a positive frame of mind.
    d. increase your personal credibility.
    e. review your speech.

11. Using parallel structure:
    a. Provides psychological closure.
    b. Means if you start with a story, end with a story.
    c. Is an organizational form.
    d. Is not very effective for some audiences.
    e. <u>All but D</u>. (177)

12. In his conclusion, Eli says, "Today we've examined how to prepare *haminados*, when they are eaten, and how to eat them. This is an example of a _____
    a. signpost.
    b. transition statement.
    c. internal preview.
    d. internal summary.
    e. <u>review</u>. (176)

13. To signal you are coming to the end of your speech, do all BUT _____
    a. <u>Say, "in conclusion" or "finally."</u> (176)
    b. Use nonverbal actions.
    c. Pause and shift your posture.
    d. Use verbal cues.
    e. All of the above are creative ways to signal you are coming to the end of your speech.

14. Merilee says, "If you have ever sent or read a text while driving, please raise your hand." Merilee is using what kind of attention-getting strategy?
    a. a rhetorical question
    b. a vivid question
    c. <u>a participatory question</u> (196)
    d. an audience assessment
    e. a preview statement

FILL IN THE BLANK: These questions test <u>knowledge</u>, <u>comprehension</u>, and <u>application</u>.

1. When you ask a _____ question, you expect the audience to answer in their minds, not out loud. <u>rhetorical</u> (169)

2. The part of the introduction where you give some form of your thesis statement is the _____. <u>preview</u> (174-175)

3. The most common phrase, although perhaps not the most creative, used as a transition from the body to the conclusion of a speech is _____. <u>"in conclusion"</u> (176)

4. Using a rhetorical question in your conclusion is one way to _____. <u>End memorably</u>. (177)

5. "Tell the what you've told them" is a good axiom to keep in mind when preparing your ____. <u>review of main points</u> (176)
6. Using an element from your introduction to close your speech provides your audience with _____. <u>psychological closure</u>. (176-177)

7. _____ is the way of life of a specific organization, which includes its history, traditions, heroes, folklore, vocabulary, rituals, and ways of doing things. <u>Organizational culture</u> (172)

8. _____ ask for an overt response, such as a show of hands. <u>Participatory questions</u> (169)

SHORT ANSWER: These recall question tests <u>knowledge</u> and <u>comprehension</u>.

1. List and explain 4 different techniques to gain attention in your introduction. (Ask a question, provide a vivid description, begin with a quotation, use an audio or visual aid, tell a funny joke or story, refer to a current event, begin with an example, start with startling numbers.) (169)

2. List and explain the 4 parts of a conclusion. (Signal the ending, review main ideas, provide psychological closure, end memorably.) (177)

ESSAY QUESTIONS: These questions test <u>knowledge</u>, <u>comprehension</u>, and <u>application.</u>

1. Identify four listener questions that a good introduction attempts to answer. Then explain ways to answer each.

2. Discuss the important components in the introduction and the conclusion, and give examples of each.

3. Discuss at three methods a speaker can use to begin a speech. Give examples of each method, followed by the benefits and drawbacks of each.

4. Using your upcoming speech as a topic, write the text of three different attention-getters you could use, identifying the reasons you might choose each one.

Chapter 11

OUTLINING YOUR SPEECH

TRUE-FALSE: These questions test <u>knowledge</u>, <u>comprehension</u>, and <u>application.</u>

1. A heading provides a brief overview of your entire speech. <u>True</u>. (184)

2. A content outline is a synonym for a script, written out in outline form. <u>False. Outlines don't contain every word</u>. (184)

3. A skeleton is a good metaphor for a content outline. <u>True</u>. (184)

4. A content outline shows the speech's structural and logical elements. <u>True</u>. (184)

5. Outlines should include a heading that identifies your purpose and central idea. <u>True</u>. (184)

6. In content outlines, use an <u>A.</u> for your first point, an <u>a.</u> for your first subpoint, and an <u>(a)</u> for the subpoint that follows. <u>False. Alternate numbers and letters</u>. (185)

7. You should highlight information you want to emphasize on your content outline, and refer to it as you speak. <u>False. Make a speaking outline consisting of key words only</u>. (191-192)

8. Your speaking outline should be a key word outline. <u>True</u>. (189-190)

9. Writing your introduction word for word on your speaking outline is a good strategy for helping you get over your nervousness at first. <u>False. Use key words throughout</u>. (189-190)

10. A key word outline is a key factor in maintaining eye contact with your audience. <u>True</u>. (191)

11. Note cards have so many advantages over a speaking outline, that you should almost always use them instead. <u>False. Speaking outlines are fine</u>. (191-192)

12. To visualize your alternative pattern speech, it may be helpful first to sketch out a diagram of the pattern you've chosen. <u>True</u>. (194)

13. Because B. J. is more of a "right brain thinker," he is less likely to choose an alternative pattern. <u>False. It's the other way around</u>. 193)

14. Your cognitive style is unique to you; it's related to your brain hemispheric dominance. <u>True</u>. (193)

15. A linear form of outlining is right-brained. <u>False. It is more left-brained</u>. (193)

MULTIPLE CHOICE: These questions test <u>knowledge</u>, <u>comprehension</u>, and <u>application.</u>

1. The pharmacy student in introduction of the chapter found that the process of creating an outline _____
   a. was a waste of her time except for her most detailed speeches.
   b. was the major reason she didn't want to take the course.
   c. <u>helped her learn skills she could transfer to other courses. (183)</u>
   d. was most useful when she used a traditional organizational pattern.

262

2. When you create your content outline, first _____
   a. <u>identify your organizational pattern and major ideas</u>. (184)
   b. write out your introduction.
   c. write out the first point with all its supporting material.
   d. make a bibliography of all your references.
   e. write out a script of your speech.

3. _____ is NOT an essential part of an outline's heading according to the text.
   a. <u>The speaker's name</u>. (184)
   b. The finalized central idea
   c. The specific purpose statement
   d. A title
   e. A general purpose statement

4. Making one point (causes) about equally weighted with the second point (effects) is an example of the principle of _____
   a. <u>coordination</u>. (185-186)
   b. subordination.
   c. indentation.
   d. alternation.
   e. parallel points.

5. Content outlines should have all these elements EXCEPT _____
   a. an introduction, body, and conclusion.
   b. alternating numbers and letters.
   c. single sentence main points.
   d. <u>major ideas written out in phrases</u>. (184-189)
   e. written out transition statements.

6. Which outlining principle means to use a consistent pattern to vary numbers and letters?
   a. coordination.
   b. subordination.
   c. <u>alternation</u>. (185)
   d. parallel points.

7. Which is NOT a characteristic of a speaking outline?
   a. <u>Write major points in complete sentences</u>. (191-192)
   b. Write out your transition statements.
   c. Write out quotations completely.
   d. Use key words to jog your memory.
   e. Make it shorter than your content outline.

8. Key word outlines use full sentences in only two places:
   a. The introduction and the conclusion.
   b. <u>Transition statements and direct quotations</u>. (189)
   c. Main ideas and transition statements.
   d. Vivid examples and main ideas.

9. Alternative outlines ____
    a. are linear in design.
    b. <u>are carefully prepared</u>. (194)
    c. require a drawing of some sort.
    d. take less time to prepare than speaking outlines take.
    e. go to the platform with you.

10. Which one is NOT part of your cognitive style?
    a. your distinctive way of thinking
    b. your distinctive way of remembering
    c. your distinctive way of perceiving information
    d. <u>your distinctive way of communicating</u>   (193)
    e. your distinctive way of solving problems

FILL IN THE BLANK: These questions test <u>knowledge</u>, <u>comprehension</u>, and <u>application.</u>

1. A _____ includes every word you say. <u>script</u> (184)

2. The principle of _____ refers to organizing the most important point and developing lesser ideas beneath each. <u>subordination</u> (185-186)

3. A(n) _____ is a record of your speech ideas, materials, and their relationship to one another. <u>outline</u> (184)

4. The principle of _____ means you give your major points the same basic value or weight. <u>coordination</u> (185)

5. _____ use key words for points, using just enough key words to jog your memory. <u>Speaking notes</u>. (189)

SHORT ANSWER: These questions test <u>knowledge</u> and <u>comprehension.</u>

1. Explain the following principles of outlining: coordination, indentation, and subordination. <u>(Coordination means points are weighted fairly equally; indentation means that points are lined up in a way that visually shows their relationship to one another; subordination is the placement of supporting points under major points.)</u> (185-186)

2. List three advantages of note cards. <u>(The book lists four: less noticeable; small enough to handle easily; sturdy; frees one hand to gesture when they're used without a podium.)</u> (190-191)

3. Give three examples of how content outlines and speaking outlines are different. <u>(Content outlines are full sentence, content outlines are formal, content outlines contain headings and standard formatting formats.</u>

ESSAY QUESTIONS: These questions test <u>comprehension</u>, <u>application</u>, and <u>synthesis.</u>

1. A student once protested that she was graded down on her outline, saying, "This is a public speaking class. We should only be graded on our speeches!" How should her professor justify the requirement of a graded outline? What's the value of outlines? Why is it important for a beginning speaker to follow a fairly standard procedure?

2. Compare and contrast content outlines and speaking outlines.

3. You are making the choice of whether to use note cards or a speaking outline. Which would you use? Give a detailed explanation comparing and contrasting the relative merits of each.

4. Rough out a content outline for a speech on campus parking. Include a heading and standard formatting.

Chapter 12

CHOOSING EFFECTIVE LANGUAGE

TRUE-FALSE: These questions test <u>knowledge</u>, <u>comprehension</u>, and <u>application.</u>

1. Your language choices reveal aspects about you such as your income and educational levels, gender, and ethnicity. <u>True</u>. (197)

2. In rhetoric, the canon of style involves how you use language, not how you walk, talk, or dress. <u>True</u>. (198)

3. Languages remain fairly stable and unchanging over a period of time. <u>False. They change</u>. (197-199)

4. Dialects are variations of a language. <u>True</u>. (199-200)

5. We should avoid ambiguous words whenever we can. <u>False. That would be almost impossible</u>. (199-200).

6. The word 'pot' has one meaning consistent across cultures. <u>False. The text points out there are are at least five meanings depending on the context used</u>. (200)

7. The connotative meaning of a word is what the word names or identifies. You can find these meanings in dictionaries. <u>False. This is the denotative meaning</u>. (199-200)

8. Euphemisms are words, often with negative connotations, that speakers such as politicians use to demean other persons or groups. <u>False. These are epithets</u>. (201).

9. It's OK to use technical jargon in your speeches if you translate it. <u>True</u>. (200)

10. Vocabulary distinctions such as steward-stewardess exclude females by making them invisible. <u>False. Women are visible but nonparallel</u>. (209).

11. Mrs. Derek Johnson sounds "natural" but Mr. Karen Johnson sounds funny because in English the terms for married men and married women are nonparallel. <u>True</u>. (209)

12. James turned 50 and his co-workers gave him a party complete with black, "over the hill" balloons and cards. The balloons carried an ageist and dismissive message. <u>True</u>. (207)

13. Using alliterated main points is an effective way to help listeners remember the major ideas of a speech. <u>True</u>. (205)

14. An example of alliteration is "A good rule for making visual aids is: *simplify, simplify, simplify*." <u>False; it's repetition</u>. (204-205)

15. Jesse Jackson's quotation, "Just because you are born in the slum doesn't mean the slum is born in you," is a type of repetition more specifically known as antimetabole. <u>True</u>. (205)

16. "Winter hit us hard" is an example of personification. <u>True</u>. (206)

17. *Code switching* refers to a computer specialist's ability to repair both Macs and PCs. <u>False. Code switching refers to a bidialectic person's ability to speak one dialect with one group and another dialect with another group</u>. (199)

18. It is OK to call the repair person from Information Technology a *computer nerd* because everyone knows it is just a joke. <u>False. This is an example of dismissive language</u>. (209)

19. "The bouncer at the bar was a gorilla" is a simile. <u>False. It is a metaphor</u>. (206)

20. Archetypal symbols are those cultural memories that a specific culture names. <u>False. Archetypal symbols are understood by all humankind</u>. (206-207)

21. My friend speaks English, French, Russian, and Spanish; she is bilingual. <u>False; she's multilingual</u>. (209)

22. One way to adapt to linguistically diverse audiences is to build redundancy into your speech. <u>True</u>. (210)

23. We commonly have negative emotional responses to speakers who are not fluent in the language. <u>True</u>. (211)

24. It is all right to laugh at the language skills of nonnative speakers of English--if they laugh. <u>False. Their laughter may simply be to relieve tension</u>. (211)

MULTIPLE CHOICE: These questions test <u>knowledge</u>, <u>comprehension</u>, and <u>application.</u>

1. The principles for language usage are found in the canon of ____
   a. invention.
   b. disposition.
   <u>c. style</u>. (198)
   d. memory.
   e. delivery.

2. When Carmen speaks to a group of bilingual (Spanish-English speaking) clients, she uses Standard English for some sentences and phrases and Spanish for others. This is called _____
   a. connotative meaning.
   b. dialect.
   c. jargon.
   <u>d. code switching</u>. (199)
   e. ESL (English as a Second Language).

3. The _____ meaning is what the word names or identifies; the _____ meaning includes the emotional overtones the word implies.
   a. connotative . . . denotative
   <u>b. denotative . . . connotative</u> (199-200)

4. The word "weed" is _____ because it has many meanings.
   a. jargon
   <u>b. ambiguous</u> (199-200)
   c. vague
   d. connotative
   e. denotative

5. The _____ of a word involves the emotional overtones and other associations that cluster around a word.
   a. cultural memory
   b. denotative meaning
   c. connotative meaning (200-201)
   d. dialectal variation
   e. jargon

6. When one politician attacks another with names, they use words with negative connotations called _____
   a. epithets. (201)
   b. euphemisms.
   c. jargon.
   d. labels.
   e. ambiguous terms.

7. My sister is *thick* is a(n) _____ for *overweight*.
   a. connotation
   b. denotation
   c. ambiguous word
   d. euphemism (201)
   e. epithet

8. When Carlos, an engineer, attended a meeting of physicians, he could barely understand them because of their specialized _____
   a. dialect.
   b. vague words.
   c. code switching.
   d. verbiage.
   e. jargon. (200)

9. According to the text, one bonus to using inclusive language is _____
   a. you can increase your credibility. (208)
   b. you have a better chance of getting a well-paying job.
   c. you have eliminated negative connotations from public discourse.
   d. you will be perceived as being politically correct.
   e. all of these.

10. Saying "my husband is a male nurse" violates which principle?
    a. Avoid language that privileges one group over another.
    b. Avoid undue emphasis on differences. (208-209)
    c. Avoid dismissive language.
    d. Avoid non-parallel language.
    e. Avoid creating invisibility.

11. Use of verbiage violates which guideline for language usage?
    a. Be accurate.
    b. Be appropriate.
    c. Be clear.
    d. Be concrete.
    e. Be concise. (203)

12. Which shows these items in order from abstract to concrete?
    a. vehicle, transportation, car, luxury model, Jaguar
    b. Jaguar, luxury model, car, vehicle, transportation
    c. transportation, vehicle, luxury car, car, Jaguar
    d. transportation, vehicle, car, luxury model, Jaguar (203-204)
    e. luxury model, vehicle, car, Jaguar, transportation

13. Margaret used _____ to make the main points in her speech about opera more memorable. Here's her preview: Attending an opera is educational, emotional, entertaining, and easy to do.
    a. repetition
    b. alliteration (205)
    c. antimetabole
    d. parallelism
    e. hyperbole

14. "Ask not what your country can do for you; ask what you can do for your country" (JFK) is a type of reverse repetition known as _____
    a. antimetabole. (205)
    b. anaphora.
    c. antistrophe.
    d. anadiplosis.
    e. oxymoron.

15. "The mountain stood guard, brooding over the city below" is an example of _____
    a. alliteration.
    b. simile.
    c. repetition.
    d. personification. (205)
    e. hyperbole.

16. Hannah speaks Hebrew, English, and Russian; Andrew speaks ebonics and standard English; she is ____ and he is ____ .
    a. multidialectical . . . bidialectical
    b. bilingual . . . bidialectical
    c. multilingual . . . bilingual
    d. multilingual . . . bidialectical (209)

17. Which is NOT a tip for speaking through an interpreter?
    a. Use simple language.
    b. Provide your interpreter with an outline beforehand.
    c. Pause after paragraphs to let the interpreter translate. (211)
    d. Shorten your speech.
    e. Look at the interpreter as she or he interprets.

MATCHING: These questions test <u>comprehension</u> and <u>application.</u>

Directions: Select the type of language BEST illustrated in the examples below. (Note: You may use some more than once, some not at all.)

    a. alliteration (205)
    b. repetition (204)

     c.   personification (206)
     d.   metaphor (206)
     e.   simile (205)

1.   Let us bind up the nation's wounds. <u>c. personification</u>

2.   A college trustee contributes three things to the institution: wealth, wisdom, and work. <u>a.</u> <u>alliteration</u>

3.   You'll find many nuggets of truth in this little volume of poetry. <u>e. metaphor</u>

4.   Words well spoken are like apples of gold in bowls of silver. <u>f. simile</u>

5.   He's a collector of good books, of good music, of good friends. <u>b. repetition</u>

6.   The fingers of dawn brushed lightly across the rooftops of the town. <u>c. personification</u>

7.   I felt like a rat running a maze. <u>f. simile</u>

8.   We should patrol the information highway. <u>e. metaphor</u>

9.   We are a people in a quandary about the present. We are a people in search of our future. We are a people in search of a national community. (Barbara Jordan) <u>b. repetition</u>

FILL IN THE BLANK: These questions test <u>knowledge</u>, <u>comprehension</u>, and <u>application.</u>

1.   _____ are words or phrases that substitute agreeable or inoffensive terms for those that might offend, embarrass, or suggest unpleasant things such as bodily functions and death. <u>Euphemisms</u> (201)

2.   "Drive the ball for the first down and avoid the safety" is an examples of_____. <u>Jargon</u> (210)

3.   Jesse Jackson's phrase, "My constituency is the desperate, the damned, the disinherited, the disrespected, and the despised," is an example of _____. <u>alliteration</u> (200)

4.   _____ is the ability to put yourself in the other person's shoes and imagine what it would be like to give a speech in a second language. <u>Perspective taking</u> (211)

SHORT ANSWER: These questions test <u>knowledge</u>, <u>comprehension</u>, and <u>application.</u>

1.   Identify and explain four types of non-inclusive language. <u>(Students choose from the following: language that privileges one group over another; stereotyping; language that creates invisibility; language that demeans; dismissive language; language that unduly emphasizes differences.)</u> (208-209)

2.   What is meant by linguistic diversity? Define, then give three examples of this <u>communication principle</u>. <u>It means audiences may speak more than one language or dialect</u>. (209)

ESSAY QUESTIONS: These questions test <u>comprehension</u> and <u>application.</u>

1. Discuss how you can use language in a diverse culture to make your message clear. Use specific examples from your personal, family, group, high school, etc., to illustrate how your language is a verbal code that serves to mark your cultural experiences.

2. Explain how the language that speakers choose has political and social effects that influence listener's perceptions regarding groups and issues.

3. Because language choices arguably have power to influence others, create guidelines for ethical language use.

4. List, define, and provide examples of ways you can make your language choices more colorful and interesting.

5. Describe some areas of linguistic difference that occur in classrooms or in society. Then give tips on how you can be a better listener to a speaker who comes from a different speech background.

Chapter 13

PRESENTATION AIDS

TRUE-FALSE: These questions test <u>knowledge</u>, <u>comprehension</u>, and <u>application.</u>

1. Used correctly, visual aids can help your audience to understand your topic. <u>True</u>. (219)

2. Your listeners learn and remember better when they use one sense to take in information. That's a major reason visual aids are important. <u>False</u>. <u>Research shows that people take in information better when using two separate but parallel senses</u>. (219)

3. Presentation aids are important for explaining topics that can't be explained in words alone, like the use of color in Picasso's early paintings. <u>True</u>. (229)

4. An audience will appreciate the decorative additions of your presentation aids. <u>False. presentation aids should not be used as decorative additions. They are a powerful means of support</u>. (219)

5. Demonstration speeches almost always need visual support. <u>True</u>. (219)

6. A skeleton in an anatomy and physiology class is a three-dimensional visual aid. <u>True</u>. (220-221)

7. Passing an object around is recommended; this enables each listener to have direct experience with it. <u>False. It detracts from the speech</u>. (224-225)

8. Some types of visual aids are illegal to bring into the classroom. <u>True. Guns are in this category</u>. (221)

9. The six-by-six rule is one way to keep your graphs from being cluttered. <u>False. The rule is relevant for lists</u>. (222)

10. One drawback to lists is that speakers are tempted to write out their main points and then read them to the audience. <u>True</u>. (222)

11. A flowchart is a smaller section of an organizational chart. <u>False. They are two different types of charts</u>. (222)

12. To show the demographic make-up of your entire student body, a bar graph is better than a pie graph would be. <u>False. Pie graphs show parts of the whole best</u>. (223)

13. You want to compare the average number of cups of coffee people drink per day in Seattle to the amount drunk in New York, in San Francisco, in Miami, and in Santa Fe. You could use a bar graph or a pictograph with little coffee cup images. <u>True</u>. (223)

14. A floor plan of a building is a type of drawing. <u>True</u>. (225)

15. Geographic maps are outdated more quickly than political maps are. <u>False. It's the other way around</u>. (225)

16. Each type of presentation technology has advantages as well as disadvantages. <u>True</u>. (220)

17. Skillful use of an overhead projector can add to your personal credibility. <u>True</u>. (228-229)

18. Simple is better when designing slides. <u>True</u>. (232)

19. Most people use PowerPoint slides effectively. <u>False. Most presenters use them ineffectively</u>. (227)

20. Document cameras have been called the 21st century overhead projector. <u>True</u>. (228)

21. Document cameras can project objects, photographs, small objects, and printed pages. <u>True</u>. (228)

22. Chalkboards are the most useful means of display for student classroom speeches, because they are so readily available. <u>False. They have several drawbacks</u>. (228-229)

23. Interactive whiteboards can link to document cameras or computers with markup software, so that you can overwrite material and save your markups. <u>True</u>. (229-220)

24. Handouts should be placed on desks face up. <u>False. Place them face down, then have audience turn handouts over when they are being used</u>. (231)

25. A flip chart can substitute for a chalkboard. <u>True</u>. (230-231)

26. Handouts are widely used in businesses. <u>True</u>. (231)

27. A chalkboard is better than a handout for showing an unfolding process. <u>True</u>. (229)

28. A poster is better than a slide for displaying a picture of the Mona Lisa in a large auditorium to an audience of 500. <u>False. The slide would be more visible to a large group</u>. (230-231)

29. A serif font looks like handwriting. <u>False. Serifs are lines on tops of letters</u>. (233-234)

30. Sans serif fonts work well on PowerPoint slides. <u>True</u>. (234)

31. For variety, change the fonts on every PowerPoint slide you create. <u>False. This can be distracting</u>. (234)

32. Red is a good color to use for visuals because it has similar associations across cultures. <u>False. It has different meanings in China, India, the U.S., and so on</u>. (234)

33. To avoid a cluttered look, use a maximum of three main colors on all of your visuals. <u>True</u>. (234)

34. If you press the "s" key on a PowerPoint presentation you will bring up a blank slide. This allows you to display a visual only when you use it. <u>False. It is the "b" key</u>. (227)

35. A good general rule about using visuals is to have a plan B in case something goes wrong. <u>True</u>. (235)

36. By carefully selecting short video segments, you can clarify your ideas dramatically and memorably. <u>True.</u> (225-226)

37. Document cameras are becoming more common in classrooms and businesses nationwide. <u>True</u>. (228)

MULTIPLE CHOICE: These questions test <u>knowledge</u>, <u>comprehension</u>, and <u>application.</u>

1. Presentation aids are all BUT:
    a. <u>Decorative additions.</u> (217)
    b. A powerful means of support.
    c. Video clips.
    d. Emeril making 'kicked up' Mac n' Cheese.
    e. None of the above.

2. Which question is NOT important in an audiovisual aid plan?
    a. What is difficult to convey in words alone?
    b. <u>What looks cool</u>? (220)
    c. Where would visual aids be helpful?
    d. What ideas need emphasis?
    e. Where does audience attention lag?

3. Which are three-dimensional visuals?
    a. models, photographs, videos
    b. overhead projectors, objects, handouts
    c. tables, lists, charts
    d. <u>people, models, objects</u> (220-221)
    e. posters, overhead projectors, chalkboards

4. _____ best displays this information: 36% of the student body is classified as Anglo; 32% are African Americans; 12% are Latino; 15% are Asian in origin; 5% are Native Americans.
    a. A line graph.
    b. A bar graph
    c. <u>A pie graph</u> (223-224)
    d. A pictograph

5. _____ best displays this information: In 1981, the faculty numbered 305; in 1985, 342; in 1990, 412; in 1995, 456.
    a. <u>A line graph</u> (223)
    b. A bar graph
    c. A pie graph
    d. A pictograph

6. The least effective way to display a photograph is _____
    a. on an overhead transparency.
    b. transferred to a handout.
    c. projected using a slide.
    d. enlarged and mounted on posterboard.
    e. <u>passed around among audience members.</u> (223-224)

7. Political maps _____
    a. don't become as outdated as geographical maps.
    b. show mountains, deserts, and other natural features.
    c. are hard to display on an overhead projector.
    d. <u>show borders between nations and states.</u> (225)

8. Which is NOT an advantage of overhead transparencies?
   a. They are simple to make.
   b. They are inexpensive.
   c. It is easy to make professional-quality transparencies.
   d. They require no equipment to display. (227-228)
   e. You can use them in place of a chalkboard.

9. To use an overhead projector skillfully you should _____
   a. turn the projector on before you display your first visual, but leave it on throughout your speech so that lights going on and off won't distract the audience.
   b. use a pointer to point at the screen rather than touch the screen with your hand.
   c. display each line as you discuss the point it makes. (228-229)
   d. ignore your trembling hand as you point out something on the transparency; audience members know you're scared, so why hide it?

10. Chalkboards are especially good for _____
    a. brainstorming sessions. (229-230)
    b. displaying maps and drawings.
    c. increasing your competence in your audience's eyes.
    d. displaying professional-looking lists.
    e. use in large auditoriums.

11. When you plan to use posters on a regular basis, _____
    a. make new ones for each presentation.
    b. use hand lettering in several colors.
    c. store and transport them in a portfolio. (230)
    d. roll them up and store them so they take up little space.
    e. use them with larger audiences.

12. Handouts are common in _____
    a. classroom speeches but not in committee meetings.
    b. sales speeches but not in business settings.
    c. committee meetings but not in classroom speeches. (231)
    d. doctors' lectures but not sales speeches.

13. You probably won't want to use slides if you _____
    a. will be speaking in a large auditorium.
    b. have access to an overhead projector instead.
    c. want to project an image-based visual.
    d. want a well-lit room so that people can take notes on your talk. (227-228)

14. Computer programs that help you prepare a set of lists, tables, graphs, and so on are called _____
    a. word processing programs.
    b. graphics programs.
    c. presentation software programs. (227)
    d. scanners.

15. When designing a text-based presentation aid, do all BUT:
    a. Use all capital letters. (233-234)
    b. Use serif fonts on handouts because they're easier to read.
    c. Use title or sentence case.
    d. Use italics.

16. Which is NOT a suggestion for using visual aids successfully?
    a. <u>Use as many visual aids as possible</u>. (235)
    b. Be sure the visual aid can be seen.
    c. Follow the six by six rule.
    d. Have a backup plan in case of mechanical failure.
    e. Display visuals only when you use them.

MATCHING : These questions test <u>knowledge</u>, <u>comprehension</u>, and <u>application.</u>

<u>Directions:</u> Select the visual aid that will BEST go with the speech topic or idea. (Note: You may use some more than once, some not at all.)

    a. a model (221)
    b. an object (221)
    c. a map (224)
    d. a list (222)
    e. a graph (223)

1. This is my great-grandma's pendant. <u>b. an object</u>

2. There are five stages of relationship development. <u>d. a list</u>

3. Migration moved from east to west. <u>c. a map</u>

4. The size of our university's endowment has continually increased across the years. <u>e. a graph,</u> <u>specifically a line graph</u>

5. A new political reality resulted in Germany after East and West Germany reunited. <u>c. a map</u>

6. Espresso is easy to make. <u>b. an object</u>

7. Let's compare the numbers of men and women enrolled in each major in the College of Liberal Arts. <u>e. a</u> <u>graph--specifically a bar graph</u>

8. Today, I will point out several areas in the human brain and describe what they do. <u>a. a model</u>

FILL IN THE BLANK: These questions test <u>knowledge</u>, <u>comprehension</u>, and <u>application.</u>

1. Something done in stages or in steps is easily displayed on a _____. <u>list</u> (222)

2. What is the six by six rule? <u>On visuals, use no more than six lines, six words per line.</u> (222)

3. A(n) _____ chart shows hierarchies and relationships. <u>Organizational</u> (233)

4. _____ are line drawings or graphic designs that explain rather than realistically depict an object or process. <u>Diagrams</u> (224-225)

5. _____ maps show mountains, deserts, and lowlands. <u>Geographic</u> (225)

6. Software programs such as PowerPoint by Microsoft, which help you create an entire package of visuals, are called _____ software programs. presentation (227)

7. The bottom line on objects is they should be _____, _____, and _____. accessible, legal, practical (221)

SHORT ANSWER: These questions test <u>comprehension</u>, <u>application, analysis</u>, and <u>evaluation.</u>

1. List and explain uses of 2-D visual aids. (<u>List can include lists, charts, graphs, photographs, drawings, diagrams, and maps. Examples will vary.</u>) (222-225)

2. Describe four types of graphs and explain the use of each. (<u>Line graphs show variables that fluctuate over a period of time; bar graphs compare data from several groups; pie graphs show divisions of a population or parts of a whole; picture graphs or pictographs compare data that relate to objects or people.</u>) (223)

3. When might a visual aid be unethical? Discuss two examples. (<u>If the visual aid fails to meet the standard of doing no harm psychologically or physically. If the visual aid is something the audience would find shocking or offensive. Examples will vary.</u>) (228)

4. List and discuss four tips to using posters. (<u>Use yardsticks or rulers to make straight lines, use more than one color, for a professional look use computer generated text, transport them in a portfolio.</u> (230)

ESSAY QUESTIONS: These questions test <u>comprehension</u>, <u>application, analysis</u>, and <u>evaluation.</u>

1. Compare and contrast the advantages of overhead projectors with chalkboards and posters as means of display.

2. Describe ways that technology--computers, photocopiers, audio and video technology, and the like--can assist you in producing effective visual aids.

3. Come up with a presentation aid plan for a speech on "How to Make Toast: Plain and Fancy," using at least three different types of aids. Discuss why you chose these types of presentation aids and how they will enhance or support your presentation.

4. Think of at least three speakers you have seen who either used visuals effectively or ineffectively. Describe what they did and explain why it was effective. Explain what they could do to use visual aids more effectively.

Chapter 14

DELIVERING YOUR SPEECH

TRUE-FALSE: These questions test <u>knowledge</u>, <u>comprehension</u>, and <u>application.</u>

1. Delivery is the way you perform your speech. <u>True</u>. (241)

2. Erving Goffman compares self-presentation to a mythic tale of knights and chivalry. <u>False. He compares it to a dramatic performance</u>. (245)

3. A speaker who has a physical feature--such as above-average weight or height or use of crutches—is right to assume that listeners will focus on that feature rather than on the words of the speech. <u>False. They may notice such features but rarely focus on them alone</u>. (245)

4. Maggie thinks she can do her speech in sweats because it is a classroom speech and how you dress doesn't really much matter. <u>False. Clothing should be appropriate and not distracting.</u> (245)

5. There are ethical implications in impression management. <u>True</u>. (245)

6. Facial expressions can reveal emotions. <u>True</u>. (247)

7. A person who extends his words is said to have a drawl. <u>True</u>. (249)

8. Fortunately, in the United States, we tend to see all regional dialects as equally acceptable. <u>False. We tend to judge some as inferior</u>. (249)

9. You can't tell someone's social status based on how they pronounce words. <u>False</u>. How someone pronounces words gives listeners an idea of his or her social status. (249)

10. YanHong Krompacky argues that America is built on accents, and accents function as symbols of U.S. freedom and prosperity. <u>True</u>. (249)

11. Research shows that speakers with a faster rate are more credible than those who use moderate speed. <u>False. Faster rates are linked to some traits of credibility, but a moderate rate is linked to others</u>. (250)

12. Ruth says "er" and "um" a lot during her speech. The technical term for these is *vocalized pause*. <u>True</u>. (266)

13. The confident speaking style is characterized by a calm, slow, soft, and less intense manner. <u>False. This is the conversational style</u>. (241)

14. The confident speaking style is more effective than the conversational style. <u>False. Both can be effective</u>. (252)

15. The great advantage of speaking extemporaneously is that it is spontaneous and spur-of-the-moment, and you don't really have much time to get nervous. <u>False. That's impromptu delivery</u>. (243)

16. One important reason that manuscript delivery is not as effective in the classroom is that it tends to limit the speaker's eye contact with his or her audience. <u>True.</u> (241-242)

17. Memorizing the introduction of your speech is particularly effective because you are most nervous at the beginning. <u>False.</u> <u>Your stress may cause you to forget.</u> (242)

18. Using a TelePrompTer is one way of using manuscript delivery. <u>True.</u> (242)

19. Posture can show confidence and pride or sadness and defeat. <u>True.</u> (247)

MULTIPLE CHOICE: These questions test <u>knowledge</u>, <u>comprehension</u>, and <u>application.</u>

1. Bonnie just got braces on her teeth at age 40. She wants to avoid speaking because of her teeth; she should keep in mind that _____
   a. her audiences will probably tune her out because of her weight.
   b. neatness is more important than looks in this culture.
   c. people won't really notice her weight.
   d. <u>people will notice her braces, but they'll focus less on it as she proceeds.</u> (245)

2. The cultural proverb "Cleanliness is next to godliness" exemplifies the U.S. emphasis on _____
   a. relatively permanent physical features.
   b. <u>good grooming.</u> (245)
   c. dressing for success.
   d. skillful use of accessories.
   e. ethical dimensions of speaking.

3. All of these suggestions about clothing are good to keep in mind EXCEPT _____
   a. remember that clothing choices influence audience perceptions.
   b. <u>select more casual clothing than normal so that you feel comfortable as you speak.</u> (245)
   c. check out the clothing expectations for the particular occasion.
   d. choose simple accessories of the best quality you can afford.
   e. in general, choose conservative clothing.

4. _____ are especially useful in conveying emotions.
   a. posture.
   b. <u>facial expressions.</u> (247)
   c. gestures.
   d. walking.

5. Gestures include all BUT:
   a. posture.
   b. walking.
   c. a small eyebrow lift.
   d. extending your hands to show a distance.
   e. <u>all of the above are gestures.</u> (246)

6. Jessica says *pahking* for *parking.* This is a difference in _____
   a. pronunciation.
   b. <u>articulation.</u> (248)
   c. stress.
   d. accent.

7. Aristotle identified these characteristics of the voice:
   a. volume, pauses, and inflection.
   b. <u>rate, pitch variation, and volume.</u> (250)
   c. inflection, pauses, and rate.
   d. pitch variation, volume, and inflection.

8. The conversational speaking style is _____
   a. <u>slower and softer, with good gestures and eye contact.</u> (252)
   b. rapid, louder, with good eye contact.
   c. rapid, softer, with good gestures and eye contact.
   d. slower and loud, with sweeping gestures.
   e. slower and softer, with minimal pitch variation.

9. Andrae communicates in a way that is personally effective and socially appropriate. The best term for this is _____
   a. <u>communicative competence.</u> (252)
   b. self-confidence.
   c. cynical.
   d. sincerity.
   e. credibility.

10. Tonya, who on the spur of the moment tells an amusing story at a farewell dinner, is using _____ delivery.
    a. <u>impromptu</u> (243)
    b. memorized
    c. manuscript
    d. extemporaneous

11. A major challenge with manuscript delivery is _____
    a. rehearsing the words you wish to accent.
    b. timing the speech.
    c. storing the speech for future reference.
    d. <u>delivering the speech conversationally.</u> (241-242)

12. The most inactive delivery is
    a. <u>manuscript.</u>(241-242)
    b. memorized.
    c. impromptu.
    d. extemporaneous.

13. Tom writes out his speech on note cards and then takes the cards to the podium where he reads from them, as conversationally as possible. He's using _____ delivery.
    a. impromptu
    b. memorized
    c. <u>manuscript</u> (241-242)
    d. extemporaneous

14. Which is NOT a tip for using a teleprompter?
    a. Rehearse with the teleprompter before you speak.
    b. Adjust the speed of the lines to your speaking rate.
    c. Think of it as reading the credit lines at the end of a movie.
    d. <u>Deliver the speech so that it sounds memorized, not read.</u> (242)

FILL IN THE BLANK: These questions test <u>knowledge</u>, <u>comprehension</u>, and <u>application.</u>

1. _____ is the way you present yourself in order to have your listeners evaluate you in a certain way. <u>Impression management</u> (245)

2. Speakers who don't believe their own messages, and instead try to create false or misleading impressions are _____. <u>cynical</u> (246)

3. Sounds such as "uh" or "um" are called _____. <u>filled pauses</u> or <u>vocalized pauses</u> (251)

4. A _____ is the screen located beneath the camera lens that projects your script line by line when you give a filmed speech. <u>teleprompter</u> (242)

5. Carefully preparing your speech, rehearsing, and then choosing the exact words during your delivery is the _____ type of delivery. <u>extemporaneous</u> (243-244)

6. _____ refers to the way you actually say words. _____ is the way you say individual sounds. <u>Pronunciation, Articulation</u> (248)

7. _____ is stopping purposely to make a point. <u>Effective pauses</u> (251)

8. _____ is personally effective and socially appropriate. <u>Communicative competence</u> (252)

9. _____ delivery used to be the norm. <u>Memorized</u> (242)

10. _____ project your manuscript line by line so you can read and look directly at the audience. <u>Teleprompters.</u> (242)

SHORT ANSWER: These questions test <u>knowledge</u>, <u>comprehension</u>, <u>application</u>, and <u>evaluation.</u>

1. Discuss how gestures, posture, facial expression, and eye contact can communicate emotion. (Answers will vary. 266-251)

2. Compare and contrast a conversational and confident delivery style. (<u>They're alike in that they have good eye contact and gestures, but the conversational style is softer, slower, and less intense.</u>) (252)

3. Identify four types of delivery and tell when each is appropriate. (<u>Impromptu--when you speak spur-of-the-moment or when you must think on your feet; memorized--when you give the same speech repeatedly; manuscript--formal occasions and speaking on media when exact timing is important; extemporaneous--most classroom and professional speaking.</u>) (241-244)

4. Explain how to make the most of your appearance. (<u>Make the most of clothing and accessories. Control gestures. Make eye contact. Vary vocal behaviors.</u>) (241)

5. Explain the concept of *communicative competence*. (<u>The ability to communicate in a manner than is personally effective and socially appropriate. Answers will vary.</u>) (252)

ESSAY QUESTIONS: These questions test <u>knowledge</u>, <u>comprehension</u>, and <u>application.</u>

1. Your friend has come to you for advice on improving her delivery skills. She says she is not sure how to dress and she is afraid she will have weird mannerisms as she speaks. What would you tell her about effective delivery?

2. List and describe the four types of delivery, telling the strengths and weaknesses of each. Give examples where each might be appropriate.

3. Compare and contrast the idea of a *confident* style and a *conversational* style. Give examples of each, then discuss when and where each type of style might be effective.

4. Congratulations. Your school's recruiting department wants to film scenes from real classrooms to feature in a promotional tape for potential students. They want to feature YOU in a classroom speech. Tell what factors you'll consider and what you'll do present yourself well on film.

5. Analyze the impression management skills of a public figure who presents himself or herself well in public situations. (Or, if you prefer, choose someone who is ineffective in public.) Examine nonverbal elements such as vocal characteristics, gestures, eye contact, clothing, and so on.

Chapter 15

TELLING NARRATIVES

TRUE-FALSE: These questions test <u>knowledge</u>, <u>comprehension</u>, and <u>application.</u>

1. People from all cultural groups use narrative as a form of reasoning. <u>True.</u> (256-259)

2. Laura Simms is an applied storyteller because her stories have practical uses in helping people adjust to difficult situations. <u>True.</u> (259)

3. The purposes of narratives are similar to those of public speaking in general: to inform, to persuade, and to entertain. <u>True.</u> (261)

4. Scientific narratives function mainly to provide examples. <u>False. They function mainly to explain.</u> (256)

5. A story explaining the history of your college is an example of a narrative that aims to explain ultimate realities. <u>False. It explains society and its institutions.</u> (256)

6. Narratives that explain social realities are factual and agreed upon by members of a culture. <u>False. They are often disputed and revised.</u> (257)

7. Ojibway poet, Lenore Keeship-Tobias, says that non-natives who borrow native stories are committing cultural theft. <u>True.</u> (257)

8. Telling a story is one way of providing good reasons for your ideas. <u>True.</u> (261)

9. Deliberative speaking gives people information and motivates them to act wisely. <u>True.</u> (258)

10. Aristotle classified narrative reasoning as deliberative speaking. <u>True.</u> (258)

11. "The rhetoric of possibility" is the phrase the text uses to describe narratives that explain ultimate realities about things such as heaven or the afterlife. <u>False. The rhetoric of possibility more commonly describes visions and possibilities for future life on this earth.</u> (260)

12. Although some stories are told mainly to entertain, all narratives have profound meanings. <u>False. Jokes and silly stories, for example, are not necessarily profound.</u> (256)

13. Identifying your speech purpose is less important for stories than for, say, a pro-con speech or a problem-solution speech. <u>False. It's important to decide whether you want to use the story to inform, persuade, or entertain.</u> (261)

14. Characters in narratives should be real in order to be convincing. <u>False. Talking animals and personified cars can convey cultural values and ideas convincingly.</u> (262)

15. The plot of the story is the challenge or conflict that tests the characters. <u>True.</u> (262)

16. A narrative should be literally true in order to function as a good reason or proof. <u>False. Fictional stories can be persuasive.</u> (266)

17. Characters in a narrative can be either real or imaginary. <u>True</u>. (262)

18. Constructed dialogue is especially effective when communicated through lively vocal behaviors. <u>True</u>. (263-264)

19. Lists are an effective way of increasing rapport between a speaker and an audience. <u>True</u>. (264)

20. The exemplum is a narrative speech built around a myth. <u>False. It's a speech created around a quotation or proverb.</u> (265)

21. One major test of narrative reasoning is coherence, meaning that it is understandable and holds together logically. <u>True</u>. (266)

22. Narrative merit means that the story faithfully represents how the world works. <u>False. This means it is worth telling</u>. (266)

23. Emotionally moving narratives can motivate listeners to intervene, to make a difference, and to improve the lives of people. <u>True.</u> (258)

24. Stories can be persuasive. <u>True.</u> (258)

MULTIPLE CHOICE: These questions test <u>knowledge</u>, <u>comprehension</u>, and <u>application.</u>

1. According to the text, narratives are so common that we live in a _____ world.
    a.   morally fashioned
    b.   mythical
    <u>c.   story-shaped</u> (255)
    d.   well-explained
    e.   religiously based

2. Walter Fisher used the term *homo narrans* to mean that _____
    a.   we live in a story-shaped world.
    b.   the narratives of the world are numberless.
    c.   ordinary citizens as well as international leaders use narrative reasoning.
    <u>d.   humans are, by nature, the storytelling animal.</u> (256)

3. _____ is how the story hangs together.
    a.   narrative fidelity
    <u>b.   narrative coherence</u> (266)
    c.   constructed dialogue
    d.   narrative game
    e.   narrative schema

4. Which is NOT true of applied storytellers?
    a.   They tell narratives for practical reasons, not just for entertainment.
    b.   They tell stories in homeless shelters, hospitals, houses of worship, and so on.
    c.   They tell stories to promote world peace and social improvements.
    <u>d.   They tell only centuries-old stories.</u> (259)
    e.   They believe that hearing and telling divergent stories can help us grow.

5. People who die and are resuscitated often tell their after-death stories in order to _____
   a. explain physical realities.
   b. explain social realities.
   c. explain ultimate realities. (257)
   d. provide a positive example.
   e. support a cultural myth.

6. Consultant Annette Simmons says you should have at least three stories: _____
   a. one to explain your past, one for your present, and another describing your future.
   b. one to explain who you are, one to tell why you are speaking, and one to describe your vision. (257)
   c. one for your beliefs, one to explain your attitudes, and one to explain your values.
   d. one to teach, one to inspire, and one to persuade.
   e. one to explain natural phenomena, one for social realities, and one to explain ultimate things.

7. When you _____, you speak to provide information that will help listeners make wise decisions regarding future courses of action.
   a. give exemplary narratives
   b. use the rhetoric of possibility
   c. engage in deliberative speaking (258)
   d. prepare an exemplum

8. Sonia tells her neighbor a fictional story of how a registered sex offender living in their neighborhood "could be" a threat to their children. This illustrates _____
   a. a personal testimonial.
   b. a positive model.
   c. a negative model.
   d. persuasion.
   e. the rhetoric of possibility. (260)

9. Which of these is NOT a place to provide detailed descriptions?
   a. at the beginning of the speech
   b. at points that disclose intimate information (263)
   c. when you are driving the point home
   d. during the key action of the plot

10. As Talia tells her story, she says, "I approached him, laughing, and said, 'Are you alright?' He responded, over the noise in the lunchroom, 'Yeah, just my pride is damaged.'" This is an example of _____
    a. narrative merit.
    b. a persuasive narrative.
    c. a detailed description.
    d. constructed dialogue. (263-264)
    e. the climax of the plot.

11. The exemplum pattern must include all these components EXCEPT _____
    a. a quotation.
    b. a humorous story that illustrates the quotation. (265) [the story need not be humorous]
    c. a paraphrase of the quotation.
    d. a stated lesson or point.
    e. the source of the quotation.

12. Which is NOT a test of narrative reasoning?
    a. The story should be coherent and hang together logically.
    b. <u>The characters should be interesting</u>. (266)
    c. The story should be worth telling.
    d. The story should faithfully represent the way the world works.

FILL IN THE BLANK: These questions test <u>knowledge.</u>

1. The Latin phrase for humans as a species characterized by their storytelling is _____. *homo narrans* (256)

2. People who tell stories for practical reasons such as promoting peace are called _____. <u>applied storytellers.</u> (259)

3. Aristotle defined _____ speaking as the type of speaking that gives people information and motivates them to make wise decisions regarding future courses of action. <u>deliberative</u> (258)

4. The _____ shows how things might be, not necessarily how they are. <u>rhetoric of possibility</u> (260)

5. The part of the narrative that describes the challenges facing the characters, and the way they respond to those challenges is the _____ of the story. <u>plot</u> (262)

6. A(n) _____ is a narrative speech organizational pattern that builds the speech around a quotation. <u>exemplum</u> (265)

7. _____ means a story is understandable and hangs together. <u>Narrative coherence</u> (266)

8. _____ means a story is worthwhile or important. <u>Narrative merit</u> (266)

9. Telling a story that describes the world as it is is _____. <u>Narrative fidelity</u> (266)

SHORT ANSWER: These questions test <u>knowledge,</u> <u>comprehension,</u> and <u>application.</u>

1. Identify three types of realities that humans attempt to explain through narratives; provide examples for each. <u>(1) explanations of natural phenomena; 2) explanations of society and its institutions; 3) explanations of ultimate things. Student examples will vary</u>.) (256-257)

2. List in order the elements of an exemplum and briefly describe each component. <u>The elements are: State a quotation or proverb; identify and explain its source; rephrase or paraphrase it; illustrate it with a narrative; apply the lesson to the audience. Descriptions of each component will vary.</u> (265)

3. Identify and explain three tests you should consider when evaluating the merits of narrative reasoning. <u>(1) Is the story coherent or understandable? 2) Is the story true or a faithful representative of reality? 3) Is the story worth telling?)</u> (266)

4. Introduce and discuss a folktale from your culture. What elements would you use to analyze the story? <u>What is the purpose of the story, are the characters real or imaginary, what is the plot, how does the storyteller incorporate vivid language and use of details, dialogue and lists. Student answers may vary</u>. (264)

ESSAY QUESTIONS: These questions test <u>knowledge</u>, <u>comprehension</u>, and <u>application.</u>

1. Explain the work of applied storytellers.

2. Choose a current event that is an unfolding narrative. Give details about the purpose, characters, and plot of the story and then apply the tests of narrative reasoning to the story as it is being told to the public.

3. Select an occupation that interests you and describe ways that practitioners of that occupation use informative, persuasive, and entertaining narratives in their work.

4. Explain Lenore Keeshig-Tobias's argument against non-natives using native stories.

5. Let's say you are asked to tell a story to children in a fourth grade public school in your community. Decide on a specific story you will tell and then describe how you will use the guidelines for narratives in preparing for your speech.

Chapter 16

INFORMATIVE SPEAKING

TRUE-FALSE: These questions test <u>knowledge</u>, <u>comprehension</u>, and <u>application.</u>

1. In "information imbalance," some people know an overwhelming amount of information and others know very little. <u>True</u>. (272)

2. The "Arab Spring" showed how information can be used to deny people their rights. <u>False. It showed how information can empower a citizency</u>. (272)

3. An information imbalance means that the speaker presents one-sided information about a subject. <u>False. It means that some people have information and others don't</u>. (272)

4. Reni's audience isn't familiar with Kenneth Burke's principle of *dramatism*. Choosing analogies, both figurative and literal, is a good strategy for him to use. <u>True</u>. (274)

5. When your listeners need to refresh their memories, your narrowed purpose will be to counter their misunderstandings. <u>False. It is to review</u>. (275)

6. When you inform with the purpose of countering misunderstandings, you'll probably get more emotional reactions than when you update information. <u>True</u>. (275)

7. The first step in planning a demonstration speech is to plan the visual support that's needed. <u>False. First think through all the required steps.</u> (275)

8. Timing during rehearsal is especially important for "how-to" speeches. <u>True.</u> (276-277)

9. All "how-to" speeches require a demonstration. <u>False. Giving instructions or tips (e.g., how to resolve conflict) doesn't.</u> (276-277)

10. Park rangers or tour guides commonly give descriptive speeches. <u>True</u>. (278)

11. Details and vivid language in speeches about events allow listeners to mentally place themselves at the event. <u>True</u>. (274)

12. Reports answer the question, "What have we learned about this subject?" <u>True</u>. (280)

13. Information should be new when giving an informative speech. <u>False. Review material can also serve as an informative speech</u>. (275)

14. Generally, chronological, topical, or narrative patterns best fit a biographical report. <u>True</u>. (280)

15. The goal of investigative reports is persuasion. <u>False. The purpose is to provide listeners with factual information so they can form their own conclusions.</u> (473)

16. Pro-con organization works well for investigative reports. <u>True</u>. (281)

17. Terez organized her speech on "destiny" by first providing the denotative meaning and then giving connotative meanings for the word. This was an effective pattern. <u>True</u>. (283)

18. An explanation of a complex concept is really a translation speech. <u>True</u>. (284)

19. Individuals and groups tend to agree on theories, concepts, and abstract ideas. <u>False. Often there are irreconcilable differences</u>. (285)

20. Audiences commonly complain that informative speeches are boring. <u>True</u>. (285)

21. Jargon is a major hazard for informative speakers. <u>True</u>. (285)

22. When audiences see information as relevant to their personal lives, they're more likely to listen and learn effectively. <u>True</u>. (285)

MULTIPLE CHOICE: These questions test <u>knowledge</u>, <u>comprehension</u>, and <u>application</u>.

1. Article 19, mentioned in the chapter, recognizes the potential danger of _____
   a. The Information Age.
   b. Information overload.
   c. a global right to information.
   <u>d. an *information imbalance*</u>. (272)

2. Potential danger in the form of _____ exists when some people or groups have a great deal of information and others have little.
   a. an electronic superhighway
   b. an information overload
   <u>c. an information imbalance</u> (272)
   d. disconnected fragments of information
   e. misconceptions

3. The audience had never before heard about detoxihol; the speaker should do all these things EXCEPT _____
   a. define terminology.
   <u>b. expect to counter negative emotional responses</u>. (274)
   c. use figurative and literal analogies.
   d. tell who, what, where, when, and how type information.

4. Odell's audience knows quite a bit about entertainer George Clinton; what general strategy should Barbara use in her speech about him?
   a. Present who, what, where, when, and how information.
   <u>b. Find novel information about one aspect of his life</u>. (274)
   c. Find scientific information about him.
   d. Get another subject entirely.

5. What are the correctly ordered steps for planning a demonstration speech?
   a. think through the steps; plan visual aids; work on the content
   b. work on the content; plan visual aids; think through the steps
   <u>c. think through the steps; work on the content; plan visual aids</u> (276-277)
   d. work on the content; plan visual aids; think through the steps

6. A description speech answers which audience question?
   a. How is it done?
   b. <u>What's it like? (278)</u>
   c. What have we learned about this?
   d. How does it work?

7. A speaker who is countering misinformation should
   a. use humor where appropriate.
   b. incorporate handouts.
   c. <u>prepare for emotional responses, often negative.</u> (275)
   d. utilize presentation software like PowerPoint.
   e. take care to dress professionally.

8. Which title is best for a report?
   a. How to Choose a Wedding Caterer
   b. Loyalty: What Is It?
   c. Theories of Global Warming
   d. <u>Educational Vouchers: Pros and Cons (280-283)</u>

9. Luke's speech on dadaism answers which audience question?
   a. How is it done?
   b. What's it like?
   c. What have we learned about this?
   d. <u>What does it mean? (284)</u>
   e. How does it work?

10. Which is NOT a guideline for speeches about concepts?
    a. <u>Choose a topic that is not very difficult.</u> (283-284)
    b. Break complex ideas into their component parts.
    c. Avoid technical jargon.
    d. Use comparisons to things listeners already understand.
    e. Supply concrete examples.

11. The speaker identifies specific parts of her topic that might be difficult for the audience to grasp; she is
    _____
    a. <u>doing an obstacle analysis of the audience.</u> (285)
    b. planning discourse consistency.
    c. personalizing her material for her audience.
    d. striving to be interesting.

12. _____ is saying the same thing more than once; _____ is saying the same thing, but a different way each time.
    a. <u>Repetition . . . redundancy</u> (286-287)
    b. Redundancy . . . repetition

13. Alliterating main points is one way to create _____
    a. repetition.
    b. redundancy.
    c. <u>discourse consistency.</u> (286)
    d. interest.

FILL IN THE BLANK: These questions test <u>knowledge</u>, <u>comprehension</u>, and <u>application</u>.

1. Because of the explosion of knowledge in the past few decades, our era is sometimes called the _____. <u>Information Age</u> (272)

2. Article 19 of _____ says that the right to information is universal. <u>the Universal Declaration of Human Rights</u> (272)

3. Two general topic categories on which people are more likely to disagree are _____ and _____. <u>concepts</u> and <u>issues</u> (275)

4. _____ answer the question, "What have we learned about this subject?" <u>Reports</u> (275)

5. When you show someone how to do something, you are _____ _____. <u>doing demonstrations</u> (276-277)

6. When you tell them how to do the procedure, you are _____ _____. <u>giving instructions</u> (276-277)

7. Chevie's speech on the *Har Nof* neighborhood of Jerusalem is a speech _____ _____. <u>describing places</u> (278)

ESSAY QUESTIONS: These questions test <u>knowledge</u>, <u>comprehension</u>, and <u>application</u>.

1. Discuss the importance of information, not only in our society, but across the globe.

2. Explain how you would give a speech about a controversial issue that informs without being persuasive.

3. Let's say your assignment calls for you to give an informative speech that requires a visual aid. List at least four categories of informative topics and give an example of a visual that would be effective in each of the categories.

4. A question set in the future: You've been asked to design a set of transparencies for a co-worker to use in a workshop on the topic of how to make informative speeches less boring. Sketch the set of transparencies you'd make.

5. What does it mean to engage a citizenry with information? Give specific examples of how societies have changed due to the increase in the availability of information.

Chapter 17

FOUNDATIONS OF PERSUASION

TRUE-FALSE: These questions test <u>knowledge</u> and <u>comprehension.</u>

1. Aristotle's artistic proofs include *ethos, pathos,* and *logos.* True. (292)

2. A Euro-American speaking style is not typically emotionally expressive. <u>True.</u> (297)

3. When you choose a subject for your persuasive speeches, it is not particularly important to select a topic that matters to you. <u>False. You should care about the topic.</u> (295)

4. "Earthquakes can be predicted" is an example of a claim of fact. <u>True. It is a debatable point.</u> (293)

5. "Eating foods rich in antioxidants will slow the aging process in your body" is an example of a claim of fact. <u>True. It is a disputable prediction that assumes a causal relationship.</u> (293)

6. "Moderate consumption of wine decreases a woman's chances of getting a heart attack" is an example of a claim of definition or classification. <u>False. It's a disputable factual claim—causal relationship.</u> 293-294).

7. "War will have devastating consequences on the Middle East for decades" is an example of a policy claim. <u>False. It's a disputable claim of fact—prediction.</u> (293-294)

8. "The Green Bay Packers will win the SuperBowl" is a claim of fact. <u>True.</u> (293-294)

9. Links that allow your audience to connect your evidence with your claim are called assertions. <u>False. They are called warrants.</u> (293)

10. "The lyrics of the rapper, Eminem, are immoral" is an example of a value claim. <u>True.</u> (293)

11. "Brand X of dog food is better than Brand Y dog food" is an example of a policy claim. <u>False. It's a value claim.</u> (293)

12. Since not all listeners will agree with you, you should have *rebuttals* prepared ahead of time. <u>True.</u> (293)

13. "Every university should offer a study abroad program" is a policy claim. <u>True.</u> (293)

14. A persuasive speech has a single purpose, so it is important to identify that purpose clearly at the outset. <u>False. A single speech will probably have multiple claims.</u> (293)

15. When your audience is unconvinced and therefore does not act, you should begin by using motivational appeals to make them want to act. <u>False. You start with logical, convincing appeals.</u> (300)

16. When audiences are apathetic, use emotional appeals to make them care about your topic. <u>True.</u> (300)

17. Topics considered appropriate for public debate vary across cultures. <u>True.</u> (294)

18. Figurative analogies are also called metaphors. <u>True</u>. (301)

19. In Maslow's Hierarchy, security and safety needs need to be satisfied before one can move to other needs. <u>False. Basic needs are the first level of need to be satisfied</u>. (299)

20. When you focus on your listeners' values, try to avoid using emotional appeals. <u>False. Try to get listeners to identify with the topic</u>. (295)

21. A demagogue is a speaker who depends more on logos than on ethos or pathos. <u>False. It's the other way around</u>. (301)

22. Toulmin's Reasoning Model attempts to explain how we make sense of the world. <u>True</u>. (292)

23. Overall, perceived behavioral control, not our attitudes or our subjective norms, influences our decision to act. <u>False. Attitudes have more weight</u>. (292)

24. With audiences that reject your proposals, approach the subject indirectly by establishing common ground. <u>True. </u>(295)

25. When you face listeners who are neutral toward your claim, ask why. <u>True. </u>(307)

26. Reasoning by metaphor compares things that are generally different but share a similarity. <u>True.</u> (301)

27. Cultures conceptualize issues practically the same way. <u>False. Cultures conceptualize issues differently</u>. (294)

28. Ethos means the emotional appeals in a speech. <u>False. Ethos is speaker credibility</u>. (295)

29. Logos refers to the rational proofs in a speech. <u>True</u>. (300)

30. Pathos should be used positively. <u>False. Pathos can be used to generate negative or positive emotions</u>. (298-299)

MULTIPLE CHOICE: These questions test <u>knowledge</u> and <u>comprehension.</u>

1. Aristotle identified three elements of rhetoric, including all BUT_____
   <u>a. warrants</u>. (292)
   b. ethos.
   c. pathos.
   d. logos.
   e. none of the above.

2. Which of the following is NOT included in Toulmin's Reasoning Model?
   a. Warrant
   b. Backing
   c. Claim
   <u>d. Experiment </u>(292)
   e. Grounds

3. Which is NOT a question to ask yourself when you choose a persuasive topic?
   a. What ideas or issues would I argue for or against?
   b. <u>What ideas or issues do I feel neutral toward?</u> (295)
   c. What changes would I like to see in society?
   d. What can make life more meaningful for myself and others?

4. "Driving an SUV is wrong" is _____
   a. a claim of fact.
   b. an opinion.
   c. <u>a value claim.</u> (293)
   d. a policy claim.
   e. a debatable point.

5. "A high protein diet is better for you than a high carbohydrate diet" is a _____ claim.
   a. factual
   b. definition or classification
   c. <u>value</u> (293)
   d. policy

6. "The U.S. government should stay out of Mexican politics" is _____
   a. a claim of fact.
   b. an opinion.
   c. a value claim.
   d. <u>a policy claim.</u> (293)
   e. a debatable point.

7. If you use a warrant that isn't broadly understood, you should _____
   a. use culturally appropriate topics.
   b. find an audience that will agree with your claims.
   c. use words like *always* and *never.*
   d. <u>collect more backing for support.</u> (293)

8. Persuasive speeches can be made about _____
   a. claims of fact but not value claims.
   b. claims of value or policy, but not both in the same speech.
   c. claims arguing for but not against status quo policies.
   d. <u>factual, value, and policy claims.</u> 293)

9. Max wants to convince his audience that zinc is an excellent cold remedy. He should do all these things EXCEPT _____
   a. begin with logical appeals.
   b. carefully build a factual case with credible evidence.
   c. <u>emphasize emotional appeals.</u> (298)
   d. prove his competence by being knowledgeable.

10. Petra's audience knows they should cut the fat in their diets; however, they are apathetic and continue to eat a lot of high-fat foods. They are _____
    a. unconvinced.
    b. <u>unmotivated.</u> (298)
    c. inconsistent.
    d. consistent.
    e. hostile.

11. Jackson's audience believes that smoking is harmful to their health, but they all smoke. He wants them to match their behaviors to their beliefs. He should _____
    a.   use narratives or testimonials that show how other students were able to quit smoking. (293)
    b.   relate personally to the smokers in the group.
    c.   pile on fact after fact showing the dangers of smoking.
    d.   use comparatively few emotional appeals.

12. Ethos, pathos, and logos are part of _____
    a.   Aristotle's persuasive theory. (292)
    b.   the Theory of Reasoned action.
    c.   classical Roman rhetorical theory.
    d.   cognitive dissonance theory.
    e.   Athabaskan theory of behavior.

13. A college president is speaking to a group of people who have donated scholarship funds for many years; she wants them to continue to do so. Her goal is _____
    a.   to demonstrate good sense.
    b.   to develop logos.
    c.   to develop ethos.
    d.   to develop good character.
    e   to express good will. (295)

14. Reasoning by analogy is done _____
    a.   through figurative analogies.
    b.   through literal analogies.
    c.   by testing claims.
    d.   all of these. (301)
    e.   none of these.

15. Making a generalization from specific examples is called:
    a.   deductive reasoning
    b.   inductive reasoning (302)
    c.   causal reasoning
    d.   problem-solution reasoning
    e.   a logical fallacy

16. African-American scholars argue that _____ reasoning is typical of African and African-American speaking.
    a.   metaphorical (301)
    b.   causal reasoning
    c.   deduction
    d.   parallel case

17. A speaker who argues that a scholarship program for debaters would succeed in your college because a similar program worked well in another college is using _____
    a.   a syllogism
    b.   induction
    c.   cause to effect reasoning
    d.   effect to cause reasoning
    e.   parallel case reasoning (301)

18. A speaker who argues that a scholarship program for debaters would succeed in your small private college because a similar program worked well in a major state university should consider if the _____
    a. case is a metaphor or a literal analogy.
    b. two situations are alike in essential details. (302)
    c. cases contrast enough to be meaningful.
    d. situation is fundamentally dialogically enough to be convincing.

19. Carol has a friend who likes University X. On a visit to campus she meets forty students, all but one of whom likes the university--and that one simply doesn't like school. She concludes from these examples that University X is a good school. This is _____
    a. parallel case reasoning.
    b. using a syllogism.
    c. induction. (302)
    d. deduction.
    e. argument from analogy.

20. "Madeleine L'Engle writes good books. This is a book by Ms. L'Engle; therefore, it will be good." This is an example of _____
    a. reasoning from analogy.
    b. deduction. (304-305)
    c. induction.
    d. reasoning from cause to effect.
    e. reasoning by parallel case.

FILL IN THE BLANK: These questions test <u>knowledge</u> and <u>comprehension.</u>

1. The three forms of proofs identified by Aristotle are _____, _____, and _____. *logos, pathos, ethos* or <u>rational proofs, emotional proofs, credibility</u> (292)

2. The Greek word meaning appeals to emotions is _____. *pathos* (292)

3. The Greek word meaning proofs that come from the character of the speaker is _____. *ethos* (292)

4. The justification or reasoning you use to connect your evidence with your claim is a(n) _____ . <u>warrant</u> (293)

5. Words and phrases (such as "usually") that limit the scope of your claim are _____. <u>qualifiers</u> (293)

6. _____ is another name for figurative analogy. <u>Metaphor</u> (301)

7. _____ is another name for literal analogy. <u>Parallel case</u> (302)

8. _____ refers to the verbal arguments you make relating to your subject. <u>Logos</u> (300)

9. _____ reasoning starts with a number of examples and results in a conclusion or generalization. <u>Inductive</u> (302)

SHORT ANSWER: These questions test <u>knowledge</u>, <u>comprehension</u>, and <u>application.</u>

1. Draw, label, and explain Toulmin's model of reasoning. (<u>Students' drawings and labels should look very much like Figure 17.1 in the text. Explanations should include: claims are disputable assertions that need support; grounds, data, or evidence support the claim; the warrant connects the evidence to the claims; qualifiers limit the scope of the claim; and the rebuttals are counterarguments</u>.) (292)

2. Discuss Aristotles's artistic proofs. How are each used in a speech? (<u>At minimum, students should be able to identify ethos, pathos, and logos, and give an example how each is used in a speech. Student answers will vary</u>.) (292)

ESSAY QUESTIONS: These questions test <u>comprehension, application, analysis,</u> and <u>synthesis.</u>

1. Show how claims, evidence, warrants, qualifiers, and rebuttal are all important in creating reasonable arguments.

2. The text identified four types of rational proofs. Choose three types, describe them, and give tests and examples for each.

3. Develop an example in which you show the connection between inductive and deductive reasoning.

4. You use emotional appeals in an argument with your roommate. Your roommate says you're overreacting and that you should be "rational" about your disagreement. Explain how emotions can act as good reasons.

5. Aristotle believed that ethos is the most important form of reasoning. Explain why this might be so and describe ways to increase a speaker's *ethos*.

6. Discuss differences in reasoning between the dominant Euro-American patterns and those of co-cultural and international groups. Explain why it is important to be aware of these differences.

7. After class you meet a classmate for coffee; she is having trouble finding a topic for a persuasive speech. Give her guidelines for finding a good speech subject.

8. Identify three types of claims and give examples of each.

9. Describe ways that beliefs and actions overlap to create four types of audiences. Then discuss strategies to use with each group of listeners.

10. Elizabeth wants to target her listeners' values and get them to agree that boxing is an immoral sport. How would you advise her on ways to accomplish her speaking goal?

11. Explain the Theory of Reasoned Action by giving an example to show how it works in actual situations.

12. The text presented a number of persuasive patterns. Choose <u>two</u> from this list and discuss them in detail: direct method, comparative advantages, criteria-satisfaction, negative method. Describe the pattern. When might you choose it? Why would it be better than another pattern? Give examples.

Chapter 18

PERSUASIVE SPEAKING

TRUE-FALSE: These questions test <u>knowledge</u>, <u>comprehension</u>, and <u>application.</u>

1. Don't think of an argument as a war of words; instead, think of arguments as intentional, purposeful activities that involve reason and judgment. <u>True</u>. (318)

2. It is easy to be believable if you are not attached to your topic in some way. <u>False</u>. <u>Choose a topic that you believe in strongly or stirs strong emotions in you</u>. (315)

3. If you want your audience to stop eating meat, your persuasive goal is to actuate. <u>True</u>. (326)

4. When you argue for the *status quo*, you are appealing for change. <u>False. You argue for "what is."</u> (318)

5. "Every university should offer a study abroad program" is a policy claim. <u>True</u>. (318-320)

6. A persuasive speech has a single purpose, so it is important to identify that purpose clearly at the outset. <u>False. A single speech will probably have multiple claims.</u> (316-320)

7. When your audience is unconvinced and therefore does not act, you should begin by using motivational appeals to make them want to act. <u>False. You start with logical, convincing appeals.</u> (322)

8. When audiences are apathetic, use emotional appeals to make them care about your topic. <u>True</u>. (321)

9. Dissonance is a motivational factor that often prompts people to change in order to avoid inconsistency. <u>True</u>. (326)

10. The following is a good strategy: Your instructor wants to explain her grading system. She first sets up criteria for "A" and "B" and "C" and "D" speeches. Then she shows how a specific speech fits the criteria for a particular category. <u>True</u>. (318)

11. Discussions of value claims are generally less emotionally laden than discussions of classification claims. <u>False. It's the other way around.</u> (309)

12. When you focus on your listeners' values, try to avoid using emotional appeals. <u>False. Try to get listeners to identify with the topic.</u> (317-318)

13. The Theory of Reasoned Action (TRA) assumes that we are emotional and that we generally look for emotional reasons to act. <u>False. It assumes we are rational.</u> (327-328)

14. According to the Theory of Reasoned Action, as we reason, we rely on subjective norms, which are our perceptions of what the people who are significant to us think we should do. <u>True</u>. (327-328)

15. Overall, perceived behavioral control, not our attitudes or our subjective norms, influences our decision to act. <u>False. Attitudes have more weight</u>. (327)

16. With audiences that reject your proposals, approach the subject indirectly by establishing common ground. <u>True.</u> (321)

17. When you face listeners who are neutral toward your claim, ask why. <u>True.</u> (321)

18. When listeners accept your criteria, it's easier for them to accept your evaluation. <u>True.</u> (318)

19. The problem-solution pattern is better for persuasive speeches than for informative. <u>False. It all depends on the purpose for the speech.</u> (328)

20. Monroe's Motivated Sequence is a modification of the comparative advantages pattern. <u>False. It's a modified problem-solution pattern.</u> (328)

21. The visualization and action steps of Monroe's Motivated Sequence make it an especially good pattern for a sales speech. <u>True.</u> (329)

22. The criteria-satisfaction pattern is less appropriate for arguing a value claim. <u>False. It's very good for value claims.</u> (324)

23. Emotion can be reasonable; reason can have emotional underpinnings. <u>True.</u> (320)

24. Ethos, pathos, and logos are separate entities. <u>False. They combine to form good reasons.</u> (328)

MULTIPLE CHOICE: These questions test <u>knowledge</u>, <u>comprehension</u>, and <u>analysis.</u>

1. Which is NOT a question to ask yourself when you choose a persuasive topic?
   a. What ideas or issues would I argue for or against?
   b. <u>What ideas or issues do I feel neutral toward</u>? (315-316)
   c. What changes would I like to see in society?
   d. What can make life more meaningful for myself and others?

2. "Driving an SUV is wrong" is _____
   a. a claim of fact.
   b. an opinion.
   c. <u>a value claim.</u> (317-318)
   d. a policy claim.
   e. a debatable point.

3. "A high protein diet is better for you than a high carbohydrate diet" is a _____ claim.
   a. factual
   b. definition or classification
   c. <u>value</u> (317-318)
   d. policy

4. "The U.S. government should stay out of Mexican politics" is _____
   a. a claim of fact.
   b. an opinion.
   c. a value claim.
   d. <u>a policy claim.</u> (318-319)
   e. a debatable point.

5. "Tuition costs should stay the same" is _____
   a. a factual claim.
   b. an opinion that most students hold.
   c. a value claim.
   d. <u>a policy claim *for* the status quo.</u> (318)

6. Persuasive speeches can be made about _____
   a. claims of fact but not value claims.
   b. claims of value or policy, but not both in the same speech.
   c. claims arguing for but not against status quo policies.
   d. <u>factual, value, and policy claims.</u> (316)

7. Max wants to convince his audience that zinc is an excellent cold remedy. He should do all these things EXCEPT _____
   a. begin with logical appeals.
   b. carefully build a factual case with credible evidence.
   c. <u>emphasize emotional appeals.</u> (322)
   d. prove his competence by being knowledgeable.

9. Inconsistency between actions and beliefs is a good motivator for change, according to _____
   a. Aristotle's persuasive theory.
   b. the Theory of Reasoned action.
   c. classical Roman rhetorical theory.
   d. <u>cognitive dissonance theory.</u> (326-327)
   e. Athabaskan theory of behavior.

11. In the Theory of Reasoned Action _____
   a. attitudes include a mental and an emotional component.
   b. subjective norms are perceptions of what significant people think we should do.
   c. perceived behavioral control is our opinion about whether or not we can do something.
   d. <u>all of these.</u> (327-328)
   e. a. and c. only.

12. Roslyn is trying to decide whether or not to lose weight. According to the Theory of Reasoned Action, she is most likely to _____
   a. have a fairly negative attitude toward diets.
   b. <u>be strongly influenced by her fiancée who wants her to drop a few pounds.</u> (327-328)
   c. feel that losing weight is nearly impossible for her.
   d. believe that a few extra pounds actually make her more attractive.
   e. all of these.

7. Which is NOT a factor in the influence of culture on reasoning?
   a. Various groups conceptualize issues differently.
   b. What is considered a "good reason" varies.
   c. <u>Some cultures do not use reasoning strategies.</u> (328)
   d. The norms for framing a discussion are different.
   e. Cultures differ on issues considered appropriate for discussion.

FILL IN THE BLANK: These questions test <u>knowledge</u> and <u>comprehension.</u>

1. _____ are standards we use to make judgments. <u>Criteria</u> (318)

2. Unmotivated audiences fail to act on their beliefs due to _____ or indifference. <u>apathy</u> (320)

3. _____ theory says that humans try to avoid inconsistency, and they strive to return to a place of psychological balance. <u>Dissonance or cognitive dissonance</u> (326-327)

4. The theory that links attitudes, subjective norms, and perceived behavioral control is _____. <u>the Theory of Reasoned Action (TRA)</u> (327-328)

5. The three forms of proofs identified by Aristotle are _____, _____, and _____. *<u>logos, pathos, ethos</u>* or <u>rational proofs, emotional proofs, credibility</u> (314)

6. The Greek word meaning appeals to emotions is _____. *<u>pathos</u>* (315)

7. The Greek word meaning proofs that come from the character of the speaker is _____. *<u>ethos</u>* (315)

ESSAY QUESTIONS: These questions test <u>comprehension,</u> <u>application,</u> and <u>synthesis.</u>

1. Explain the Theory of Reasoned Action by giving an example to show how it works in actual situations.

2. The text presented a number of persuasive patterns. Choose <u>two</u> from this list and discuss them in detail: direct method, comparative advantages, criteria-satisfaction, negative method. Describe the pattern. When might you choose it? Why would it be better than another pattern? Give examples.

Appendix A

SPEAKING IN SMALL GROUPS

TRUE-FALSE: These questions test <u>knowledge</u> and <u>comprehension.</u>

1. The ability to work well in small groups is valued throughout the world. <u>True</u>. (335-336)

2. According to a recent study, the ability to work in teams is the most important skill that employers seek. <u>True</u>. (335)

3. Group work is always preferable to individual effort. <u>False. There are disadvantages to group work</u>. (336)

4. Small groups enhance learning for many people. <u>True</u>. (335)

5. Working in small groups is a good motivating factor for many people. <u>True</u>. (336)

6. Small group work is inherently dialogical. <u>True</u>. (340)

7. Most well-functioning groups require less time when compared to that of an individual working alone. <u>False. They take more time</u>. (336)

8. Men are from Mars and women are from Venus —which means that men and women have vastly different communication styles. <u>False. The genders are probably more alike than different.</u> (336-337)

9. Sophie didn't really want to agree with the group, but as she was the only woman, decided to go along. This is indicative of the tendency of women to speak out in groups only when it is vital. <u>False. Women tend to defer to men in groups</u>. (336-337)

10. In small groups, women interrupt more than men do. <u>False. Men interrupt more</u>. (336-337)

11. Science students who team up to investigate and report on a subject are developing valuable occupational skills. <u>True</u>. (337)

12. It's vital to elect a leader during the first group meeting. <u>False. It's possible but not vital</u> to designate a <u>leader</u>. (37-338)

13. The person who plays the gatekeeper role is the one who makes sure that quiet people participate and dominant people give others a chance to contribute. <u>True</u>. (337)

14. John Dewey's problem solving steps are unique to the United States. <u>False. People in other places like Africa use a five-step process</u>. (338)

15. The problem-solving method in the text is strictly linear and structured. <u>False. It's structured, but not strictly linear</u>. (339-340)

16. In the first stage of the problem-solving method, you should formulate a factual question rather than ask a value or policy question. <u>False. State the issue as a policy question</u>. (339)

17. It's a good idea to avoid emotionally charged language in the statement of the problem. <u>True</u>. (339)

18. When you analyze the problem, ask what you <u>must</u> do and what you <u>want</u> to do. <u>False. Do this in the criteria-setting stage.</u> (339)

19. A mind map is especially useful as a way to record information generated in a brainstorming session. <u>True</u>. (339-340)

20. When you select the best solution, you judge the possible solutions against the criteria you set. <u>True</u>. (339-340)

21. Although all members of a group contribute to a final report, one designated spokesperson does the speaking. <u>True</u>. (340)

22. A panel discussion is more dialogical than a symposium. <u>True</u>. (340-341)

23. Tom's committee has formulated a policy for dealing with vandalism on campus. He prepares and delivers a speech on the history of the problem; Lisa talks about the effects of vandalism; Marietta's speech deals with the criteria selected and the solution the group's decided upon. They are a participating in a panel discussion. <u>False. It's a symposium.</u> (341)

MULTIPLE CHOICE: These questions test <u>knowledge</u> and <u>comprehension</u>.

1. Which is NOT an advantage of group work?
    a. You'll get a deeper level of involvement with your topic.
    b. Group work is a means for co-creating meaning.
    c. You can pool resources with others.
    d. <u>Groupthink allows group members to come to consensus</u>. (336)
    e. A group is more creative than an individual.

2. One late night during summer, your group of friends convince you to join them going skinnydipping in the pool. You don't want to, but finally go along with the group. Later, you find out others didn't want to go either. Your group of friends fell victim to _____
    a. time pressures.
    b. <u>groupthink</u>. (336)
    c. the co-creation of meaning.
    d. slackers.
    e. dominators.

3. Compared to men, women in groups tend to do all these things EXCEPT _____
    a. personalize their information with examples and stories.
    b. suggest more topics.
    c. <u>talk more</u>. (336-337)
    d. help one another and build relationships between people.
    e. provide fewer explanations.

4. Stella always asks the group members who don't speak up what they think about a given idea. She also makes sure that one special person doesn't dominate the discussion. Stella is acting as the group
    _____.
    a. recorder
    b. leader
    c. agenda setter
    d. <u>gatekeeper</u> (337)
    e. brainstormer

5. The final group meeting exists mainly for _____
   a. congratulating one another on a job well done.
   b. organizing the material that people have gathered.
   c. finalizing details. (338)
   d. making sure that everyone did her or his part.
   e. preparing audio and visual aids.

6. Which is the BEST statement that defines a problem?
   a. What should we do about the problem of campus vandalism? (339)
   b. Why is vandalism occurring on campus?
   c. Should we do something about vandalism on campus?
   d. How can we get rid of these irritating campus vandals?
   e. Who are the campus vandals and why are they vandalizing?

7. When you analyze the problem, you should discover the _____ relating to the issue.
   a. facts
   b. causes and effects
   c. values
   d. all of the above (339)
   e. a. and b. only

8. Which step of the problem-solving method involves asking what is required and what is desired?
   a. Define the problem.
   b. Analyze the problem.
   c. Set criteria for deciding on a solution. (339)
   d. List possible solutions.
   e. Select the best solution.

9. In which step of the problem-solving method is brainstorming especially useful?
   a. Define the problem.
   b. Analyze the problem.
   c. Set criteria for deciding on a solution.
   d. List possible solutions. (339)
   e. Select the best solution.

10. _____ is a reporting format in which group members assign one person to present the group's findings.
    a. A final report (340)
    b. A panel
    c. An announcement
    d. A symposium

11. _____ is a reporting format in which group members divide the topic into parts, and each member selects one part and prepares and delivers a speech on it.
    a. A final report
    b. A panel
    c. An announcement
    d. A symposium (341)

FILL IN THE BLANK: These questions test <u>knowledge</u> and <u>comprehension.</u>

1. _____ results when members pressure one another to conform in order to avoid conflict. <u>Groupthink</u> (336)

2. Deborah Tannen uses the label, _____, for women's talk that stresses relationships as well as information. <u>"Rapport Talk"</u> (336-337)

3. The problem-solving method discussed in this chapter was developed by_____. <u>John Dewey</u> (338)

4. The issue should be stated as a _____ question. <u>policy</u> (339)

5. _____ is a common way for groups to generate ideas by presenting a number of ideas without evaluating them. <u>Brainstorming</u> (339-340)

6. A _____ is a format for group reporting in which all members of the group discuss the issue in dialogical interactions with a moderator who guides interactions. <u>Panel or panel discussion.</u> (340)

7. A _____ is a format for group reporting in which each member of a group selects one aspect of the topic and prepares and delivers a speech on it. <u>symposium</u> (341)

8. Stan likes to keep a written record of the group meeting. He serves as the group _____. <u>Recorder</u> (341)

ESSAY QUESTIONS: These questions test <u>knowledge</u> and <u>comprehension.</u>

1. You've been assigned to do a group project with some of your classmates. You're reluctant to do this assignment, because you've had some bad group experiences in the past. Psych yourself up for this project by describing the advantages of working in a group; then identify some ways you can all work to deal with the inevitable disadvantages of group work.

2. Compare and contrast your own speaking patterns with the conversational styles or tendencies that Deborah Tannen identified as associated with men and women.

3. Let's say your campus has parking problems. You've been asked to serve on a committee to recommend a solution to the board of trustees. Use this problem as a case study for explaining the five steps in the problem-solving method discussed in the text.

4. Identify and explain three methods of presenting your group's findings.

5. Your group has worked together all semester. Give examples of three different ways to present your group's findings.

Appendix B

SPEAKING ON SPECIAL OCCASSIONS

TRUE-FALSE: These questions test <u>knowledge</u> and <u>comprehension.</u>

1. The integrative function of ceremonial speaking binds an organization's members together around shared goals. <u>True</u>. (342)

2. Introductions function to integrate newcomers into a group. <u>True</u>. (343)

3. Each succeeding generation of an organization must create its own myths, symbols, and ceremonies, because we drop these relics from former generations. <u>False. We pass on rituals, etc., to new generations</u>. (345)

4. It's easy to say good-bye to highly unpopular individuals. <u>False. Changes always require adjustment</u>. (334)

5. The roast the other department members gave Jim at the moment of his retirement was appropriate. <u>True</u>. (344)

6. Essential to announcements are details regarding who, what, when, where, how. <u>True</u>. (344-345)

7. When you present an award, it's a good idea to talk about the award itself. <u>True</u>. (346)

8. When you work in international organizations, it's a good general rule to give awards to individuals who achieve more than their peers. <u>False. Some cultures honor groups more than individuals</u>. (346)

9. When an actor wins an Oscar award, they should give a lengthy speech thanking everyone who helped them succeed. <u>False. Acceptance speeches should be brief</u>. (346)

10. A criteria-satisfaction pattern or a statement of reasons pattern both work well for speeches of nomination. <u>True</u>. (347)

11. Commemorative speeches that highlight and reinforce important cultural values are called tributes. <u>True</u>. (347)

12. Nominations are short persuasive speeches. <u>True</u>. (346-347)

13. The purpose of commemorative speeches is to inspire. <u>True</u>. (347)

14. Norma got choked up during the eulogy she delivered, but the audience responded well, because given the circumstance, she behaved appropriately. <u>True</u>. (349-350)